Monetary Evolution, Free Banking, and Economic Order

Studies in the History, Methods, and Boundaries of Economics

Series Editors
Axel Leijonhufvud and Donald N. McCloskey

Monetary Evolution, Free Banking, and Economic Order, Steven Horwitz

Carl Menger and the Origins of Austrian Economics, Max Alter

The Making of an Economist, Arjo Klamer and David Colander

FORTHCOMING

A History of Balance-of-Payments Theory, John S. Chipman

Search, Symmetry, and Arbitrage: A Unified Approach to the Social and Life Sciences, John J. McCall

The Hand Behind the Invisible Hand, Karl Mittermaier

Monetary Evolution, Free Banking, and Economic Order

Steven Horwitz

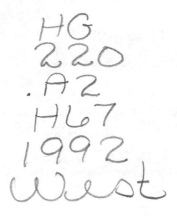
Westview Press
BOULDER · SAN FRANCISCO · OXFORD

Studies in the History, Methods, and Boundaries of Economics

Copyright © 1992 by Westview Press, Inc.

Published in 1992 in the United States of America by Westview Press, Inc., 5500 Central Avenue, Boulder, Colorado 80301-2877, and in the United Kingdom by Westview Press, 36 Lonsdale Road, Summertown, Oxford OX2 7EW

Library of Congress Cataloging-in-Publication Data
Horwitz, Steven.
  Monetary evolution, free banking, and economic order / Steven Horwitz.
    p. cm. — (Studies in the history, methods, and boundaries of economics)
  Includes bibliographical references and index.
  ISBN 0-8133-8514-8
  1. Money—History. 2. Monetary policy—History. I. Title.
II. Series.
HG220.A2H67 1992
332.4'9—dc20
                                                    92-36838
                                                    CIP

Printed and bound in the United States of America

The paper used in this publication meets the requirements of the American National Standard for Permanence of Paper for Printed Library Materials Z39.48-1984.

10   9   8   7   6   5   4   3   2   1

To my parents

For their love, their trust, and their support

Contents

Acknowledgments

My acknowledgments begin where I was first exposed to many of the ideas I grapple with in this book—the University of Michigan. My main intellectual debt is to Don Herzog, who forced me time and time again to step back and try to examine my own prejudices. To this day, I hear his voice, and it keeps me honest. A number of people and institutions at George Mason University also played integral parts in the process of writing this book. My greatest debt is to the Center for the Study of Market Processes, which supported my work both spiritually and financially, and to its director, Jack High, and his executive assistant, Colleen Morretta. Thanks also go to the Institute for Humane Studies at GMU and its vice president for academic affairs, Walter Grinder, for financial and spiritual support. An F. Leroy Hill Summer Faculty Fellowship in 1990 provided me with the time and resources to do some further reading and research. The Graduate School at George Mason also contributed financial support for the completion of this project.

Various other friends and colleagues at George Mason provided me with a large degree of intellectual interaction and stimulation that I hope emerges in the pages of this book. The students at George Mason made my time there the most enjoyable and rewarding intellectual experience of my career. In particular, I owe more thanks than I can possibly express to two of my friends—Peter Boettke and David Prychitko. Much of what I have to say has evolved out of countless hours of discussion, criticism, and just plain fun with them. It is a pleasure and an honor to count them as both my friends and my intellectual allies.

I would also like to thank Richard Wagner, Mark Jacobs, and Phil Wiest for their comments on an earlier draft. I want to especially thank Karen Vaughn, not only for her comments and suggestions but also for her personal support as department chair for the four years I was at George Mason. The degree to which she helped cultivate the atmosphere of intellectual excitement at GMU is greatly underappreciated.

My friends and colleagues at St. Lawrence University also deserve thanks for their support. Particular thanks go to Jeff Young and Howard

Bodenhorn for their comments and discussion on sections of an earlier draft. I also want to acknowledge the university for providing financial support for various stages of this project and thank Laurie Olmstead for her expert and efficient skill in preparing the camera-ready copy.

No book is solely the product of the author's mind. Therefore I would like to acknowledge a number of other people whose comments or conversations have somehow contributed to the ideas within. Thanks go to Kurt Schuler, Larry White, Richard Timberlake, Gary Madison, Jeffrey Friedman, Jeremy Shearmur, Tyler Cowen, Bill Woolsey, Bill Butos, and Roger Koppl. I also wish to thank seminar participants at George Mason, New York University, Trinity University, and St. Lawrence for their comments. I hope this book in some way reflects a little bit of the wisdom of all of the aforementioned and in some way returns something to them.

I would also like to extend a special thank you to the anonymous reader from Westview Press whose painstakingly detailed comments and suggestions have immeasurably improved the content of this book. Others at Westview have contributed to the final product in important ways. Senior editor Spencer Carr and project editor Deborah Lynes greatly smoothed the transition from manuscript to book and Diane Hess's copy editing greatly enhanced the readability of my prose.

Three other individuals deserve special recognition. I owe a great deal to George Selgin for my knowledge of monetary theory. Both inside and outside the classroom he has taught me more about monetary theory and about how to write economics than anyone. His intellectual commitment and the depth of his scholarship continually challenge me to improve my own. Though George was instrumental in the conception of this project, the results reflect numerous changes since then. Despite the changes, it is George's intellectual guidance that permeates the pages that follow.

I would also like to acknowledge Don Lavoie, who served as chair of the original dissertation committee and who has been my teacher in the truest sense of the word. Don's ability to get me to see what was implicit in my own ideas and his willingness to let me explore those implications define what it means to teach. His concern for the set of ideas that drive this study was a constant source of inspiration.

Finally, I want to thank my wife, Jody, for bearing with me through the writing and completion of this study. Her constant support, her love and her patience, and her ability to make me laugh and relax when I needed it most were probably much more than I deserved. For all of those reasons, and many more, she and my son, Andrew, are a constant reminder that my work is still only the *second* biggest love of my life.

Steven Horwitz

Introduction

The Delphic demand "Know thyself" meant, "Know that you are a man and no god." It holds true as well for human beings in the age of the sciences, for it stands as a warning before all illusions of mastery and domination. Self-knowledge alone is capable of saving a freedom threatened not only by rulers but much more by the domination and dependence that issue from everything we think we control.

—H. G. Gadamer (1981, p. 150)

Why Money?

There is perhaps no economic good that is so important, yet so mysterious and misunderstood, as money. Economists have long recognized the various benefits of a monetary economy, but much argument remains over the origin of money, its exact functions, and the proper institutional arrangements for its supply. One fundamental question concerns the relative roles of the individual, social interaction, and the state in defining and maintaining a monetary order. Neoclassical economic theorists have tried to trace the derivation of money and describe its functions with mathematical models of atomistic, utility-maximizing agents and have paid little, if any, attention to the social context within which those agents act.[1] The standard neoclassical view also gives the state several key responsibilities, including originating the monetary unit, producing or overseeing the production of the unit's material representatives, designing and enforcing a supply policy, dealing with monetary crises, and generally using these powers to promote economic growth.

To the extent that economists have generally accepted and promoted this view, the state itself has, in turn, widened the actual scope of its involvement in monetary affairs.[2] This book is an attempt to show that the traditional view of the state's role in securing a monetary order is seriously exaggerated *and* that traditional maximization models are not

1

helpful in determining precisely what, instead, constitutes the basis of monetary and economic order. The ways in which private initiative interacts with social institutions and contexts have been downplayed or completely overlooked by traditional approaches. Some of the literature on the origin and functions of money and the burgeoning literature on alternatives to central banking are beginning to question this strategy. In addition, recent work in the philosophy of the social sciences provides a framework for questioning the validity of the type of formalistic and objectivistic approaches to studying human action normally employed by neoclassical economists. This study will pursue and extend all of these themes into new areas.

There are two major motivations for this study: one involving the subject itself and the other involving the particular approach being taken. Why should we be so concerned with one good, money, among the many present in a modern economy? The answer, I believe, is because of the centrality of money to the socioeconomic order. Virtually all exchanges in organized markets have to take place via the medium of exchange. As Robert Clower (1970, p. 100) points out in his well-known formulation, "Goods buy money, money buys goods—but goods do not buy goods in any organized market." For this reason, money touches everything in the economy. Money's pervasiveness is one reason for the constantly reappearing analogy to blood and the common appropriation of the term *circulation.*

Many economists of differing methodological and ideological perspectives have also argued that money and its institutions play a fundamental role in generating the crises that have plagued Western economies in the modern era. If we are indeed going to "know our-selves" and solve the problems of the twenty-first century, we need to understand money and the role it plays in human society. If money can be better understood, perhaps steps can be taken to mitigate or eliminate monetary crises and alleviate their terrible human costs. For these reasons, further discussion of these topics is important. If an orderly monetary system is the basis for an advanced, productive, and orderly economy, we need to examine what constitutes the basis of monetary order.

A Note on Methodology

The particular approach taken here differs from the standard one in the monetary economics literature. This choice does not necessarily imply that the standard approach is invalid; rather I argue that exploring alternative ways of looking at particular problems may help to discover connections and implications that could not be obtained with standard methods. More specifically, maximization models may not be sufficient to explain why actors in the economy behave the way they do. As philosophers of science (Gadamer 1985; Dallmayr and McCarthy 1977) and a few economists[3] realize, formal modeling, statistical significance, and other apparatuses of the scientific method are not the only ways of generating valid theoretical and empirical insights in the social sciences. By traveling a road not frequently taken, I hope to find both new trails and new forms of life and subject them to economic analysis in the same way those found in more familiar lands have been analyzed. In doing so, we can see whether these new forms of life are ultimately compatible with the flora and fauna that economists have traditionally scrutinized.

The starting point for this investigation comes from S. Herbert Frankel (1977, p. 2), who begins his book on the philosophy of money by summarizing some colloquial descriptions of money and the problem that modern social science faces in explaining them:

> The definitions, or descriptions, that have been applied to money are legion. They range from those which carry the implication that it is the root of all evil to those that regard it as manna from heaven. Some have argued that it does not matter, others that it matters too much. Money has been described as a political, or sociological, phenomenon, as a mechanism, as a mirror, as a religion, as a myth, as a means of communication which reduces complexity and as a distortion which increases it, as the curse of the miser and the elixir of the spendthrift, as a means to all ends and as an end in itself, as barren and as all-powerful, as inert or neutral, and as "the drink which stimulates the economic system to activity," as the tool of social progress and as an obstacle to it. . . . Such definitions, descriptions, implications, or epithets always imply or involve a moral or philosophical issue. This is not generally recognized *because Cartesian forms of thought still dominate our thinking* [emphasis added].

In the chapters to follow, I will explore many of the issues Frankel raises, but more important, I want to utilize an alternative, *non-Cartesian* philosophical approach that will recognize and explore the philosophical issues involved.

Frankel's book is an excellent, albeit brief, description of the nature of money as a social institution. However, by sticking to verbal analysis, Frankel opposes the dominant formalist-positivist methodology of late twentieth-century neoclassical economics. Because Frankel provides no philosophical defense for the nonformal style of his book, it will continue to be viewed as just unscientific rambling—neither theory nor empirics—in the eyes of most neoclassical economists. Unless Frankel's type of work can be backed up by an appeal to some philosophical framework that recognizes nonmathematical, nonstatistical investigations as legitimate and can grapple with the philosophical issues involved, the knowledge gained from such investigations will continue to go unrecognized by economists and other formalist social scientists.[4]

This study offers such a defense by undertaking two tasks in the course of its examination of money. First, this study can be seen as another example of how nonformalist approaches can illuminate valid and important questions in the social sciences. To the extent that it has something to contribute, this study will show that nonformalist approaches can provide meaningful and relevant knowledge. A second goal is to explicitly link the study of money to the emerging "interpretive turn" in the social sciences.[5] The interpretive philosophical tradition provides good reasons for believing that formalistic approaches to questions of human action can, at best, see only one side of the story. The essentially human part of the social world can be found only through the continued examination of past and present human actions and texts.

The two main philosophical authorities that I rely on are Michael Polanyi (1958) and Hans-Georg Gadamer (1985). Polanyi's focus is on overturning objectivistic models of the natural sciences. We cannot, he argues, envision a scientific process without the participation of knowing human scientists. Once we admit the presence of human knowers, we have to take account of the ways in which humans know. Many of the ways we acquire and use knowledge are tacit (or inarticulate) and thus cannot be described in the explicit way demanded by positivist-objectivist models of science. As a result, Polanyi concludes that in understanding the natural sciences, as in understanding any other human endeavor, we have to admit the importance of factors such as belief, faith, confidence, and commitment in searching for truth. Models of science that have no place for these factors cannot accurately describe real-world scientific processes.

Gadamer's emphasis is somewhat different. His two targets are historicist approaches that deny the truth claim of the social sciences and formalist methods that presume to reconstruct such truth objectively from a state of pure Cartesian doubt.[6] For Gadamer, the human sciences do indeed have a claim to truth, but that claim cannot completely be discovered by method; the human sciences must involve a dialogue with the texts, traditions, and institutions that form a social order. The fact that certain practices, institutions, and objects have survived, or that certain art is considered "classical," cannot be examined from the throes of Cartesian doubt. We come of age with certain interpretive frameworks with which we view the world. These are what Gadamer terms our "prejudices." We cannot totally escape these prejudices, but by providing us with a framework for interpretation, they enable us to understand the social world. These prejudices contain a truth claim that we can begin to understand only by interacting with others and the objects of society.

For the purposes of this study, the approaches of Polanyi and Gadamer have two sets of consequences for my methodology. First, my theorizing will not involve constructing a formal model, and my historical evidence will not be arrived at by using statistical empiricism. On the theoretical side, the argument is that many of the most important aspects about money cannot be discovered by the use of mathematical modeling. In fact, the use of such models is one reason that neoclassical economics has had such difficulty in dealing with monetary issues. The inherent limits of what can be expressed in functional mathematics mark the limits of our ability to use mathematical models to get at the questions of human meaning embedded in social institutions such as money. Instead, my "method" will be to look at what others have had to say about money and try to develop those lines of thought in light of newer work in economics and the social sciences. The goal is to search for the meaning of money and its surrounding institutions.[7]

Empirical evidence will be provided by means of traditional historiography rather than econometric studies. The main reason for using traditional historiography is that the questions I ask about U.S. monetary history are not about the data but rather about what the data mean. I use the theoretical framework developed within this study to offer a different interpretation of the generally agreed upon "facts."

Second, I will consciously integrate work from outside the sphere of economics. As indicated previously, philosophy will play a role, but so will the work of sociologists such as Georg Simmel and Alfred Schutz, as well as contributions from political science and history. Two thinkers in particular, Karl Marx and F. A. Hayek, provide examples of the kind of interdisciplinary approach I wish to take. Both of their works span the social sciences and both stress the need for integrating a multiplicity of disciplines when studying the crucial questions in social theory.

Spontaneous Order Theory as an Analytical Framework

The interpretive approaches of Gadamer and Polanyi also have something to say about the specific theoretical approach taken here. As noted previously, any attempt to understand social events necessitates that the observer begin from some point of departure. However, in the post-Kuhnian world of the philosophy of science, it is generally recognized that such a point *cannot*, and need not, be Archimedean. It is impossible for the social scientist to step completely outside the world she studies and view it from a scientific Mount Olympus.[8] In Polanyi's (1958, p. 311) terms, doing science requires a commitment to a theoretical framework:

> To accept commitment as the only relation in which we can believe something to be true, is to abandon all efforts to find strict criteria of truth and strict procedures for arriving at the truth. A result obtained by applying strict rules mechanically, without committing anyone personally, can be nothing to anybody.

However, it must also be understood that frameworks themselves must be open to discourse and challenge from the scientific community. To argue that one's perspective is unchallengeable or outside the social process of science is to engage in one of the worst forms of dogmatism.

Nonetheless, the denial of an Archimedean point does not imply that any and all perspectives are equally valid, or that discussion of the validity of frameworks is ruled out. Such a view is also a form of dogmatism in its refusal to listen to, or admit the possibility of, reasons for preferring one perspective to another.[9] Though we may lack some point outside of human discourse for judging our truth claims, we can still offer better or worse *reasons* for accepting or denying particular positions: "Truth becomes the rightness of an action; and the verification of a statement is transposed into giving reasons for deciding to accept it, though these reasons will never be wholly specifiable" (Polanyi 1958, p. 320).

In both extreme dogmatic positions—what we will, following Bernstein (1983), call objectivism and relativism—the scientific process is arbitrarily cut off, either by a claim to extrahuman truth or by the accusation that no manner of truth is possible.[10] Both views fail to recognize that the truths that are possible are ultimately human truths in that they are bound up in the process of human interaction and the development of human traditions and human history. Only continued scientific discourse on both the various frameworks of scientists and their results are capable of discovering such truths.

The importance of commiting to a framework is even greater when doing comparative analyses. Given that this study is an exercise in comparative monetary systems, there must be something with which to compare things. The goal of this study is to compare both current and historical monetary economies to a theoretical evolutionary economy outlined in the chapters to follow. It is this latter system that forms this study's framework for comparing alternative monetary regimes and the economic orders that result from them.

It should be understood that this spontaneous evolutionary process does not describe the history of any actual economy. Rather it is what is known, in the tradition of the Austrian economists, as a "thought experiment."[11] The particular way these evolutionary explanations unfold can best be described as "spontaneous ordering processes" in the tradition of the Scottish moral philosophers.[12] These evolutionary accounts explain how social institutions arise unintentioned as a result of the actions of individuals. By tending to their own needs, people unintentionally develop highly advanced, and highly useful, institutions that serve the public good. We will explore the nature of order-based explanations and then use them to trace the origin of money, the evolution of banking, and various innovations taking place in advanced banking systems. These explanations serve as a framework from which we will survey historical, actual, and potential alternative monetary orders. The evolutionary nature of spontaneous-order approaches forces us to examine not just current monetary institutions but the very origins of money. Advanced financial institutions, like other social institutions, reflect a path dependency, so to understand where actual financial institutions have evolved to and where they might go, we need to see where they came from. This also necessitates using a framework that can span the entire evolutionary process.

Peter Rutland (1985, p. 53, emphasis in original) gives a summary of this use of what he calls utopian strategies:

> Utopian writers are, after all, essentially nothing more than social critics, interested in providing a commentary on certain aspects of existing society. They merely use the description of a non-existent, utopian society as a way of illuminating the present, a distancing device which opens up the possibility of rational observation and analysis. One should not, therefore, assume that utopianism refers solely to the future: on the contrary, one can even argue that it is just as much an interpretation of *past* events as it is a prediction about future ones.

It can be argued that this device of utopian writers is analogous to Marx's strategy through much of his writings. Marx's analysis of capitalism takes place from the vantage point of the socialist future. If we stand in Marx's future world, his analysis of capitalism may be quite accurate, but one could question his whole project by forcing him to defend the validity of his particular point of departure. If Marx's future world is not achievable by human actors, then we ought to be entitled to ask what the value of Marx's analysis is for human problems.[13] Implicit in any critique is an alternative, and implicit in any view of history is a future. Unfortunately, by not giving us more details about where we are headed, Marx effectively closes off discussion of that future and therefore shields his own prejudices from entering the critical conversation.

For these reasons, I want to reemphasize that both my perspective (spontaneous-order theory) and the future it implies (a society of voluntarily interacting persons) are themselves open to criticism. Though it is not my purpose in this study to defend either on their own grounds, I am certainly open to criticism based on alternative perspectives. Instead I want to argue that the value of using these evolutionary processes as a framework derives from the fruitfulness of their results, and that the viability of the ideal monetary order described within is implied by the failures of attempts to stifle it. If this study sheds valuable light on the issues it addresses, and if the alternative it implies is humanly achievable, that would justify the procedure employed. Other methods can, and do, provide other light, but the use of spontaneous-order theory appears to me to be significantly more helpful, and the vision it implies seems more viable, so it is to it that I throw my Polanyian commitment.

Knowledge and the Spontaneous Evolution of Monetary Institutions

What I argue in the chapters to follow is that the bits and pieces of knowledge possessed by individual economic actors are the starting point for monetary economies and economic order. The argument is that these bits of private knowledge are not inaccessible and that social institutions, like money, *make private knowledge available socially.* Some economists have made this point about the price system. Prices, by reflecting the decisions of others, allow us to utilize bits and pieces of private knowledge that would otherwise be inaccessible (see Hayek 1945 and the discussions in Chapters 2 and 3). It is indeed such private knowledge that underlies a monetary economy; but as the economic order evolves, this private knowledge becomes increasingly socially usable. As a result, money and markets allow us to do things as a society that no individual could do alone because they allow us to make use of the tacit knowledge of others in ways that no other institution can. No single individual knows completely how to create and marshal all of the resources needed to construct a skyscraper from the very beginning to the very end, but as a society, with the help of money and the price system, we manage to build them. The basis of monetary order may indeed be the private knowledge of acting humans, but the *essence* of a monetary order is how that private knowledge becomes social and how such social knowledge makes an advanced, complex, and prosperous society possible.

My argument is ultimately a synthesis of a number of distinct ideas from a variety of sources. I intend to paint a picture of monetary and economic order with very broad strokes. All the chapters can be read as exploring some very basic questions about how human beings form, and are formed by the socioeconomic order.

The inspiration for the specific approach of this study derives from the renewed interest among monetary economists in the theory and history of free banking.[14] The reopening of investigation into the operation of a system of competitive note issue, and its corresponding critique of central banking, has broadened the scope of monetary economics. This renewal, combined with a revival of interest in the work of Hayek and, more broadly, in the Austrian school, on the role of knowledge in the market process form the intellectual backdrop for this study.[15]

The dispersed and tacit nature of human knowledge implies that centralized intentional direction of economic processes is highly problematic, if not impossible. The origin and evolution of money and banking support this view. I argue that the evolution of money is a knowledge-extracting and -creating evolutionary process that enables actors to embed a specific good with near-perfect liquidity. Money, as the outcome of this embedding process, becomes a social institution that enables the further evolution of the market process. Money works in much the same way as language in making social communication possible. Money has an advantage over language in that monetary exchange allows for the communication of tacit forms of knowledge in addition to the explicit knowledge communicated by language. This communicative function of money makes possible the heightened complexity of an economy based on monetary exchange, and this complexity requires new institutions of coordination.

As actors acquire and use money balances, a demand for storage facilities arises. This demand leads to the evolution of banking and the creation and use of bank liabilities as money substitutes as well as to other financial innovations. The process of financial evolution is also a discovery process that extracts and creates knowledge, enabling a further level of complexity and coordination among traders. Because we cannot accurately predict the future needs of these traders, any attempt to design financial institutions will be inferior to the results of the spontaneous process of evolution. Markets have built-in feedback processes that ensure the survival of those practices and institutions that facilitate welfare-enhancing exchanges. How these feedback processes play themselves out in financial evolution is the subject of Chapters 3 and 4. For now, we can simply say that a freely evolved banking system will reflect more socially necessary, and usable, knowledge than any consciously designed system could.

Precisely because of their epistemological advantages, free banking systems are better at providing macroeconomic stability and order than is central banking. Using evolutionary free banking systems as a benchmark, I then examine the history of the United States National Banking System (1863-1913) and the creation of the Federal Reserve System (Fed). Interpreted through the framework of free banking, the historical evidence indicates the failure of conscious regulation and direction. The evidence also helps to show where elements of spontaneous order emerged before the Fed was created and how this spontaneity was eventually squelched. The history of the creation of the Fed, and its related problems, illustrate how a less formalistic approach to money and knowledge, such as that of the Austrians, can help to understand the advantages of spontaneous market institutions and the difficulties involved with conscious design and regulation.

The world of the twenty-first century needs to come to grips with the notion that the institutions that are arguably the center of modern Western society, money and finance, are not the product of human design. We need to understand how these institutions did originate and evolve, and how their very spontaneity better enables them to contribute to both orderly market processes and general human welfare. Given that human actors neither created nor control them, monetary institutions have to be treated with a respectfulness deserved by all social institutions and traditions, such as language and law, that facilitate social order. Our attempts to design the undesigned, and undesignable, surely reflect modernity's hubris; and the results of attempts to design the financial system have been, and will continue to be, as disastrous as the failure of the more comprehensive attempts at economic planning in Eastern Europe and the former Soviet Union.

The outline of the book is as follows. Chapter 1 is an overview of previous attempts to explain the origin and use of money, particularly those of neoclassical economists. Chapter 2 offers an alternative evolutionary framework for viewing socioeconomic processes (order analysis), a framework that represents an attempt to take account of many of the factors missing from neoclassical theory. The third chapter applies the ideas of evolution and order to the origin and function of money, arguing that money plays a role analogous to language in extending social communication. The fourth chapter extends the analysis of the evolution of monetary order to the evolution and development of monetary institutions such as banks and the money substitutes and other services they produce. Chapter 5 is an interpretation of the history of pre-Federal Reserve banking in the United States as evidence for the views presented earlier. I conclude by arguing that the evolutionary concept of monetary order I have presented is crucial for understanding debates over economic policy and issues concerning capitalism and socialism more broadly.

Notes

1. The term *atomistic* here refers to models that treat agents as self-contained entities, unaffected by other persons or the culture in which they act. The critique of atomism should not be construed as a rejection of methodological individualism, properly understood. Madison (1990, p. 48) argues that methodological individualism "maintains, not that the individual exists prior to the social or that the social can be 'reduced' to the individual, but that an understanding of social orders . . . can best be achieved by viewing them in the light of the activities of myriad *individual agents.*"

2. Of course, increased state intervention does not need the blessings of economists. It is also in the self-interest of political actors to raise revenue through monetary intervention. The history of central banking and bank regulation reveals seigniorage, not just the ideas of economists, to be the dominant force behind increased government intervention. See the various histories in Vera Smith (1990).

3. See the important contributions of McCloskey (1983, 1985). Also see Boettke (1990b), Prychitko (1990 and 1992) and the papers collected in Klamer, McCloskey, and Solow (1989) and Lavoie (1991).

4. Ludwig Lachmann has argued that the lack of a general philosophical framework to defend their approaches plagued a number of nonformalist thinkers in the history of economic thought. He makes specific reference to Robbins, Knight, and Shackle, all of whom had difficulty defending their methodological approaches because they "had no reservoir of general ideas to fall back on" (personal correspondence with Bruce Caldwell, cited in Caldwell 1991, p. 143). The context of those remarks was an attempt by Lachmann to explain why modern subjectivist economists should attempt to forge links with interpretive philosophers and social theorists.

5. For a selection of readings concerning the recently rediscovered importance of interpretation in the social (and natural) sciences see Dallmayr and McCarthy (1977). Excellent introductions to many of the same issues can be found in Bernstein (1983), Weinsheimer (1985), and Rabinow and Sullivan (1986).

6. From thence follows the title of Gadamer's book, *Truth and Method.* A more explicit title might have been "The Truths in Tradition and the Limits of Method." This title would have placed his real point in the forefront: Not all that is true can be discovered by scientific method.

7. The meaning of a social institution like money should not be restricted to money's meaning in the plans of individual actors; it should also include how its meaning emerges in the unintended consequences of those actions. See Lavoie (1990) and Prychitko (1992) for a discussion of these issues. This distinction can be seen as analogous to Yeager's (1986) discussion of "individual" and "overall" viewpoints in monetary theory.

8. In fact, attempting to do so would deprive us of the very tools of thought we possess as humans: "A presuppositionless thinker would not be a thinker at all, but a *tabula rasa;* he would not have raised himself to the 'vantage point' of God, but would have reduced himself to the helpless pre-socialized state of an infant" (Johnson 1990, p. 187).

9. This version of relativism is one among many strands within the broad discourse movement in the social sciences. The so-called deconstructionist view differs from interpretive approaches because it attempts to show that *any* perspective is simply a result of the social, economic, or personal milieu of the author. This relativist position rightly implies that there are no extrahuman standards for judging truth, but it wrongly extends that denial to *human* standards as well. As a result there is no point to debating the truth of various perspectives and propositions, because all are equally valid within the asserter's frame of reference. Gadamer (1985), Polanyi (1958), and others in the interpretive schools of the discourse movement are attempting to salvage some notion of human truth against positions of this kind. See the discussion in the introduction to Rabinow and Sullivan (1986). Also see the excellent defenses against deconstructionism by Bernstein (1983), Warnke (1987), Madison (1988), and Johnson (1990).

10. The term *objectivism*, which will be a critical target throughout this study, should not be confused with Ayn Rand's philosophy of Objectivism. Though the two share much, especially their rhetorical outlooks, Rand's philosophy is in some ways closer to the approach this study uses. See Johnson (1990) for more on the relationship between Rand and interpretive philosophy.

11. The use of thought experiments as the method of economics is defended in Mises (1966, pp. 236-37), who refers to them as "imaginary constructions" and in Hayek (1978c, p. 41), where he argues: "The usual procedure of classical economic theory [is] to put together, from what we know of our common experience of the conduct of men in relevant situations, a sort of mental model (or thought experiment) of what is likely to happen if many men are exposed to new alternatives."

12. The first attempt to use this way of proceeding in economics is, of course, Adam Smith's metaphor of the invisible hand in *The Wealth of Nations* (1976). Some of Smith's colleagues in the Scottish Enlightenment had also applied this same kind of approach to social analysis. Included among their texts are Bernard Mandeville's (1970) *Fable of the Bees*, which explained how private vices could actually be public virtues; Adam Ferguson's work on social theory; and David Hume's sociophilosophic writings. Hayek (1973, p. 20) attributes his definition of spontaneous order ("of human action but not of human design") to Ferguson. Overviews of Scottish Enlightenment thought can be found in Bryson (1968) and Hamowy (1987). One of the more notable later developers of spontaneous-order theory in economics is Carl Menger, whose spontaneous-order theory of money forms the foundation of Chapters 3 and 4.

13. Arnold (1990, p. 5) describes what he calls the "alternative institutions requirement" of any radical critique: "The radical critic needs to specify a set of alternative social institutions that . . . at least do not have the problems that face existing institutions." Arnold goes on to argue that Marx's radical critique fails this requirement as his particular set of institutions leads to problems similar to those Marx finds with capitalism.

14. On theory see Selgin (1988b), Dowd (1989), Glasner (1989), L. White (1984), Hayek (1978b), V. Smith (1990), and Klein (1974). On history see L. White

(1984), V. Smith (1990), Rockoff (1974), Rolnick and Weber (1983), and Dowd (1992), among others.

15.   On knowledge and the market see Hayek's collections of 1948 and 1978a as well as Lavoie (1985a, 1985b, and 1986a).

1

Problems with Formal Models of
Monetary Exchange

Despite its pervasive presence in the economic and social landscape, money has posed numerous problems for modern economic theory.[1] What to the outsider must seem like the most obvious, most common, and most fundamental aspect of modern economies, the use of money, is to the economist a source of much discomfort and disruption. In short, the properties of real-world moneys throw a monkey wrench into the neoclassical theory of economic exchange. Neoclassicism's most refined set of tools, general equilibrium theory, allows little place for money as a generally accepted medium of exchange, arguably its most important function. In spite of this, theorists have continued to try to use the mathematical and geometrical formalizations of equilibrium theory to construct explanations of the real-world origin and use of money.

Such attempts have met with very limited success, and continued efforts in this direction are likely to be constrained by the inherent limits of the formalistic conception of theory held by neoclassical economists. After overviewing the main problem involved in constructing a general equilibrium theory of money, we will proceed to examine critically several previous attempts to do so. This critical analysis will also indicate the broad outlines of an alternative approach to monetary exchange, one that will be explored in succeeding chapters.

The Fundamental Problem

At the bottom of the problem of explaining money is the nature of the tools that the standard economist uses. General equilibrium theory is accepted by a majority of economists as their scientific approach to the study of human behavior.[2] When such economists analyze a person, institution, or situation it is the constructs of general equilibrium theory that classify their observations and results. To understand why general equilibrium (GE) theory and money are so incompatible, a brief summary of the theory is in order.

Many GE theorists would argue that they are attempting to give a scientific rendering of Adam Smith's "invisible hand." Smith argued that if left to their own devices, individuals would be led "by an invisible hand" to produce beneficial outcomes they neither designed nor intended. GE theory can be thought of as describing the end result of such a process; that is, what would the world the invisible hand leads to look like? It would be a world where all possible benefits from exchange have been exhausted. People would be unable to improve their current outcomes without harming another's. This implies that all markets would need to be cleared. No excess supplies or demands of any commodities could exist. No one would face frustration trying to buy or sell at prevailing prices. Put another way, we can imagine a vector of prices such that the market for every good would be cleared. Is it possible to discover or describe such a vector of prices, and what kinds of assumptions would have to be true in order to arrive at it? These kinds of questions have motivated the development of GE theory.

For general equilibrium to exist, several other things must be true. First, agents must both have perfect knowledge of their own tastes and preferences and know and take as given all of the opportunities available to them in the market. Second, utility functions must obey certain regularity conditions. Third, no trading can take place until the GE price vector is found. These assumptions are necessary to ensure that no false trading takes place. Incomplete knowledge, that is, false trading, would allow for nonmaximizing situations, incompatible with the overall view of a perfectly equilibrated market. Agents in this model match their own preferences (through curves of indifference generated from self-knowledge of their utility functions) with the trade-offs available in the market. Each agent maximizes his utility subject to this budget constraint. At such a point of maximum utility, the agent by definition has equalized the ratio of the marginal utility of each of his goods to its price: $(MU_x/P_x) = (MU_y/P_y) = (MU_n/P_n)$, and so on. This simply indicates that the agent cannot gain any utility by shifting a dollar's worth of consumption to any other good given the array of prices.

It should be noted that the assumption of perfect knowledge by definition implies that there is no uncertainty of any kind.[3] Agents know what the future will bring, they know what they will buy and sell and when they will buy and sell it. Like a frictionless surface in physics, GE theory puts no barriers in the way of action and reaction. The existence of economic "frictions" would imply that potentially mutually beneficial exchanges fall by the wayside because the costs of exchanging prevent them from taking place.

General equilibrium is a model where agents with perfect knowledge maximize known and given utility functions subject to a known and given budget constraint made up of known and given wealth and prices. There are no costs to transacting, no costs to acquiring information, no uncertainty about the future, none of a number of real-world factors that are part and parcel of a real-world economy. More important, because of these assumptions, the world of GE also has no place for firms (all "production" is a functional response to prices of inputs and outputs), no historical time (all maximization takes place at a point along a discrete time vector, and perfect knowledge precludes the mental changes that are our way of recognizing the passage of time), and no place for money.[4]

Fundamentally, there is no need for money in general equilibrium. The GE world is a barter world because trading is in a significant sense predetermined by the assumption of given knowledge. Agents know what they want and they know what they have. This perfection of knowledge permits barter exchanges to occur. As Hahn (1970, p. 3) has noted, "The Walrasian economy that we have been considering . . . is essentially one of barter." Because the GE price vector is found prior to any exchanges, there is no need for a medium of exchange to enter the picture. Goods would not differ in their liquidity, obviating the need for money, which is defined by its superior liquidity. Each good has its own rate of return, and by hypothesis each good is perfectly liquid. This implies the view that money is "barren" (it has no yield of its own),[5] and sense can be made of Keynes's (1937, pp. 115-16) quip "Why should anyone outside a lunatic asylum wish to use money as a store of wealth [in that model]?" The very model that economists consider to be the foundation of their analysis of prices produces a world where the use of money, the object with which real-world prices are formed, is meaningless. Indeed, then, it should not be a surprise that attempts to find a role for money in GE models have met with only marginal success.

Recognition of the paradox of a general equilibrium theory of money is not absent in the literature. Paul Davidson (1978, p. 140), for one, argues that "in a neoclassical world of perfect certainty and perfect markets . . . it would of course be irrational to hold money." Axel Leijonhufvud (1968, pp. 79-80, n. 25) offers the following observation: "The current status of 'pure' monetary theory is a curious one: The preferred analytical tool of many of its most distinguished practitioners is the general equilibrium model. But money cannot be 'important' in theories which devote attention only to equilibrium situations." Karl Brunner and Allan Meltzer (1971, p. 785) note that "the standard theory of exchange, or price, however, provides no hint as to why dominant mediums of exchange emerge." The basic problem is best summarized by Ross Starr (1972, p. 608): "The standard theory [is] a model of exchange in which money does not appear. This poses a dilemma. How do we make money appear without making the standard theory disappear?"

Neoclassical economists seem to be caught on the horns of a dilemma. Their theory cannot explain one of the obvious facts of the real world. So do they keep the theory and ignore the world or restructure their theory to explain the world? At least to this point the vast majority of neoclassical monetary theorists seem to have taken the former way out. The latest advances in monetary theory, especially overlapping-generations and legal restrictions models, seem to be heading off into ever more esoteric territory and are deriving "moneys" that bear little resemblance to anything seen in any existing economy.[6]

Is Partial Equilibrium a Way Out?

The focus of the previous section was on *general* equilibrium theory's difficulties in explaining money. Not all of the economics profession works with GE's tools. Many prefer so-called *partial* equilibrium analysis, which concentrates on particular markets, firms, or industries while holding constant the systemwide effects that interest GE theorists.

Although this approach may be more fruitful than GE for some microeconomic analyses, it is not an improvement when we try to deal with macroeconomic problems. By its very nature, money touches everything, and trying to isolate its effects in individual markets ignores fundamental aspects of what money is all about. Impounding systemic effects in a ceteris paribus clause throws the baby out with the bathwater.

Ultimately, partial equilibrium analysis must either collapse to sectoral GE analysis or be inconsistent. To the extent that partial equilibrium deals with money, firms, and uncertainty (i.e., all the things absent from GE), partial equilibrium analysts can no longer assume that they are dealing with equilibrium situations and so cannot reach welfare conclusions that require equilibrium. If instead partial equilibrium analysts choose to assume away those things, then partial equilibrium analysis is reduced to sectoral general equilibrium and provides no additional or interesting insights. In either case, it is not a way out.[7]

Classical Foundations of Neoclassical Monetary Theory

Previous attempts to understand monetary exchange are numerous and varied and date back to the beginnings of scientific economics. Authors such as Adam Smith and J. B. Say recognized the advantages of money over barter, and most realized that those advantages cannot be captured in oversimplified comparative statics experiments. The benefits of money can best be seen from a dynamic or evolutionary perspective on economic exchange. In general, money allows social actors to more easily achieve their ultimate ends by eliminating the need for a double coincidence of wants in order to exchange.[8] Under barter, an exchange partner must "have what you want" and "want what you have." Money reduces this necessity to a simple double coincidence of "desired exchanges" rather than wants (Jones 1976, p. 761). Money allows us to exchange for a good(s) that we do not directly want but will use to exchange for the goods we ultimately want.

Smith (1976, pp. 26-27) noted the double-coincidence problem and argued that people held certain quantities of desirable goods as a means of overcoming it. Say (1971) anticipated many of the insights of modern monetary theory in his discussion of the essential properties of money. Say (p. 218) had a similar description of the process of overcoming the double-coincidence problem and gave a particularly lucid account of the relative importance of individuals and governments in the development of monetary exchange. William Stanley Jevons's *Money and the Mechanism of Exchange* (1969) contains what many consider to be the seminal discussion of many of the problems of modern money theory.

The starting place for most of GE monetary theory is with the work of Leon Walras, the founder of GE approaches. Most Walrasian models simply introduce money as an (n)th good in a general equilibrium system. Added on as an additional good, money can be neatly fit into GE models. Contrary to GE, however, the real-world problem is that money is not simply a good that shares the same qualities as all other economic goods.[9] The basic point is that money, by definition, is the most liquid good in the economy. GE models, by hypothesis, contain goods with equal liquidity. How then can a theory of equally salable goods make room for a good of extremely high salability?

Problems with the Forgone-Interest View of Money Demand

The lineage of monetary theory, like much of economics in general, begins to diverge in the twentieth century. The focal point of these diverse paths is in the work of Alfred Marshall (1842-1924). One lineage runs from Marshall to Hicks and much of the neoclassical synthesis and monetarism. The other half of Marshall leads to Keynes and the various post-Keynesian approaches to money. Because most of the Keynesian literature is based on criticisms of the neoclassical approach, the distinctly Keynesian arguments will be saved for the end of this chapter.

The next major contribution in neoclassical monetary theory is from Sir John Hicks. In his 1935 article "A Suggestion for Simplifying the Theory of Money," Hicks tried to offer a synthesis of value theory and monetary theory. Attempts at such a synthesis have been at the root of much of modern monetary theory and attempts to explain the origin of money. Hicks (1935, p. 18) poses the basic question that pervades modern theory:

> What has to be explained is the decision to hold assets in the form of barren money, rather than interest- or profit-yielding securities. . . . So long as rates of interest are positive, the decision to hold money rather than lend it, or use it to pay off old debts, is apparently an unprofitable one.

To explain this apparent problem, Hicks invokes a broad concept of transactions costs. Because investing in interest-earning assets is costly, it is conceivable that the interest minus the transaction cost might be negative, making money a better "investment." Hicks can continue to assume that money yields no positive return by arguing that no return can be better (in opportunity-cost terms) than the negative return possible from some costly interest-earning assets. He explains the holding of money without recourse to any explanation of what money does; he shows only that other assets are worse choices due to the costs involved. What follows for Hicks is an exhaustive analysis of these costs and the roles they play.

The problem with this approach, and the bulk of monetary theory descending from it, is that it starts off on the wrong foot by assuming that money is "barren," that is, that it yields no return. The barrenness view has a long history tracing back to Aristotle but runs into difficulties when one reconsiders exactly what is meant by *yield* or *return*. Although it is undoubtedly true that money does not yield an objective, pecuniary return as do interest-earning assets, it does yield a subjective, nonpecuniary return.[10]

The yield provided by money is subjectively evaluated "availability services," that is, money provides services to its possessor by being readily available. Because it is perfectly liquid, and acceptable anywhere, money is held so that its purchasing power is available when needed. The need for liquidity arises because exact knowledge of the timing and amount of income and expenditures is impossible. Money is a bridge over this uncertainty, a "stock of wealth" available in an accessible form. One could imagine the problems involved with trying to both know and time income and expenditures exactly so that one could simply liquidate nonmoney assets at the precise instant that their value is required for expenditures. Money removes this necessity. Even if it turns out that not all of one's money balances are needed this month, the fact that money is available to be spent if needed gives it a positive yield.

Money is not the only good that provides these availability services. For example, one would not say that a fire truck standing in the garage, or an umbrella under one's arm, is wasteful or barren. Obviously when it is needed, a fire truck renders firefighting services, but when standing it is available, waiting to be needed. Imagine that standing fire trucks were considered to be barren, leading to fire companies lending the trucks for other uses and intending to get them back in time for any fires that might arise.[11] The obvious difficulty would be knowing when fires would occur and timing the loans of the trucks to work around the fires. Our inability to exactly predict the occurrence of fires is an example of the kind of uncertainty that availability services (such as those provided by standing fire trucks) can overcome.

The problem with the barrenness view derives from the explicit or implicit general equilibrium framework adopted by its modern-day protagonists: It is difficult to fit subjective yields into GE's models. The structure of GE deemphasizes the importance of the subjective perceptions of human minds; GE theorists prefer to work with the objective traces of those perceptions, such as indifference curves.[12] If the return is not measurable in some way, it is difficult to fit into the mathematical models of general equilibrium.[13]

All of these arguments gloss over the more important point that the yield on money held is fundamentally no different from the yield on *any other good*. All goods have subjective yields, and the ultimate explanation for purchases of any goods is that they provide services to their possessors.[14] Although the specific services money provides differ from those of other goods in that money is neither a production good nor a consumption good, the fact that its services are subjectively evaluated makes it like other economic goods.[15] The expected services of the money sacrificed to purchase a good is traded off against the perceived value of the good. GE models are an attempt to objectify utility into indifference curves and budget constraints. Outside of this model, however, value emerges from the interplay of human minds with other human minds in the buying and selling of the market. How much any individual values a particular good is best (although often not completely) known by that individual.[16]

For money, the trade-off is between its availability services (which are dependent on its purchasing power, among other things) and the services provided by either interest-earning assets or other useful goods. The money-versus-goods trade-off is simply a question of service yields, but the money-versus-other-financial-assets trade-off is more complex. This is because many other financial assets have a moneyness about them and can be used as media of exchange (e.g., demand deposits).

One can argue that the money-assets trade-off takes place along continuum representing a trading off of availability or moneyness (liquidity) versus interest.[17] The expectation would be that those assets that possess a fair amount of moneyness would have lower objective (interest) yields, offset by their increased availability yields.[18] Demand deposits might be a good example here. Assets with less moneyness would have correspondingly higher interest yields. The inconveniences of using most money market mutual funds as regular checking accounts might be reflected in their higher interest yields as compared to regular demand deposits. Finally, items such as Treasury bills or corporate bonds, which have almost no moneyness, may have the highest (risk-adjusted) interest yields of all. The rational moneyholder will try to equalize availability and interest yields on all of these various margins. The important point is that the holding of money is no more problematic than is the purchasing of any other good: The decision to hold money is a decision to use some wealth to purchase availability services. The cost of holding money is either the forgone services of unbought goods or the forgone services from the interest-plus-partial-availability returns on nonmoney financial assets.[19]

Unfortunately, the literature following Hicks remains confined to the narrow money-bonds trade-off. Keynesian textbook models (e.g., Froyen [1986, p. 132ff.]) portray money versus bonds as the only choice to be made under the wealth constraint. Paul Samuelson (1947, pp. 122-24) continued the Hicksian view when he argued that in the absence of any uncertainty or transaction costs ("frictions"), it is unclear why anyone would hold money when alternative positive returns are available. In fact, Samuelson suggests that in the absence of such frictions, either money must somehow offer a positive return, or the rate of interest will have to fall to zero. There is no other way to explain away the disparity of returns on money and bonds.[20] With neither of these alternatives appearing very palatable, most theorists have gone on to suppose that this paradox can be explained only by some sort of transaction costs and/or uncertainty.[21]

Transaction Costs Explanations of Monetary Exchange

Karl Brunner and Alan Meltzer (1971) offer an important neoclassical attempt to explain the function of money in anything resembling a real-world economy. Their starting point is to "explain the use and holding of money" (p. 784) given that some theorists have argued that the use of money may, under certain circumstances, reduce social welfare. The difficulty in doing so is that "the standard theory of exchange, or price . . . provides no hint as to why dominant mediums of exchange emerge" (p. 785). The (n)th good can be any good imaginable because clearing the (n)th market requires no specific properties whatsoever. As

Brunner and Meltzer also note, logically, this is equally likely to be any good, and the particular good selected has no effect on the allocation of real resources (pp. 785-86).

In contrast, Brunner and Meltzer want to show why particular goods emerge as money and to explain what services money provides. The key to the use of money, they argue, is that information is decentralized and distributed unevenly among traders. This is the transaction cost necessary to explain away the paradoxes thrown up by strict GE theory. Because information is dispersed, it is costly to acquire. More specifically, they argue that the marginal cost of acquiring information about a good depends on the good in question and that there are noticeable patterns of distribution of the extent of these costs across groups of goods. In addition, the marginal costs of information acquisition diminish as goods are used more frequently. The existence of information costs and the frequency condition together provide the foundation for an explanation of the use of money.

Brunner and Meltzer also point out that if a good is used more widely, not only will it be less costly to learn about it but its price will also have a smaller dispersion than less frequently used goods. Once recognized, these informational costs can be added on to the standard theory of consumption (p. 787). Specifically, the neoclassical utility maximizer has two additional options: (1) he can devote resources to increasing his information about the quality of goods (hoping that the expected utility gained through higher quality outweighs the cost of information acquisition) or (2) he can attempt to make sequences of exchanges by acquiring goods with low marginal information costs and subsequently exchanging them for the ultimate desiderata. These are referred to as the "real costs of transacting or exchanging" (p. 787). Agents can now use these transaction chains to more easily acquire their ultimate wants. The question of how long such chains should be is found by comparing "the marginal cost of acquiring information to the marginal cost of rearranging the transaction chain and to the benefits obtained from these and alternative uses of resources" (p. 788). In other words, can utility be most increased by acquiring new information or by more efficiently using existing information to obtain ultimate goods?[22]

Brunner and Meltzer next model the various informational aspects of exchange and conclude that traders have incentives to arrange their transaction chains to use goods whose qualities are better known because this will lower the total amount and variance of resources spent in finding efficient transaction chains (p. 792). This also implies, given the first condition, that particular goods will tend to be used in these chains and that knowledge about these chains is substitutable for more detailed knowledge about market conditions and qualities of goods (p. 792). Indirect exchanges become informational shorthands.

To demonstrate that this process must converge toward a small number of media of exchange, Brunner and Meltzer invoke their second condition—that frequency of use decreases the marginal cost of information acquisition about a good. As some transactors begin to use certain goods in their chains, they are induced to use the goods again, as the first usage lowers subsequent costs. More important, this induces others to use the goods in question, which in turn lowers the relevant costs. The result is "clustering and the convergence of individuals' chains toward a common pattern" (p. 793). By relaxing the GE assumption of zero transaction costs, Brunner and Meltzer are able to explain the reasons people use money.

Like much of the other literature, Brunner and Meltzer's work views money as the logical outcome of individualistic utility maximization processes. In short, their contribution is really to argue that the constraints of the maximization process should take account of information-related transaction costs, thus allowing for chains of transactions. Money then does nothing more than allow atomistic agents to more efficiently achieve utility maxima. This approach, as is true of GE in general, ignores fundamentally social aspects of money and monetary exchange.

Also absent are any discussions of either the effects of money use on social relationships (other than in terms of greater social efficiency due to a greater number of mutually beneficial exchanges) or how such social outcomes might feed back to affect the kinds of choices that individuals make. Finally, it is difficult, as we shall argue, for static approaches like Brunner and Meltzer's to explain evolutionary processes such as a monetary order. Clearly, reaching the point of using money is not the end of the story. As will be argued in the next few chapters, the use of money so transforms the economic landscape that claiming that it allows individuals to better achieve their ends is not nearly enough.[23]

Other transaction costs approaches to the use of money fall victim to many of the same problems. Jurg Niehans (1971, p. 779) explicitly introduces a broad concept of transaction costs in order to generate a money economy. Niehans's argument has many of the same problems discussed earlier, but it has an additional one worth noting. For a model to generate a unique medium of exchange, different goods have to have different transaction costs. Niehans (p. 779) models these costs by "assessing arbitrary positive values to transaction costs rates in a random fashion." This assumption leaves the economist unable to explain why any *given* good will emerge as money. Why have gold and silver done so historically? What is it about these particular goods that have made them so suitable, and does that have implications for how we, today, should arrange our monetary institutions? Niehans would argue that their transaction costs are lower, but the logical response is to ask why. He cannot explain *why* particular goods become money, only *that* certain ones *will*. More specifically, the whole transaction costs approach seems to associate "moneyness" with some physical property of goods rather than with the "social nature of money, in the sense that you want it because other people want it" (Nagatani 1978, p. 116).

In another variation on this theme, Perlman (1971) introduces a form of transaction costs that would generate money in a general equilibrium model. He (p. 239) concludes that "the holding of money . . . is a perfectly valid equilibrium phenomenon given that there are transaction costs." But, are such transaction costs simply an ad hoc addition to general equilibrium models? It certainly is true that the real-world has transaction costs, in some sense of the term, but how useful is GE when each explanation of real world phenomena requires introducing a different auxiliary assumption? As noted earlier, the past twenty years of economic theory has seen the rise of this approach. We now have transaction costs explanations of money, firms, and unemployment, all of which reduce the power and elegance of GE theory. It will be argued further on that these approaches point out failures of GE rather than advantages of introducing transaction costs.[24]

Information, Decentralization, and the Functions of Money

One advantage of general equilibrium theory, and its application to money, is that it purports to explain systemic outcomes as the results of individual choices. Beneficial exchanges need not be created or planned by some overarching agency but can emerge naturally from the optimizing behavior of human agents. Such decentralized explanations are congenial to those who think in general equilibrium terms.[25] It is natural that some GE theorists would then focus on the ability of money to allow exchange to take place at a more decentralized level than moneyless GE models, which rely on an auctioneer to set the terms of trade. Although this fundamental insight seems acceptable, its particular manifestations in the literature have been less than satisfactory.

One modern attempt along these lines is by Ostroy and Starr (1974). They argue that "the function of a common medium of exchange is to allow the decentralization of the trading process" (p. 1094). The advantage of money is that it allows more mutually beneficial exchanges to take place by decentralizing the trading process via the informational gains obtained in monetary economies. Ostroy and Starr begin by assuming that all exchanges must be some type of quid pro quo trade. The problem then is that traders have to obtain the information necessary to coordinate all of the exchanges. For Ostroy and Starr, the lack of a double coincidence of wants is a communication problem.

To trade one commodity for another, one has to know that there is another person willing to trade reciprocally. The problem is knowing about a potential trade and then being in the physical and temporal location needed to execute it. When money is introduced, agents need to know only that potential traders accept the medium of exchange. Ostroy and Starr (p. 1094) argue that "the informational requirements of barter imply the need for a central coordination of trade" but that money's role is to allow this to happen in such a way that "no such communication is necessary."

Their model of the trading process involves a price vector (formed prior to the process of exchange, presumably through some tattonnement procedure), a matrix of excess demands, and a matrix of initial endowments. The price vector is known so that traders can know if their exchanges satisfy quid pro quo (p. 1094). The model explicitly excludes credit arrangements and goods destruction (pp. 1095-96). They also define decentralization such that a decentralized trade is one that individual traders make based on a small amount of widely known information that they themselves may be presumed to know. The key to money's role is that it brings a slackness to the trading process. The money commodity will be such that people will hold stocks greater than what is minimally sufficient for direct use. This slack acts as a surrogate for any missing information involved in exchanges, which leads to the decentralization of exchange (p. 1108). Money is a good that can be held in inventory in order to reduce the informational costs of barter and better reduce nonmoney excess demands.

Ostroy's (1973) own work focuses on these informational properties of monetary exchange. His main argument is that Walrasian models exclude the possibility of decentralized exchange and beg all of the informational questions. This is why it makes sense that GE models have no money: "It does no good to append what is a trading constraint to a model which ignores trade" (p. 597). When we introduce trade with other people, instead of trade with "the market," questions of information have relevance and the need for money becomes clear. Monetary exchange is a way for information about excess supplies of goods to be passed along to other traders (p. 603). Money performs this function by acting as a placeholder until a satisfactory reciprocal excess demand can be found: "When money is used, the parties to the transaction are admitting their inability to predict with whom and how the account will be settled" (p. 604). That money can lie in wait reduces the amount of information necessary to make exchanges. One need only have a double coincidence of desired exchanges, not wants.

Starr's (1972) own work also deals with money's ability to overcome the double-coincidence-of-wants problem. He introduces a good into a general equilibrium model such that all trades with the good (1) do not worsen the sign of either party's excess demands, (2) meet quid pro quo requirements, and (3) lead to, in the long run, all excess supplies and demands equaling zero. The only good that can satisfy all three of these conditions is some generally accepted medium of exchange. Once introduced, money can perform these functions and the model can be solved. However, he offers no explanation of how money might, in fact, be introduced into the exchange process.

In light of the literature on the ability of markets and prices to communicate information, specifically in light of the debate over the possibility of rational resource allocation under central planning (to be discussed in Chapter 6), Ostroy and Starr's approach needs to be examined critically. Ostroy and Starr appear to argue that a central trade coordinator would be better at handling the informational problems associated with barter than would decentralized exchange. The advantage of money is that it lessens these informational requirements so that no central coordinator is necessary. If we reduce the problem of finding a trading partner (matching excess supplies and demands), one now need only find someone with an excess supply of the desired good and trade it for money, because money is a good that traders are always willing to accept in exchange.

Supporters of this view misunderstand the nature of information in the market and have an overly static understanding of the role of money. As is common with neoclassical approaches to informational questions, the problem to be overcome is one of getting agents to acquire information that is "out there" and available.[26] The implied solution is to append information as one more good agents desire and to rework the utility maximization problem.[27] The difficulty this approach (like that of the writers in the previous section) runs into is that most contemporary theories of knowledge argue that "out there" is precisely what knowledge is not. Rather knowledge emerges from the interaction between human minds and the social institutions and traditions that constitute society. Properly functioning social institutions are ones that enable us to utilize the knowledge of others by making available the contents of their minds.

To model the role of money as assisting in the acquisition of already existing information appears to beg the question of how that information came to be. A more fruitful exploration of money could examine how money might make possible the *coming-into-being* (rather than the acquisition) of information. By easing the process of exchange, money allows us to better express our wants and better deploy our skills and abilities in the market. The process of monetary exchange brings knowledge into existence that might otherwise not be knowable to other agents. It will be argued in the third chapter that this aspect of monetary exchange is far more important than money's ability to facilitate the acquisition of existing information.

In an important sense, this point is a question of statics and dynamics. If the market were frozen at a point in time, one could argue that money's role is to reallocate information more efficiently, but in a dynamic market process, money's role is far different. In fact, it seems as though rather than simplifying information problems as Ostroy and Starr think, money exponentially complicates them. The use of money brings with it a degree of division of labor and specialization that makes advanced production possible. Barter economies will be inherently static and simple societies precisely because of the problems that economists have pointed out, that is, problems of finding trading partners. But as complex as "solving the equations" of a barter economy might be for a central coordinator, the "solution" to a money economy is infinitely more difficult due to the increasing complexity that money makes possible.

Because the use of money lightens computational burdens on individuals at points in time, it makes exchange and production that much easier. Yet this increase in economic activity drives the economy to a new level of complexity, which increases these informational burdens. At the same time, though, money allows this complexity to stay reasonably coordinated by making possible profit-and-loss accounting for both firms and individuals.[28] As the economy gets more complex, it brings forth more ways of coping with that complexity—foremost among them is money. In addition, as more ways of coping with complexity emerge, they also allow the economy to sustain higher degrees of complexity. The roles and functions of money have to be examined both in terms of less objective views of information and more evolutionary views of monetary exchange and economic order. The transaction cost literature is lacking in both.

Recent Evolutionary Approaches

Dissatisfaction with the overly static nature of both monetary theory and economics in general, has lead to more evolutionary (though still within the broad confines of neoclassical theory) views of the origin and functions of money.[29] Two related contributions deserve specific attention.

The first of these attempts at an evolutionary theory was by Robert Jones in 1976. One advantage of Jones's approach is that he is concentrating on the origin of money, as well as on its development and functions. Building on the work of earlier theorists such as Carl Menger and Jevons, and the more recent neoclassical literature, Jones tries to explain how money emerges through the decentralized, individual, voluntary behavior of human actors. He begins by explicitly attempting to answer the mystery that Menger had posed many years earlier: How can self-interest explain a social convention that appears to have to be the result of some explicit social agreement? Jones (1976, p. 758) defines monetary exchange as a situation where one good is at least half of every exchange, and where every other good is not reexchanged. The former good is what we call the medium of exchange. Jones also reviews much of the literature that was discussed earlier, concluding, as was concluded here, that earlier approaches have failed to provide an explanation of how monetary trade emerges (given that it is beneficial) or have failed to specify why the necessary conditions for money's emergence tend to be so prevalent (p. 759). Jones has to make four assumptions about the nature of exchange to fuel his theory: Exchange must (1) be voluntary and bilateral, (2) be based on a set of consistent and parametric general equilibrium prices, (3) be costly, and (4) involve limited information about other specific individuals.

People come to the market with fixed trading strategies and attempt to execute trades in the least costly way possible, including by minimizing search time (p. 762). Trading strategies are based on what people think are the probabilities that any random trading partner will be willing to buy or sell a given good. These probabilities in turn, rest on two assumptions. First, it is assumed that an identical percentage of traders wish to buy a good as wish to sell it. This is a market-clearing assumption, and this probability is denoted $P(i)$. Second, there is no relationship between what another trader offers and what he desires.

Based on this, Jones denotes the probability of trading good i for good j as $P(i)P(j)$ (p. 763). These probabilities can be additive for indirect exchange, so that the probability of executing any indirect exchange sequence is the sum of the probabilities of executing each half. The most efficient medium of exchange (n) will be one that maximizes the probability of encountering it $[P(n)]$ in a random pairing of trading partners. Of course this, in turn, depends on the nature of the other good in the sequence (p. 764).

The important step in the process is realizing that traders will choose a two-step trading sequence rather than barter if $P(n) > P(i) + P(j)$, that is, if "the fraction of individuals in the market desiring to buy or sell that most common good exceeds the sum of the fractions [for] the two goods he is ultimately exchanging" (p. 765). If the subjective probabilities are similar across people, then that one good will emerge as the medium of exchange. Jones notes that this model explains the possible coexistence of barter and monetary exchange. He also captures the evolutionary process. As more people begin to demand good n as a medium of exchange, $P(n)$ rises and people begin to recognize it. The rise in probability increases the use of n as a medium: $P(n)$ is now more likely to be greater than $P(i) + P(j)$, which increases $P(n)$ again. This evolutionary advance in $P(n)$ stops when subjective estimates of $P(n)$ match the true probability of exchanging for it. Jones concludes by pointing out that the first commodity moneys would indeed be very common goods according to this scenario and "that this commonness is a *market* characteristic of goods rather than an intrinsic *physical* characteristic" (p. 775, emphasis in original). As we shall see later in our detailed examination of Menger's work, Jones's conclusion matches Menger's emphasis on subjective valuations of differing goods as leading to money and decentralized exchange.

Though in many ways Jones's analysis is superior to those that came before, several lingering problems remain. One concern is that agents have fixed trading strategies (based on parametric prices) that are decided upon before entering the market. It would seem as though these assumptions deterministically drive the results toward an outcome implied in the assumptions. Agents simply reveal true probabilities during the exchange process, but no genuine learning takes place, no new knowledge or discovery is generated, and there is no feedback process from the results to the trading strategies. Agents only incorporate new information into a fixed framework—they have no way of changing the framework. The assumption of parametric prices also restricts any learning process by preventing agents from using new information to affect prices. Movements in prices are an important way for agents to receive and communicate new information and interpretations in the market, and assuming parametric prices negates this all-important process.

Jones (p. 763, n. 8) also "characterize[s] the search for a complementary trading partner as a sequence of Bernoulli trials."[30] The assumption is made in order to facilitate the mathematics, but this both limits the individuality of the agents and further restricts their ability to learn and adjust, especially in combination with the previous assumptions. A truly evolutionary process will be an open-ended one where the set of facts at any point in the future has not been predetermined by the facts at some point in the past.[31] A theory of social institutions must be compatible with the existence of genuine novelty and new knowledge and the ways in which social actors attempt to utilize that knowledge. Though an improvement, Jones's model misses these crucial steps.[32]

Oh (1989) attempts to repair two of the shortcomings of Jones's model. Oh argues first that Jones's model ought to consider the possibility of conditional rather than fixed trading strategies. Because it does not, any level of monetization is a possible outcome. Observations of existing economies indicate that high levels of monetization seem to be much more stable, and hence much more likely, outcomes. Second, the assumption of fixed trading strategies,

> implies that the same individual can sometimes refuse to accept a certain commodity as a means of payment while he accepts that commodity at other times. Thus, in Jones' model, under an equilibrium of partial monetization, a *generally acceptable* medium of exchange does not exist. (p. 102, emphasis added)

Oh shows that using conditional trading strategies leads to a high level of monetization and that barter will always be a usable option under particular circumstances.

His key change is to allow traders to adopt strategies "that permit them to carry out exchange according to the types of encounters they meet in the market" (p. 109). This allows agents to receive feedback from their interaction in the market. Given some set of responses to attempting to pursue one strategy, the agent may decide to pursue another and will learn from its results. The assumption of conditional trading strategies brings Oh's model closer to adopting novelty and learning, though he too remains inside a world of parametric prices and Bernoulli trials (p. 105 n. 2), with all of their shortcomings. These evolutionary approaches are improvements over the static, allocative questions tackled by earlier theorists in the neoclassical tradition, but they too fall short of a satisfactory explanation of any real-world evolutionary process of monetary exchange.

The Keynesian Dissent

The line of thought explored in the previous several sections is one of two descending from Marshallian economics. Opposed to this neoclassical approach is a line of monetary thought beginning with Keynes and extending through post-Keynesians such as Paul Davidson and G.L.S. Shackle. Their starting point has been a rejection of several of the underlying assumptions of the neoclassical approach, especially those dealing with general equilibrium theory. Though this path has generated more helpful insights through its criticism than through its constructive theorizing, an exploration of its arguments will prove helpful.

The major difference found in the Keynesian literature is that money's function as a medium of exchange is derived from its function as a unit of account and store of value. Keynes (1930, vol. 1, p. 3)[33] begins his *Treatise on Money* with

> Money-of-Account, namely that in which Debts and Prices and General Purchasing Power are *expressed*, is the primary concept of a theory of money. . . . Something which is merely being used as a convenient medium of exchange on the spot may approach to being money . . . [but] Money-Proper in the full sense of the term can only exist in relation to a Money-of-Account.

With this switch in emphasis comes a difference in Keynes's (p. 4) view of the origin of money:

> It is the State or Community . . . which decides what it is that must be delivered as a lawful or customary discharge of a contract which has been concluded in terms of the money-of-account. The State, therefore, comes in first of all as the authority of law which enforces the payment of the thing which corresponds to the name or description in the contract. But it comes in doubly when, in addition, it claims the right to determine and declare *what thing* corresponds to the name, and to vary its declaration from time to time—when, that is to say, it claims the right to re-edit the dictionary. . . . It is when this stage in the evolution of Money has been reached that Knapp's Chartalism—the doctrine that money is peculiarly a creation of the State—is fully realised.

In opposition to the line of thought examined previously, Keynes bypasses explaining money as emerging from the interactions of individuals and opts for the view that in the modern world, an external authority imposes a money on society.

This approach is understandable (though not necessarily correct) when the unit of account or store-of-value function is primary. *Which* particular good serves as money is not as important as that *some* good does. By serving as a unit of account, money allows comparisons of the values of goods and permits a common denominator with which to trade them.[34] As a store of value, money allows us to defer decisions until the uncertain future without suffering a pecuniary penalty. As both Keynes (p. 7) and Shackle (1973, p. 43) emphasize, the choice of the money commodity is purely conventional and, therefore, apparently beyond explanation. For Keynes, the origin of money is the declaration that some good will serve as the unit of account (and will thus acquire value through time) and be the thing by which all debts are ultimately settled.

The broad Keynesian approach needs one more pillar on which to balance its theory of money—real-world uncertainty. As noted previously, in the real world we do not know (nor can we sufficiently predict) the course of future events. Genuine surprise and novelty are the order of the day. Given this, Keynesians see that one of the advantages of money is that it allows us to defer decision-making in the face of such uncertainty. Because we can never know which way the course of history will unfold, holding money allows us to hedge our bets by waiting until we know more before we extract from society the entitlement we earned by virtue of the sale of productive services, and the receipt of money, at some earlier point. To quote Shackle's (1973, pp. 44-45) elegant prose at length:

> The need for money as a store of value is an aspect of the basic, irremediable and permanent insufficiency of knowledge, and this insufficiency of knowledge is an aspect of time itself, which washes away knowledge (the relevance and applicability of knowledge) as the tide carries off the daily flotsam of the sea. When today's needs have become yesterday's, we must make up our minds afresh, for tomorrow and many tomorrows which are too distant yet for any decision about them. Money, when we keep it in stock, is what enables us to put off deciding what to buy.

It is the combination of money as a store of value and the existence of genuine uncertainty that leads to the Keynesian critique of traditional monetary theory. According to Paul Davidson (1978, pp. 140-41):

> In a neoclassical world of perfect certainty and perfect markets, with a Walrasian auctioneer assuring simultaneous equilibrium at a given point in time, it would of course be irrational to hold money as a store of value as long as other assets provided a certain positive yield. In the absence of uncertainty, neoclassical theory had no room for the store of value function in its definition of money; nor would money play any more important role than peanuts in a neoclassical world. . . . Why hold money if it is really not needed for transactions since in equilibrium goods trade for goods, and since the present and the future value of all economic goods can be determined (at least in a probability sense) with complete certainty?

The Keynesian argument extends from theory to broad conclusions drawn about the efficacy of markets. If one accepts the Keynesian view, then one is led to question how intertemporal coordination ever takes place.[35] As the well-known Keynesian (Keynes 1936, p. 210) critique of

Say's law argues, What ensures that today's decision not to consume (i.e., hold money) is linked with today's decision as to what to produce tomorrow?[36] The standard Keynesian answer is "very little," and the resulting policy prescription is to use government to adjust savings and investment as necessary to repair the miscoordination engendered by a money-using economy. The classical theory might work for a world of certainty and rational calculation, but in the world of the "animal spirits," various psychological propensities, and pervasive uncertainty, money's role as "a link between the present and the future" (Keynes 1936, p. 293) has to be seriously considered and worked into economic analysis.

Although much of this literature echoes points of criticism that have been directed at the neoclassical literature, it too remains unsatisfying for a variety of reasons. The root of its problems is the overly exaggerated role given to conscious intent, in this case the state, both in the origin and control of money.

The Keynesian approach really does not provide an explanation of the origin of money. We are told what money does (or should do) but not offered an explanation of how it comes to do it. To say that what the state declares as legal tender is money is to somewhat oversimplify. Historically it is clearly the case that states have only given recognition to moneys already accepted as a matter of custom by members of the community.[37] Money is, in Hayek's (1967a) terms, a "complex phenomenon" that cannot be explained simply by the intent of particular actors or groups. Instead it evolves out of a multitude of different, yet dovetailing, actions. Given this, we need to explain (as the neoclassical literature tries to) how such a complex, customary process unfolds.

If, however, Keynes is merely saying that the state can alter the terms of exchange at its pleasure by simply redefining the monetary unit or altering its supply, then other problems arise. In fact, that this is what he apparently means by defending Knapp's Chartalism is revealed in his comment about the state being able to "re-edit the dictionary." Although it is certainly true that the state can *legally* take such actions, it cannot *compel* the populace to accept them. As we shall see in Chapter 3, Keynes's analogy of money and language is appropriate, but his view of language belies his view of money. As S. Herbert Frankel (1977, p. 43) comments on this passage:

> It is not true that the State or any other authority can either enforce or write a dictionary, even if it wished to do so. A dictionary is not created by an author like a novel or scientific work. A dictionary is a collection

of words which *society* has created in the past and is continuously creating and re-creating in the present and the future. Nobody has ever been able to force a single word onto society which the individuals composing it did not wish to use.

Though perhaps overstated, Frankel's point is essentially correct. Money and language are both complex social conventions that rest on an intersubjective understanding between social actors. That understanding (in the case of money, the understanding Frankel points to is trust) has to evolve from the mutual orientation and reorientation of the various actors. Attempts to impose or alter this understanding from the outside, whether by the state or by other means of coercion, are highly problematic. The trust that engenders money is a delicate social understanding that cannot simply be mechanistically manipulated.

The entire Keynesian argument runs something like the following: In a world of certainty there would be no need for money and economic coordination would be exact. Given the existence of uncertainty, money finds a use, and economic coordination is (substantially) inexact. To make up the losses in economic coordination, we need some external force, likely government policy, to pick up the slack. Therefore, money-using economies will never be perfect and always imply the potential need for some amount of governmental adjustment.

The confusion in this argument is that it is comparing the wrong two states of affairs. Uncertainty is not going to go away any time soon, and to complain that the world is imperfect because of it is like complaining about all the problems that gravity causes. The relevant question is, What kind of money and monetary institutions best allow us to cope with uncertainty? In order to provide an answer, we must examine various social processes, including both the market process and the political process, to determine which will better solve the problem. To simply assert that where the market is imperfect, government will step in and solve the problem is to ignore the very real question of the possible imperfections of government. It is between these two sets of imperfections that we must make our choice.

Instead of comparing the real world with some world of perfect coordination, one should compare a real world with money to a real world without it. Consider savings and investment and the complicated credit systems involved with both. The existence of money and uncertainty clearly make credit systems less than perfect, but at the same time one has to acknowledge that it is the very use of money that allows for such relationships in the first place by permitting greater sophistication in tailoring production to intertemporal preferences.[38] A world without money makes credit relationships difficult and, in so doing, masks intertemporal coordination problems. We cannot begin to discuss the imperfections of monetary exchange without first acknowledging that money can bring about the kind of complex and creative relationships that concern Keynes.

The analogy to language returns here as well. We might complain that "words get in the way" and that we would be better off if we were telepathic and could directly access thoughts. We could bemoan all of the misunderstandings that occur because we have to use language. But in the end, it is only language that permits us to think and communicate in the first place. We think in language, we talk in language, we *live* in language. It would be highly questionable to argue that the imperfections of language require an external agency to come in and mandate the usage and nonusage of particular words and phrases in order to solve the problem.[39] Yet when the analogous argument is made for money, few voices are raised in objection. The lack of objection may stem from the Keynesian legacy of ignoring the question of possible imperfections of the political process, either within it or caused by it. The question to be asked is whether imperfect government or imperfect social interaction will better permit money to serve as a socioeconomic coordinator.

Conclusion

The various attempts of economists to explain the uses and functions of money have led us down a number of different paths—some more fruitful than others. The attempts of some neoclassical economists to explain money as the unintended result of some form of human action is indeed praiseworthy, as is their emphasis on information and decentralization. However, they are to be criticized for their failure to take seriously human imperfections, human knowledge, and the existence of uncertainty. In addition, by choosing to model money as the result of an atomistic, asocial maximization process rather than as part of a broader process of human action, such theorists miss some of money's most fundamental properties. By trying to explain money with the tools of general equilibrium theory, neoclassical monetary theorists wind up with a "money" that looks very little like anything that can be seen in the real world.

Keynesian theorists, however, have taken uncertainty and imperfection seriously, at least within the market process. The Keynesian argument falters by not applying these with equal force to the political process. Entrepreneurs are fallible and subject to the "animal spirits," but political actors are presumed to be immune to such distorting factors.[40] In addition, Keynesian approaches seem to not give any recognition to the things that money makes possible; money has benefits as well as costs. The real questions ought to be (1) What are money's benefits and costs? and (2) Will the political or market process better allow money to provide as many net benefits as it is capable of providing? In the attempt to more accurately characterize the costs and benefits of money, markets, and politics and to offer an alternative theoretical framework for money and the monetary economy, I will try in the chapters to follow to come to grips with both of these questions.

Notes

1. Karl Brunner (cited in King and Plosser 1986, p. 93) has noted precisely this tension: "The existence and use of money remained an embarrassing puzzle for monetary analysis. We observe over man's history that social groups without generally accepted media of exchange exhibit poor survival characteristics."

2. On general equilibrium theory see Walras (1977), Pareto (1971), Hicks (1946), Samuelson (1947), Hahn (1973) and Debreu (1959). A useful overview of the history of the theory can be found in Weintraub (1985).

3. The assumption of perfect knowledge does not, however, preclude risk as opposed to uncertainty. Risk can be defined as possible courses of events with known probabilities, such as the toss of a coin. Uncertainty refers to a situation with unknown probabilities and, perhaps, unknown possible courses of events. An uncertain event might be the likelihood of a third world war. One of the best discussions of this distinction is also one of the first; see Knight (1971).

4. The importance of the timelessness of the GE model can hardly be understated. The assumption of perfect knowledge by its nature implies certainty and timelessness. Human beings experience the passage of time as changes in knowledge. If our knowledge were indeed perfect we would never experience it changing and would not experience time in any relevant sense. The fact that we do experience this historical time due to our imperfect and evolving knowledge causes significant problems for the real-world relevance of GE. Its use of so-called Newtonian time, which lacks the irreversibility inherent in real historical time, is one major obstacle to its relevance. On the nature of time and knowledge see Bergson (1960), Husserl (1964), Schutz (1967) and Shackle (1986).

The implications of this view for the usefulness of GE are discussed in Mises (1966), O'Driscoll and Rizzo (1985), Davidson (1978), and Shackle (1982).

5. This view is normally accepted by general equilibrium theorists and by those working in a GE tradition in monetary theory (see Wallace 1983) but is questionable from other perspectives. See the contributions of Hutt (1956), Selgin (1987a) and Horwitz (1990b).

6. Examples of the New Classical view of money can be found in Wallace (1983, 1988). An example of modern monetary theory's technical wizardry and its corresponding lack of real-world relevance can be found in Engineer and Bernhardt (1991).

7. A more developed argument for the inconsistency of partial equilibrium can be found in Fink (1984-85).

8. This basic insight dates all the way back to Aristotle's *Politics.*

9. See Leijonhufvud (1968, p. 79, emphasis in original): "Cash is *the* perfectly liquid asset. This suggests the 'essential and peculiar' role that money plays. . . . Much of modern monetary theory deals with money as just one of the n goods in a general equilibrium model. It is now clear that *in general competitive equilibrium all goods are perfectly liquid.* . . . Money has no special status, and in a model which deals only with situations characterized by exchange equilibrium, money is (at most) 'just another good.'" See also Clower (1967, p. 85 and 1969, p. 101), Davidson (1978, p. 149) and Nagatani (1978, p. 106).

10. One case when money does yield a pecuniary return would be during deflation, when the real value of money increases as it is held. Obviously, inflation would constitute a negative pecuniary yield. The recently reacquired ability of banks to pay interest on demand deposits does not pose a problem for the argument that follows in the text as long as currency does not bear interest.

11. It is interesting to speculate how a GE theorist might view standing fire trucks. Either she must admit that they do yield some return, and implicitly admit that money does as well, or she must view them as wasteful and argue that they should be lent as described. Clearly it is not only money that does not fit into the GE world of objectively known perfect information.

12. For example consider the following quotes from Hahn (1973, p. 77): "Traditional equilibrium theory does best when the individual is of no importance—he is of measure zero. My theory also does best when all the given theoretical problems arising from the individual's mattering do not have to be taken into account"; and Pareto (1971, p. 120), referring to indifference curves: "The individual can disappear, provided he leaves us this photograph of his tastes."

13. Niehans's (1978, p. 20) textbook explication of monetary theory explicitly states that "no direct utility of money will be hypothesized." King and Plosser (1986) try to incorporate a subjective yield to money by referring to the benefits it provides as an economizer of information costs. These benefits trade off against any lower pecuniary rate of return money might have.

14. In the final analysis, all that a market economy produces is want satisfaction. Goods, services, financial assets, and the like are all different ways of satisfying wants. Economic activity does not change the total mass of the physical world, it only rearranges it so as to be more coordinated with human

purposes and plans. This is the creation of economic value. A related, though overly neoclassical, discussion can be found in Stigler and Becker (1977). Recognition of this idea is useful in both theory and policy, especially when addressing concerns over the supposed decline of a "goods" economy and the corresponding rise of a "service" economy. See McKenzie (1988) for an application to these issues.

15. Niehans (1978, p. 1) argues that "economists have always found it more difficult to analyze the services of a medium of exchange than those of producer and consumer goods. This is because a medium of exchange derives its usefulness from some sort of imperfection or 'friction' in the market, while the essentials of value and allocation can be understood on the assumption of perfect or 'frictionless' markets." For general equilibrium theory, the very fact of money's uniqueness is the source of its analytical difficulties. Notice also that Niehans implies that one can know the essentials of value and allocation without ever making room for money in one's theory. The argument in Chapter 3 can be read as a response to this point.

16. See Menger (1981, p. 121), Sowell (1980, pp. 217-18) and Buchanan (1969, pp. 38-50).

17. See also Hayek (1978c, p. 52): "What we find is rather a continuum in which objects of various degrees of liquidity . . . shade into each other in the degree to which they function as money." Hayek cites Fritz Machlup as coining, so to speak, the term *moneyness* for describing this continuum.

18. Begging the difficulties of measurement, if we define r as the interest yield from any asset and A as the availability yield, each individual will try to ensure that the total yields (defined as T such that T = r + A) will tend to be equal across all assets. In addition, the utility lying behind those T values will tend to be equal to the marginal utility per dollar gained from goods and services purchased. Financial assets closer to money would have a higher A/T and a lower r/T, with financial assets farther from money having the opposite relationships. For a fuller elaboration, see Horwitz (1990b).

19. To the extent that this analysis is valid, it appears to cast doubt on Keynesian models where portfolio choices are just between money and bonds. There is nothing special about the fact that bonds earn an objective interest yield that justifies distinguishing them from other utility-producing items of consumption. Money and bonds and all other goods and services are all ways of satisfying wants.

Therefore, to argue that excess supplies of money will spill over into the bond market alone is to ignore the fact that any other goods or services could also be the object of portfolio adjustments. D. H. Robertson (1963, p. 383) criticizes Keynes on these grounds: "Bonds are not the only alternative to money as a use for resources, even for the private person, still less for the entrepreneur; and a theory of money which insists on working everything through the bond market . . . seems to me to be lacking in realism and comprehensiveness." If there are more alternatives, Keynesian assumptions about interest elasticity of money demand may be highly suspect, as will be the resulting predictions about the efficacy of fiscal and monetary policy.

20. Of course this observation is the launching point for Wallace's (1983) seminal piece on the legal restrictions theory of money. Wallace (p. 4) cites this passage from Samuelson and then proceeds to flesh it out in some detail. For criticisms of the legal restrictions theory that parallel the points developed here, see Selgin (1987a) and L. White (1987).

21. The novelty of legal restrictions theory is that it associates transaction costs with legal restrictions rather than with phenomena inherent in market exchanges. For Wallace and others, legal restrictions are sufficient conditions to explain the paradox; there is no need for inherent market frictions. It is only the law that prevents us from achieving a general equilibrium outcome in the real world.

22. The context in which Brunner and Meltzer are writing should be noted here. Their analysis is parallel to the search-theory view of the labor market and other similar developments in transaction costs economics (such as Alchian and Demsetz's [1972] theory of the firm) that were happening about the same time. In the search-theory story, workers may choose to be unemployed because it is worth it to spend time searching for a potentially higher-paying job. The point is that some level of unemployment may be optimal, just as some amount of resources applied to information acquisition may be optimal for Brunner and Meltzer's agent. A classic contribution to search theory is Phelps et. al. (1970), and a criticism can be found in High (1983-84). An early version of the search-theory hypothesis was developed by Hutt (1977).

23. Armen Alchian (1977) also pursues a transaction costs approach, concentrating on informational issues deriving from Brunner and Meltzer's paper. Alchian argues that ignorance about the quality and availability of goods leads to the development of specialized brokers who allow nonspecialists to take advantage of their superior knowledge of potential mediums of exchange. Alchian's contribution is really to extend and deepen the Brunner and Meltzer argument and to offer one possible criterion explaining why particular goods become money. Aside from this it suffers from many of the same shortcomings.

24. As Cowen and Kroszner (1987, p. 577, fn. 23) argue in a somewhat different context: "The absence of money from the basic model of general equilibrium may be a virtue of the theory rather than a failure. . . . A full understanding of the reasons for money's persistence might suggest other approaches to constructing a framework for the analysis of a monetary economy."

25. It is particularly ironic, then, that GE has to rely ultimately on a central authority to guarantee its results. In GE, trade takes place only at prices generated by the Walrasian auctioneer: a central authority. The auctioneer calls out prices and watches excess supplies and demands and adjusts prices accordingly. GE exchange is ultimately centralized because control over the all-important price vector resides not in the agents but in the auctioneer. It is equally ironic that a theory designed to show the efficacy of decentralized markets operates in a manner strikingly similar to theorized socialist central planning boards. See Chapter 6 and Lavoie (1985b, chap. 5).

26. See Thomsen (1989) for a parallel criticism of the neoclassical view of information as another good.

27. This criticism applies with equal force to the informational transaction costs literature discussed previously.

28. See Cowen and Fink (1983), Boettke, Horwitz, and Prychitko (1986) and Chapter 2 for more extended discussions of the complexity and coordination issues.

29. Although the contributions discussed in this chapter are attempts to incorporate a more evolutionary view, none deals with the problems of neoclassical views of knowledge. The alternative approach suggested in Chapters 2 and 3 can be seen as an attempt to take account of both the tacit nature of much of our knowledge and the evolutionary perspective needed to see the effects of the use of money.

30. That is, that trades take place in a predetermined linear sequence.

31. An open-ended process can still be path-dependent. Path dependency allows for forms of novelty (such as genetic mutation in evolutionary biology) that strict determinism precludes.

32. Nagatani (1978, chap. 6) presents a formalized version of Menger's story that is quite similar to Jones's, and many of the same criticisms apply to both.

33. See also Keynes (1937, p. 115): "Money, it is well known, serves two principal purposes . . . [first] acting as a money of account. . . . In the second place, it is a store of wealth." This appears right before his famous remark (quoted at the beginning of this chapter) about only a lunatic using money as a store of wealth in the classical theory. Notice that seven years after the *Treatise* there is no mention of money's medium-of-exchange function.

34. See also Shackle (1973, p. 43) "It will be necessary [in the market] to have one good agreed upon as the one in terms of which all prices shall be expressed. Such a good is then serving as a *unit of account,* and this is one of the duties performed by money." Though he says it is only one of money's functions, Shackle discusses this function first and derives the others from it.

35. On the problems with Keynesian explanations of intertemporal coordination, see Garrison (1985).

36. See also Shackle (1973, p. 73): "There is no organization and no means by which the two sets of intentions [to save and to invest] are or can be *pre-reconciled.* They are essentially mutually independent, their equality, if by some chance it should occur, would indeed be the result of chance." Answers to macroeconomic questions ought to revolve around whether this problem is a permanent feature of a world of uncertainty or whether alternative institutional arrangements could better *post*reconcile ex ante savings and investment.

37. Also see Menger (1892, 1981), Mises (1980), and Marx (1906).

38. See Frankel (1977, p. 67, emphasis added): "The capitalist system depended for its functioning not primarily on inequality of consumption but on those free, individual, contractual and credit relations in a monetary economy which made efficient saving, investment and consumption decisions *possible.*"

39. One could read Orwell's *1984* as touching upon the ramifications of this type of proposal.

40. Examples of this line of thinking abound in the Keynesian literature, but consider the following two: "I expect to see the State, which is in a position to calculate the marginal efficiency of capital-goods on long views, and on the basis

of the general social advantage, taking an ever greater responsibility for directly organizing investment" (Keynes 1936, p. 164); and, "In so far as individual business men's or firms' decisions to improve their equipment depend on suggestions, rather than on demonstrative reasoning from established facts, the government can take action which offers such suggestions" (Shackle 1973, p. 82). In both cases one might ask why government agents are not subject to the same "animal spirits" and "suggestions" that economic agents are, and which of the property rights systems each is involved in is better suited to rewarding the long-run, rational decisions that Shackle sees as so important.

2

Rules, Institutions, and the
Evolution of Economic Order

As indicated in the previous chapter, an approach that emphasizes the interaction of contextual knowledge and evolution may prove more helpful than the static, objectivistic models of general equilibrium in analyzing the roles and functions of money and monetary institutions. This chapter will discuss a broad approach to economic theory that offers an alternative to general equilibrium, and that accounts for the roles of knowledge, rules, and the evolution of social and economic institutions. This approach argues that the concept of *order* provides a better theoretical framework than does equilibrium and that economic order is intertwined with the nature of human knowledge and the ongoing evolution of market processes.

Subjective Knowledge and the Austrian School

The theoretical framework that underlies the approach to economics to be explored is that of the Austrian school.[1] The uniqueness of the Austrian approach is its focus on, and extensive development of, the subjective nature of economic phenomena. Hayek's (1952b, p. 52) words, "It is probably no exaggeration to say that every important advance in economic theory during the last hundred years was a further step in the consistent application of subjectivism," could have been written only by an Austrian and certainly taken seriously by the economics profession only at a much earlier time. The most recent major developments in neoclassical economic theory stress the objective nature of two of the most important economic phenomena—knowledge and expectations.

Search theory, as developed in the late 1960s, treats knowledge as a good that is "out there" and attainable at some cost, and rational expectations theory treats expectations as mirroring the objective probability distribution of future outcomes. Although the vast majority of economists (likely excluding only some traditional Marxists) would accept the proposition that economic value is subjectively determined, very few extend that subjectivism to knowledge and expectations. The history of the Austrian approach to economics is its extension of subjectivism from the realm of value to the realms of knowledge and expectations and the implications of that extension for the coordination of economic activities.[2] If one can talk of a uniquely Austrian approach, it is a focus on both the way in which people's perceptions drive their actions and the patterns of economic order that emerge as the unintended consequences of those actions.

The origins of a distinctly Austrian school can be traced to Carl Menger's (1981) *Principles of Economics.* Menger argued that economic value is a creation of the human mind. Goods possess value because particular individuals perceive that those goods will be useful in satisfying some end. Menger recognized, as do modern Austrians, that such perceptions may be mistaken ex post, but that the factors influencing value and price are ex ante expectations and perceptions. Menger also argued that the relevant unit for understanding value is the marginal unit. A question about the value of water is not concerned with the value of all water everywhere, rather it is concerned only with the value of the concrete unit of water being applied to the end under consideration. The realization that value is both subjective and marginal shifted the focus of economic theory away from plutological notions of aggregate wealth and long-run trends to a human-centered theory emphasizing the role of all economic actors as valuers.[3]

Another aspect of Menger's thought that was to profoundly influence Austrian theory was the notion of spontaneous order.[4] In his (1985, p. 146) book on the methodology of the social sciences, he asked the following question concerning the origin of social institutions: "How can it be that institutions which serve the common welfare and are extremely significant for its development come into being without a common will directed toward establishing them?" The idea that institutions could evolve without a common will directed toward their establishment became the cornerstone of Austrian explanations of the movement from individualized economic value to patterns of social order. The market was to be viewed as an example of such an institution, and the job of the economist was to explicate its rules of operation.

Ludwig von Mises extended Menger's fundamental insights into a systematic vision of economic theory stretching from methodology to economic policy. Each of Mises's major contributions can be viewed as extending subjectivism into specific areas.[5] His (1980) book on money and business cycles was a major step forward in applying subjectivism to monetary phenomena. In 1920, he relied on the subjective nature of value and knowledge to argue that Marxian comprehensive central planning was impossible, and in 1933 he extended subjectivism to methodology by reasserting that the fundamental "data" of economics are the thoughts and perceptions of individual economic actors.

All of these extensions of subjectivism were in marked contrast to the development of neoclassical theory, which was in the throes of the Keynesian and general equilibrium revolutions. The vast majority of the profession was turning to mathematical and statistical analysis in both theoretical and empirical research, but Mises was arguing that such approaches were beside the point when dealing with the subjective nature of human knowledge. Such knowledge began inside the heads of economic actors and could not possibly be meaningfully quantified and functionalized by an observing economist. For Mises, economic theory was the logical tracing of the necessary consequences (both intended and unintended) of human action. Starting from the fundamental principle that human beings act by attempting to remove "felt uneasiness," Mises (1966) outlined a systematic approach to economic theory that was an attempt to explain virtually every aspect of economic interaction.

Though perhaps not quite as neatly and tidily as Mises believed, he had laid the foundations for the advances that would ensue. Of particular interest is that Mises integrated the new advances in phenomenological philosophy and the methodology of the social sciences being developed by Max Weber (1968), Alfred Schutz (1967), and others on the Continent into the methodology of economics. This phenomenological twist to Mises's work would later become fundamental to Austrian explanations of the relationship between knowledge and economic order and will be pursued in greater detail when applied to the specific example of money.[6]

Mises's student and associate F. A. Hayek, however, was in many ways to have a more profound impact on modern Austrian theory. It was Hayek's development of Mises's system that guided Austrian economics toward its focus on knowledge and the evolution of institutions. Hayek's journey into the intricacies of epistemology and evolutionary theory was launched by his participation in the debate over the feasibility of rational economic calculation under socialism. Picking up where Mises had left off in his 1920 article, Hayek argued through the 1930s and 1940s that both comprehensive central planning and market socialism were doomed to fail because neither could account for the nature of human knowledge and the constant change of an advanced economy.[7] Despite the force of his arguments, Hayek's case fell on uncomprehending ears. The path that neoclassical economics was taking at the time had little scope for concerns about knowledge and dynamic evolution. The practitioners of the static, perfect-knowledge models of general equilibrium simply did not see the relevance of Hayek's argument.

As a result, Hayek was led to reexamine his own understanding of just what was happening in a market economy, namely the relationship between knowledge and economic order. In two papers in 1937 and 1945 (reprinted in Hayek 1948), he argued that models of economic equilibrium, including those of the market socialists, were only valid if it could be assumed that all of the knowledge in the economy was available to one mind at one point in time. Hayek claimed that, on the contrary, knowledge in society is dispersed and fragmented among social actors and is often tacit, as discussed earlier. Given that such contextual knowledge could not be mastered by one mind, equilibrium models gloss over the fundamental social question of how knowledge is generated, transmitted, and utilized in the market. To assume that knowledge of how best to use resources is "given" to anyone is to assume away the very role of prices and market processes.

Fundamentally this was simply an extension of Menger's original subjectivism. Now it was not just economic value that was embedded in the minds of individuals but also a great deal of all the knowledge relevant for economic interaction. Hayek's next step was to describe the way in which an unhampered price system allows this contextual knowledge to be utilized by others. When actors buy and sell and otherwise act in the market, they affect prices. These ever-changing arrays of prices serve as nodes of communication, which fluctuate in response to the changing knowledge, interpretations, and judgments of economic actors.[8] With people free to exchange both consumer and capital goods, their bits and pieces of articulate and tacit knowledge are made available to others through the price system. Any kind of centralized system would not have access to the same quality and amount of knowledge because planners would be necessarily limited to knowledge that could be articulately communicated through the written or spoken word: "Markets and prices . . . help to utilize the knowledge of many people without the need of first collecting it in a single body" (Hayek 1952b, p. 177). For Hayek, the marvel of the market is its ability to allow society to utilize contextual knowledge in such a way as to allow markets as an institution to do more than any of us could ever dream of doing as individuals.[9]

The ever-changing knowledge embedded in prices leads to a different understanding of the systematic properties of market economies. Rather than using the analogy of Newtonian physics drawn by equilibrium theory, Hayek turned to biology for the concept of evolution.[10] As prices and knowledge change, so do markets. To Hayek, the value of markets lies not in their ability to allocate resources at a point in time but in their ability to adjust and reorient themselves to changes in human knowledge and natural conditions. Markets are valued more for their internal predictability (i.e., the ability to form reasonable expectations about the pattern of future events) than for approaching some kind of preconceived ideal. Hayek (1978a, p. 185) best summarized this while also indicating the fundamental difference between equilibrium and order approaches:

> We do injustice to the achievement of the market if we judge it, as it were, from above, by comparing it with an ideal standard which we have no known way of achieving. . . . We [should] judge it . . . from below, that is . . . against what would be produced if competition were prevented.

This type of order analysis is concerned not with the correspondence between the actual economy and some theoretically constructed ideal; rather it focuses on the coherence among the actions and perceptions of actors within an actual economy.

The post-Hayekian path has extended subjectivism one step further into the interpretation of economic knowledge. Ludwig Lachmann, for one, has asked why we should believe that the interpretive schemas of economic actors always ensure that they will react appropriately to the knowledge signals emanating from prices. Knowledge is not unambiguous—it has to be interpreted through the mind of the knower. It may well be the case that people will respond wrongly to the "right" signal. This argument has led modern Austrians to both reexamine the nature of human knowledge (focusing more on interpretive theory and the active nature of knowing) and refine their understanding of economic order. If such misinterpretations are possible, markets must be more than processes that increase the quality of human knowledge; they must also have ways to weed out mistakes and permit individuals to use the knowledge (whether correct or not) that markets make available. An extended discussion of how markets lead to order and why it is beneficial that they do so will occupy the remainder of this chapter.

Uncertainty, Rules, and the Emergence of Institutions

A discussion of order must recognize that human beings live in a world of uncertainty. We do not, in fact, have the perfect knowledge from which neoclassical economics derives its results. Though we may have good reasons to believe that particular events are more likely than others, we can never know with certainty what the future will bring.[11] Surprise and novelty are the essence of human existence. However confident one may be of particular outcomes, the possibility of the unconsidered or the dismissed remains.

One immediate implication of life in an uncertain world is the fragmentation of human knowledge. In addition to its imperfection, human knowledge is also scattered and dispersed among different people. Some are in a better position to correctly anticipate an uncertain future than others. Such ability rests partly on sheer luck, but mostly on what Hayek (1945, p. 80) calls the "knowledge of the particular circumstance of time and place." Not only do we each not know all, but we all know different bits and pieces.

Given the contextual nature of our knowledge, it seems reasonable to ask how anything ever gets accomplished. It would seem far more likely that a society in such a position would continually stumble around in the dark rather than build artificial hearts and write great literature. Yet these accomplishments do happen and productive social interaction is possible.[12] Hayek (1977, p. 8) argues that one major reason is the use of rules: "Rules are a device for coping with our constitutional ignorance. There would be no need for rules among omniscient people who were in agreement on the relative importance of all the different ends." As societies evolve, members discover that certain types of action tend to be more successful than others. Actors usually do not (and most importantly need not) understand why success occurs, only that it does. Once such successes occur, actors continue to behave in those ways to capitalize on their successes. As Hayek frequently indicates, this line of evolutionary argument traces back to the thinkers of the Scottish Enlightenment.

Hayek (1952a, 1978a) has also argued that the mind itself is a spontaneous order guided by rules that it, itself, cannot understand: "If . . . it is basically impossible to state or communicate all the rules which govern our actions . . . this would imply . . . the impossibility of ever fully explaining a mind of the complexity of our own" (1967c, p. 60). For human beings facing an uncertain future, the mind has evolved rules of conduct that lead to the successful execution of plans of action.[13] For societies facing unknown contingencies or interpersonal conflicts, sets of rules that we call "institutions" have evolved to settle as-yet-unknown problems—for example, property rights.

Individuals use rules when forming their expectations of the future. The essence of human behavior is goal-oriented action. At some point in time we are unsatisfied with the current state of affairs and wish to change it (Mises 1966, p. 13). People formulate goals, attempt to ascertain means appropriate to them, and then execute these plans. However, at the same time, others are doing the same, and often such plans will be mutually exclusive (O'Driscoll and Rizzo 1985, p. 80).[14] The inability to precisely know the subjectively devised plans of others and how the interaction of such plans will work itself out are major sources of uncertainty (Hayek 1937, p. 38ff.).

We have to take the actions of others into account when we formulate and execute plans, so we must have some expectations about how such others will act. The problem again is how we can form expectations about others when the contents of their plans are not accessible to us in any direct way. The plans of another are always the plans of an "other," and this "otherness" limits our knowledge.[15] In such a situation of uncertainty, one way out is the use of rules. In this case, however, rules of a particular kind are needed.

Because we cannot know the particulars of all the "others" with whom we interact, we have to formulate some kind of general behavioral rules, or ideal types.[16] Based on past experiences with particular types of people, we build up patterns of expected behavior. Out of these patterns we formulate an ideal type. As Simmel (1908, p. 11) put it:[17]

> The practice of life urges us to make the picture of a man only from the real pieces that we empirically know of him, but it is precisely the practice of life which is based on those modifications and supplementations, on the transformation of the given fragments into the generality of a type and into the completeness of the ideal personality.

For example, the ideal type "mail carrier" involves a fair bit of generalized knowledge and expectations. If the execution of a particular plan involved a mail carrier (say, paying a bill on time), then we would use our ideal type of a mail carrier to form an expectation about the relevant behavior (e.g., will the carrier come today?).

An important factor here is that the degree of specificity of an ideal type depends on the degree of our knowledge of the person or phenomenon in question (Stonier and Bode 1937, p. 419, and Schutz 1967, p. 194ff.). If the carrier in the example is the one who most frequently serves my house, then I might also form an expectation about what time the person will arrive and how reliable the carrier is in delivering important letters. For example, take a grocery store owner concerned about customers. The ideal type "customer" would most likely be even more abstract than a mail carrier is to me. At the broadest level, this ideal type would perhaps be "someone interested in buying food." However, the more entrepreneurs know about their customers, for example, that a large number of customers prefer kosher food, the more specific will be the content of the ideal typifications.

Ideal types are formed from our expectations of the rule-following behavior of others (Hayek 1967c, p. 55). An ideal type is a set of rules that describe the expected behavior of the person or institution in question. Like the rules from which they are formed, ideal types are a result of our uncertainty about the plans and particular actions of others. The more complex society is, and the more socially distant any individual becomes, the more necessary ideal types become for successful action. If we could completely know an "other" we could dispense with the use of an ideal typification of that person because we would know with certainty what she would do. Ideal types are a necessary complement to a world of individuals with dispersed and contextual knowledge.

Individual behavior, and the ideal types it leads to, is not so varied that no behavioral patterns ever emerge. The fact that certain types of behavior are successful will lead to their being imitated by others. This imitative process is self-reinforcing. As more people begin to follow the same rules of action, the incentive for any given individual to follow those rules will increase because by conforming to the emerging social norm, the individual's behavior becomes more predictable and coheres better with the behavior of others.[18] When a sufficient number of persons all follow similar rules of action, a social institution emerges. As Lachmann (1971, p. 68) phrases it,

> Successful plans thus gradually crystallize into institutions. . . . Imitation of the successful is, here as elsewhere, the most important form by which the ways of the elite become the property of the masses . . . Institutions are the relics of the pioneering efforts of former generations from which we are still drawing benefits.

When we participate in social institutions, our behavior can be understood as that of the ideal type that corresponds to the institution in question.

For example, when we use money, others can form expectations about our behavior based on the ideal type of "money user." The use of money brings with it a host of various typical behaviors, many of which will be explored in the next chapter. These ideal typical actions enable us to overcome the uncertainty involved with acting in an anonymous social order: "In reducing the uncertainty of the future which enshrouds all human action, and helping us overcome the limitations of our ignorance of the present, [the] coherence and permanance [of social institutions] are indeed of primary importance" (Lachmann 1971, p. 70). Social institutions are thus reservoirs of human knowledge that give us a measure of predictability in our attempts to execute our plans. Social institutions are, in Lachmann's (p. 50) words, "nodal points [that] . . . relieve [us] of the need to acquire and digest detailed knowledge about others and form detailed expectations about their future actions." The importance of institutions is even greater when we realize that they create situations where we *need* knowledge of others and that without the institutions, we could not even begin to obtain the knowledge in question. Institutions are embodiments of knowledge that would be relatively inaccessible if it were dispersed among individuals.

By participating in a social institution we are putting limits on the range of possible actions we might undertake. Institutions are a social form of self-constraining behavior. One might ask why individuals would agree to such constraints. The answer is that these constraints make our behavior more predictable to others and increase our chances of mutually coordinating our behavior. By adhering to rules, or to sets of rules embodied in institutions, individuals communicate knowledge to each other. Recognizable modes of behavior are "basically an information device that allows players to interpret the actions of their opponents" (Schotter 1986, p. 128). Social institutions reduce the burden of uncertainty. As they emerge out of the dovetailing of successful plan executions, institutions create the possibility of forming reasonable expectations (and therefore increasing the chance of plan coordination with others) by constraining the range of actions an individual might take to those that were historically successful. As Langlois (1986, p. 237) nicely summarizes them, social institutions are "interpersonal stores of coordinative knowledge . . . [that] serve to restrict at once the dimensions of the agent's problem-situation and the extent of the cognitive demands placed upon the agent."

Institutions are not static, however; they change and evolve. In fact, one can argue that each time we participate in social institutions, they will likely be, at least infinitesimally, changed. As Gadamer (1985) has argued more broadly, all interpretations are new interpretations. Each time we "use" an institution we are bringing something of ourselves to it, and that input of ourselves changes, if only slightly, the institution. Hayek (1973, p. 100) notes how the evolution of the legal order embodies this constant change. Judge-made law evolves through the application of precedent by judges to particular cases. Hayek says explicitly that although judges can consciously alter around the margins, "the system of rules as a whole does not owe its structure to the design of either judges or legislators." The "meaning of the law" emerges through this constant process of application and interpretation. Each time the law is applied to a new situation, its scope and meaning are more precisely defined.[19]

The importance of the mutability of institutions is that they are flexible enough to change with changes in circumstances yet maintain sufficient coherence to allow us to still form reasonably accurate expectations based on them.[20]

Striking a continual balance between flexibility and coherence characterizes both successful individual rules of action and social institutions. An insufficiently flexible social institution will be unable to adapt to changes in human behavior and nonhuman circumstances; an excessively flexible rule will be unable to provide the minimum amount of stability that is needed to guide us in an uncertain world. It is the existence of uncertainty that forces rules to sail between the Scylla of excessive rigidity and the Charybdis of excessive flexibility. This challenge was also recognized by Hume (1961, p. 457), who argued with reference to the law that "the rules of justice seek some medium betwixt a right stability and . . . changeable and uncertain adjustment." Uncertainty means that human behavior is never totally predictable, but successful social action requires that human behavior must, nonetheless, be predictable enough. Good social institutions allow for accurate expectation formation (from accurate ideal types) and successful plan execution.

To summarize, rules and institutions allow us to overcome our lack of knowledge of the particulars of the action of others. The more accurately rules allow us to form expectations and therefore execute our individual plans, the more successful are our actions in social settings. This success will feed back to the rules guiding it and will help us to select the helpful and the unhelpful. Successful rules become crystallized and regularized in social institutions and in the patterns of behavior and knowledge these institutions embody. Institutions that allow us to relate across the space that separates us as individuals (institutions that make successful social coordination possible) will tend to survive; those that fail to provide the necessary guidance in a world of uncertainty will tend to be discarded.

Coordination, Discoordination, and Economic Order

The advantage of rules and their crystallization into social institutions is that they lead to an extension of social order. For Hayek (1973, p. 36), the word *order* describes

> a state of affairs in which a multiplicity of elements of various kinds are so related to each other that we may learn from our acquaintance with some spatial or temporal part of the whole to form correct expectations concerning the rest, or at least expectations which have a good chance of proving correct.

Hayek thereby brings the concept of order into the previous discussion. The cornerstones of his concept of order are uncertainty and expectation formation (i.e., ideal types). Notice also that order is conceived as being procedural, not substantive.[21] Ceteris paribus, any given distribution of incomes (for example) may be an orderly outcome, just as any given distribution could be disorderly. What matters are the dynamic properties of the system, not its static allocative ones.

One of the justifications for this concept of order is that the complexity of some orders, and economic ones in particular, prevents us from knowing all of the details necessary to bring about any desired end state (Hayek 1973, p. 40ff.). In the absence of this knowledge of the particulars, the most we can rely on are rules of conduct. Much as we construct ideal typifications of individuals in an attempt to form accurate expectations of their behavior, so do orders depend on their elements following certain rules and utilizing particular institutions. In both cases we know little about the exact behavior of the elements in question, so we rely on rules to make that behavior somewhat predictable. To quote Hayek (1973, p. 44):

> Order will always constitute an adaptation to the multitude of circumstances which are known to all the members of that society taken together but which are not known as a whole to any one person . . . [and] for the formation of such an overall order it is necessary that in some respects all individuals follow definite rules, or that their actions are limited to a certain range.

As argued earlier, rules and institutions both increase the accuracy of our expectations and facilitate plan execution by bounding the actions of others. Social orders are characterized by the fact that people's expectation-formation processes, as assisted by rules and institutions, are reliable enough to aid them in successfully executing some substantial portion of their plans and in learning from the plans that fail.[22]

Notice that we are not defining order as completely successful plan execution, only saying that the process of expectation formation is reliable (and hopefully increasingly so through time). Austrian economists have, for a long time, rejected Pareto optimality or equilibrium conditions as standards for economic welfare.[23] Instead, they have tried to develop an alternative standard based on some notion of plan coordination. Most of these discussions have been based on Hayek (1937, pp. 37-38):

> Equilibrium in this connection exists if the actions of all members of the society over a period are all executions of their respective individual plans on which each decided at the beginning of the period . . . In order that all these plans can be carried out, it is necessary for them to be based on the expectation of the same set of external events . . . This means that the plans of different individuals must in a special sense be

compatible if it is to be even conceivable that they should be able to carry all of them out.

The main idea is that complete economic coordination (what Hayek here calls equilibrium) is a state of affairs such that all existing plans could be consistently carried out.[24] In our terminology economic coordination would require that everyone's ideal types (expectations) reflected a high degree of understanding of the behavior of others and that all plans based on them were mutually compatible. As Schotter (1986, p. 127) puts it in a more neoclassical context, whether strategies are successful in a game-theoretic situation "depends on how fine the mode structure is, that is, how sophisticated the players are in interpreting the actions of others." Despite his more formalistic tone, Schotter is nonetheless emphasizing that coordination is related to the accuracy of expectations.

Obviously, having the ability to accurately interpret and/or predict the actions of others is a strict condition for any kind of "optimal" outcome. More recently a shift has occurred, turning the discussion from coordination as a state of affairs more toward the issue of what kinds of institutional arrangements make *coordinating processes* more or less likely. In a recent paper Kirzner (1989a, p. 87, emphasis added) makes this point when he says, "We must distinguish carefully between (a) a possible norm of coordination in the sense of a coordinated *state of affairs,* and (b) a possible norm of coordination in the sense of the ability to detect and *to move towards* correcting situations in which activities have until now been discoordinated." The market is to be desired, in Kirzner's view, because its institutions increase society's ability to detect and eliminate discoordination, providing coordination in his second sense of the term. For Kirzner (1989b, chap. 4), coordination is provided by the entrepreneurial aspect of human behavior that is alert to such discoordination and can profit by removing it.

Kirzner's notion of "coordinating processes" is an improvement compared to Hayekian "coordination," but it does not go far enough. Kirzner's focus on the entrepreneur as a coordinator misses the potentially discoordinating effects of entrepreneurial behavior.[25] For example, suppose an entrepreneur invents a new process for making highly useful plastics. Certainly her invention is coordinating in that fewer resources will now have to be used to satisfy the same wants. However, this coordinating action can have disruptive effects on the plans of others. Those who use the old process now face an unexpected decision over which process to use. In addition, the new process might hamper the availability of parts and service for now-obsolete equipment. The single coordinative aspect of her invention could be outweighed by the discoordinating aftereffects.

One could respond by saying that the entrepreneur's invention reveals already existing discoordination, thus leading to the need for further coordination down the road. The problem with this response is that it isolates the discoordinating change and then argues for eventual coordination by making a ceteris paribus assumption during the process by which coordinating adjustments are taking place. Although it might be true that if everything else stays the same, actors would fully adjust to the new production process and users of the old process would make rational economic changes, this is not the point of the Lachmann's critique. By impounding these potential changes in ceteris paribus clauses, one removes the full range of market activities from the analysis of *real* market processes.[26] If we remove the ceteris paribus constraint, then all kinds of other events might occur that would prevent the coordinating adjustments from having their full force, events such as a further refinement of the production process, a change in tastes, or a change in the relative prices of inputs. Though examining coordinating tendencies may work in very specific market contexts, claims that market processes as a whole tend toward coordination, or that coordinating forces dominate, appear to run up against a constantly changing real world that undermines coordinative tendencies. In addition, only seeing "tendencies toward coordination" is a problematic argument for the desirability of market economies.[27]

If the concept of coordination is insufficient, how can we begin to describe theoretically the operation of real market processes? One approach is to move the discussion one level higher. Instead of focusing on coordination, we need to return to the concept of order. One can admit that existing market processes may not completely coordinate behavior, and that entrepreneurs' attempts at coordination may lead to further discoordination, but still see the welfare-enhancing properties of markets.

Creativity, Complexity, and Coordination

The concept of economic order encompasses more than just the coordination of economic activities.[28] In our examination of how market processes actually unfold, accounting for their coordinative abilities is necessary but not sufficient. It is true that consumers and producers individually attempt to increase their utility or profits and thus unintentionally set coordinative processes into motion. To conclude, however, that markets as wholes simply lead to coordination would be to forget that the profit- or utility-increasing actions of some have to interact with similar attempts by others. As we saw in the previous section, the constant change in human minds and the natural world will almost always prevent full coordination from being reached. Given the existence of continual discoordination, an explanation of the desirability of market processes will have to include additional elements that can be used to understand economic order. Cowen and Fink (1983) argue that in addition to coordination, the concepts of creativity and complexity should be included in order analysis. An order analysis informed by all three components looks not only at how institutions, or collections of institutions, facilitate the coordination of human action but also at how they utilize creativity and complexity to cultivate orderly economic processes.

Any process of social order will have to include some notion of coordination as discussed. Ultimately human beings attempt in the course of their activities to adjust their behavior to both their own desires and the limitations imposed by the behavior of others. For example, my desire to purchase a particular good ought to have some relationship to the willingness of others to produce it. When I walk into the store to buy milk, it should be on the shelf waiting for me. Like the verbal communication that takes place between two parties to a conversation, market coordination is an attempt to achieve some mutual understanding, or in Gadamer's (1985, p. 273) terms, "a fusion of horizons." Orderly processes will allow a high degree of such coordination to take place.

However, as pointed out, discoordination is a fact of life in the market as well. This brings in the concept of creativity. The missing piece is recognition of the way markets offer feedback to people's expectations. In the plastics example, those actors whose plans have now been discoordinated are able to acquire the new information and use it to adjust their expectations and formulate new plans. The role that profits and prices play as ex post indicators of success and failure in the market lead actors to adjust their behavior accordingly. Market discoordination also provides socially valuable knowledge. The advantage of markets is not just that there are institutional incentives for coordination but also that even discoordination can be creatively utilized by agents to learn and better anticipate the future, thus increasing the complexity of the economic order.[29] What matters in the market is not just that good or bad knowledge is generated and dispersed but also that actors are able to *utilize* the knowledge that is generated.

Discoordination and the ability to socially utilize contextual knowledge allow the market to cultivate creativity. It is through the use of such knowledge that actors alter the course of the market process in genuinely novel ways. As long stressed by writers like Shackle, human creativity, that is, the fact that some human choices are undetermined, means that outcomes in the market are not implied by any set of initial conditions. Human beings are truly creative and can thus introduce true novelty (events not implied by the previous state of affairs) into social processes.[30] The use and interpretation of knowledge is not mechanistic but is genuinely creative and novel, like the open-ended evolutionary process of the market itself. We can identify and examine two sources of creativity: discovery and imagination.

The idea of markets as allowing for discovery is most present in the writings of Hayek (1978a) and Kirzner (1973, 1979, 1989b). Both emphasize the ways in which markets lead people to discover what was not previously known. Kirzner's emphasis is on the entrepreneur's ability to perceive changes in consumer wants and react to them. This discovery of changes in the economic landscape is one source of creativity in the market process. Entrepreneurs are essentially interpreters of culture. To find profitable innovations, entrepreneurs have to discover and interpret the wants of consumers. Doing so requires that entrepreneurs have a sophisticated, or very insightful, understanding of the culture in which they operate. Examining current cultural trends, or tapping into avant garde ideas or goods, and creating the products and services to meet them are the essence of entrepreneurship. Interpreting culture is one way in which entrepreneurs discover what was previously unknown. Entrepreneurs who are better discoverers will produce new and better products designed to meet these newly discovered wants. Kirzner stresses that this is genuine discovery in that it cannot be predicted based on a previous set of affairs. Such discovery often results from discoordination but also leads toward further coordination as producers and consumers advance toward further fusions of horizons.

In fact, the very existence of creative activity in the market implies the absence of full market coordination. If markets actually did lead to full coordination, then entrepreneurial activity would eventually cease. In other words, if entrepreneurial activity actually increased economic coordination, then it would lead to the disappearance of entrepreneurs, as they would have no role in a fully coordinated economy.[31] The continuing existence of entrepreneurship gives us reason to be skeptical of claims that markets actually tend toward full coordination. More to the point, one reason markets require entrepreneurial activity is that the plans of other entrepreneurs have failed, creating the discoordination that is exploited by current entrepreneurship. On this line of argument, the advantages of markets are again related to their ability to facilitate the use of knowledge rather than increase the *quality* of knowledge. What matters is that entrepreneurs can creatively utilize the failed plans of other entrepreneurs by using the signals provided by market institutions, *not* that entrepreneurs ipso facto increase economic coordination.

The second source of creativity is more along the lines stressed by Shackle. Rather than simply speaking of "discovering what was not-yet-known," we can speak of "imagining the not-yet-existing." The creative power of imagination brings into existence what the entrepreneur imagines consumers might want in the future.[32] Whereas Kirzner and Hayek's notion of discovery seems more concerned with the present uncovering of past discoordination, the more Shacklean notion of imagination points toward the future and all of its indeterminacy. All economic actors face uncertainty and all have to use imagination to formulate plans for the future. Though our acts of imagination are bounded by physical laws and the broad limits of human behavior, they are ultimately individual acts based on people's perceptions of themselves and the world around them. Such imaginative choice offers a second source of creativity made possible by opportunities to better coordinate economic activities.

Both parts of creativity rest on the idea that acts of perception and knowing are not like making a photocopy. Knowing is not merely copying what is "out there" but consists of applying what is already in our personal contexts to what we perceive.[33] Differences between our minds (background, prejudices, previous knowledge) will mean that we each "know" the world in a somewhat different way. Discovery and imagination and the interpretive processes they involve are all concerned with minds that play an active part in the process of understanding and acting rather than ones that simply accept information and react mechanistically to its contents.

What is important about creativity and coordination is that they increase the complexity of the market process. By inducing coordination and cultivating creativity, the market will rise to an increased level of complexity with which it had better be able to cope. The further fusions of horizons and the creativity that result from discoordination will lead to new products and new procedures and institutions that will increase the complexity of the marketplace. Social orders will develop other procedures and institutions that enable us to cope with a more complex world.

For example, consider the relationship between the extension of the division of labor and the use of money.[34] In a barter economy actors will realize the gains to be made from specialization, which leads to the unintended consequence of the social division of labor. With the resulting increase in productivity, individuals have excess supplies of goods that they wish to exchange. When such exchange begins, the absence of double coincidences of wants becomes a problem and the evolution of indirect exchange via money begins. However, the evolution of money makes the further division of labor more profitable by making exchange easier and facilitating monetary calculation. The ability of entrepreneurs to see potential gains from exchange and arbitrage is the driving force. The extension of monetary exchange and the resulting division of labor will continue until the increased complexity that results proves to be too much to handle for current entrepreneurs attempting coordination. This use of order analysis leads us to a more complete understanding of Adam Smith's insight that the division of labor is limited by the extent of the market.

Coordination, creativity, and complexity all form parts of this order-cultivating process. Entrepreneurs creatively exploit gains from exchange, leading to the evolution of money and the increased division of labor. These creative acts make the market process increasingly complex, but the very results of this creativity (the use of money and profit-and-loss calculation) allow entrepreneurs to have means of coping with the increased complexity. These means of coping lead to increased coordination. Creativity engenders complexity, and increased complexity requires coordination. Through their attempts to coordinate (successful or not) at the increasing level of complexity, entrepreneurs create knowledge and increased complexity at an even higher level of order. As long as the coordinating processes are sufficient to cope with the increased complexity generated by the creative exploitation of discoordination, the process of order generation will continue. Widespread discoordination indicates that the order has become too complex and that some scaling back of the division of labor has to take place.

The kind of complexity that markets generate should be distinguished from mere "complicatedness" due to the open-endedness of processes that are complex in this sense. The difference is that complicated phenomena have some future course of events implied in their current states of affairs, whereas open-ended ones do not. A complicated phenomenon might be a very difficult math problem or a hard-to-solve mystery. In both cases, the current set of facts implies some reachable result. An example of an open-ended phenomenon would be the market process or the course of history. In both the market and history, no given state of affairs implies that any other state will be necessarily forthcoming.[35] This open-endedness prevents us from complete knowledge of the phenomena; we can understand it only in terms of the rules and patterns that constitute it.[36] More important, because there is no implied future course of events, the details of open-ended phenomena must be studied historically. Before the facts, we can at best only know of broad rules and patterns. To understand the actual course of events in open-ended phenomena, some historical distance is necessary to reconstruct what took place.

An implication of this distinction is that there is a continuum running from complicated to complex open-endedness. This distinction seems analogous to Hayek's (1973, chap. 2) distinction between organizations and orders. Organizations have a single end, and resources within an organization can be consciously directed toward that end. Orders are processes for achieving a multiplicity of ends as determined by the particular desires of individuals and organizations.[37] Within orders, conscious direction is impossible because no one person or group possesses the knowledge of all the possible ends and the appropriateness of all of the means, that is, the course of events is open-ended and path-dependent. The difference between the two can be conceived of as along a continuum of the relative roles of conscious design and spontaneous interaction.[38] Organizations can be complicated in that it may take time and effort to ultimately understand in a fairly detailed way how they work and who does what. To the degree that organizations begin to head toward orders however, they begin to move from the merely complicated to the more complex and open-ended. There must exist some threshold point at which complicatedness becomes open-endedness and frustrates attempts to consciously allocate resources. This would imply, in the case of the firm, for example, that there is some limit to just how large an organization can be.[39]

It is this intertwining of creativity, complexity, and coordination that constitutes the concept of order. An orderly process will involve all three factors. It is the market's ability to incorporate all three elements that allow it to produce orderly outcomes. Such outcomes are visible to us as the increasing complexity, creativity, and coordination that are part and parcel of an advanced (and advancing) economy.

Parallels to the Evolution of Natural Order

When adopting evolutionary approaches such as the one in this chapter, social scientists leave themselves open for the inevitable comparisons to the theory of biological evolution. As noted earlier, such comparisons are appropriate because it has been argued that Darwin's theory of natural selection and evolution was inspired by the social-evolution theorists of the Scottish Enlightenment. Social and natural evolutionary theories share a common ancestry, and it may help to flesh out this chapter's line of inquiry by briefly comparing it to Darwin's theory of biological evolution.

Darwinian evolution theory purports to explain the process by which distinct living species have come into being. Specifically, it argues that the competition for resources insufficient to enable all to survive simultaneously has led to a process of natural selection whereby certain individual animals and species are able to survive while others are not.[40] During the course of normal reproductive activity there will be some amount of gene mutation resulting from the genetic makeups of the parents. Though it is not quite right to call these mutations random events, it is important to note that activity at the genetic level bears no necessary relationship to environmental challenges, that is, changes in natural surroundings do not cause genetic change.[41] Instead, those who are born with mutations that enable easier adaptation to the environment are better able to survive and will genetically pass those advantages to their offspring. Those lacking the beneficial mutation will likely die and thus be unable to procreate. In this way, nature introduces beneficial genetic changes and weeds out those species and creatures unable to adapt to a constantly changing environment. The historical evolution of species can be traced by explaining their features as mutations that enabled successful adaptation, that is, survival of the fittest. Many of Darwin's original insights can be shown to be analogous to socioeconomic evolutionary processes.

The role played by genetic mutation in biology is analogous to the role played by creativity in social-ordering processes. Through acts of creative entrepreneurship humans can arrive at new possibilities for overcoming the challenges posed by the ever-changing demands and supplies of economic actors. In the same way, genetic mutation allows animal species to develop new means for overcoming the environmental challenges of natural scarcities.[42] The success of such changes is indicated by their ability to increase the animal's chances for survival in the environmental context in which it finds itself. This is the analog of coordination in social evolution. Much as creative acts by economic producers and consumers will survive only if they make possible an increased degree of coordination between buyers and sellers, so will genetic mutations get passed on only if they permit species to better conquer the challenges of their surroundings. Darwin (1859, p. 93) argues that

> natural selection acts exclusively by the preservation and accumulation of variations, which are beneficial under the organic and inorganic conditions to which each creature is exposed at all periods of life. The ultimate result is that each creature tends to become more and more improved in relation to its conditions. This improvement inevitably leads to the gradual advancement of the organization of the greater number of living beings throughout the world.

Later (p. 152) Darwin relates this advancement to competition: "For in the larger country there will have existed more individuals and more diversified forms, and the competition will have been severer, and the standard of perfection will have been rendered higher." He admits that neither he nor anyone else has yet to devise a satisfactory concept of "the advancement of organization" but that it must relate in some way to the "division of physiological labor" (p. 94). This would seem to be the biological version of the division of labor being limited by the extent of the market.

As with social evolution, the biological concepts of adaptation and complexity imply that the standard of success cannot be external but must instead be contextual. The notion of economic order developed earlier allowed for mistakes and imperfections when viewed in comparison to the perfection of standards such as Pareto optimality. The whole problem of these external standards is that they are, in fact, unreachable. Instead, it was argued that we should examine the internal order generated by social processes and compare it to what would have been achieved had such processes not been allowed to operate.

The same is true of Darwinian biological evolution. For Darwin, the standard of success is *not* how much a given creature or species resembles some hypothetical perfect animal. What constitutes survival is fitness to given environmental contexts. Perfection would be a mistaken standard by which to judge evolution. As Stephen Jay Gould (1980, pp. 20-21) argues,

> Ideal design is a lousy argument for evolution, for it mimics the postulated action of an omnipotent creator. Odd arrangements and funny solutions are the proof of evolution—paths that a sensible God would never tread but that a natural process, constrained by history, follows perforce.

It is the remnants of past imperfections, such as the human appendix, that provide traces of the evolutionary process. Their very existence is evidence of change and adaptation.[43]

The extent of the analogy between biological and social evolution need not imply that the acceptance of social evolution implies a kind of crude social Darwinism. This is true for two reasons. First, social evolutionary processes are not genetic. Individuals and groups who adapt in superior ways do so *not* because they are inherently physically better but rather because they have *learned* or discovered better ways of coordinating their activities. The fact that some are not as able as others to adapt to socioeconomic change does not imply that they are inherently inferior, or that they should be left to die in biological terms. Economic maladaptation is not genetic, and our ability to learn and change implies that such a condition is likely to be only temporary and that those in such a position are not a drag on the biological survival of the human race. Crude social Darwinian notions of the genetic, biological, or even moral superiority of the economically successful have no place in a sensible version of social evolution.

This leads to a second reason to abandon crude social Darwinism. Technically, social evolution is not Darwinian but Lamarckian. Whereas animals can only acquire beneficial mutations by the luck of the genetic draw, and not by consciously adjusting to new challenges, we can use our intelligence to consciously learn and discover new rules and institutions to assist our survival and *pass those changes on to our offspring.* Hayek (1973, p. 27) argues that "the error of 'Social Darwinism' was that it concentrated on the selection of individuals rather than on the selection of institutions and practices, and on the selection of innate rather than culturally transmitted capacities of the individuals." The institutions of language, science, tradition, and culture offer us ways to acquire and pass on desirable adaptations.[44] The advantages of Lamarckian processes have far surpassed Darwinian biological evolution. Stephen Jay Gould (1980, pp. 83-84) nicely captures this:[45]

> Cultural evolution has progressed at rates that Darwinian processes cannot begin to approach. . . . The crux in the earth's history has been reached because Lamarckian processes have finally been unleashed upon it. Human cultural evolution, in strong opposition to our biological history, is Lamarckian in character. What we learn in one generation we transmit directly by teaching and writing. Acquired characteristics are inherited in technology and culture. Lamarckian evolution is rapid and accumulative.

With these advantages also comes a cost: Although we are admittedly unable to completely control and direct human genetic inheritance processes, the false belief in our ability to control and direct the evolution of human cultural and economic institutions has led to the political dystopias of the twentieth century. The effects of these misguided experiments in social engineering have been no less dangerous or deadly than the worst imagined nightmares of genetic engineering. An understanding and appreciation of the evolutionary nature of social processes (assisted by the biological analogy) can give social science and public-policy makers a much needed dose of humility.

Law as an Institutional Framework

Any discussion of social order must also include an examination of the kinds of institutions that cultivate such order. Money, of course, is one such institution. Of additional importance for the cultivation of socioeconomic order is the nature of the legal order within which socioeconomic processes unfold.[46] What kinds of legal institutions make markets possible, and what kinds make them more likely to be increasingly orderly?[47] One of the characteristics of the failed attempts to design social orders has been their failure at redesigning the law. The consequence of this latter failure was the elimination of the law's central role as a cultivator of social order. Thus the dystopias of this century eventually were all plagued with the breakdown of their economies *and* their legal systems, and the moral underpinnings of both, leading to the inevitable slide toward social chaos.

A framework for this discussion is provided by Hayek's (1973) distinction between law and legislation. He argues that law consists of the set of abstract rules (which are ends-independent) observed by members of a spontaneous order. Such rules allow the elements of that order to use them for any of their particular purposes (pp. 97-98). They are rules of what not to do. The best examples of law, in this sense, would be a majority of the Ten Commandments of the Judeo-Christian tradition. Under the law, actors are free to pursue their own plans and purposes; the law, as such, does not indicate what to do.

The reason this sense of law is appropriate to spontaneous orders is that the lawmaker has little knowledge of the particular purposes of the members of a complex society and is not in a position to know whether mandating some particular type of action is appropriate. The interaction and mutual adjustment that take place in society determine which purposes are beneficial and which are not. This outcome is not the result of any one will, and the judge is not in a position to know the appropriate outcome ex ante. Society itself has no purpose, and the rules that allow it to exist serve no other purpose than to allow its members to pursue their own individual and group purposes.[48]

What Hayek refers to as "legislation," by contrast, applies to the kinds of things that would fall within our previous discussion of organizations. Legislation indicates what should be done or who or what should go where. It is relevant only when we are in a position to determine the particular positions of individuals with respect to the single end being sought. Because societies do not have the required single end, Hayek argues that the rules of a social order must take the form of law (abstract, general, universalizable rules of what not to do) and not legislation. Attempts to legislate are doomed to fail: The legislator can never know all the effects of a piece of legislation because the social order is too complex to understand all of the particulars. Legislation is relevant only for the internal workings of the political process, not for its effects on other social and economic processes. Again, in the absence of detailed knowledge of the particulars, we have to rely on rules.[49]

The advantage of law relates back to the previous discussion of order. Because Hayek's concept of law leaves individuals free to use their knowledge in the ways they see fit, with an equal respect for others' ability to do the same, it allows social actors to adjust and adapt their behavior to changes in both physical facts and the behavior of others. Bruce Benson's (1990, p. 32) study of the evolution of commercial law leads him to conclude that it "coordinated the self-interested actions of individuals, but it also coordinated the actions of people with limited knowledge and trust." An important part of the coordinative effects of the evolution of the legal order is the development and refinement of language. The individual actors within the framework of the law have a need for articulate communication, and language allows the law to be codified (or textualized) in a way that makes it accessible to a larger number of persons. As we will see with respect to money, the process of articulating and codifying the patterns that emerge from spontaneous orders has to assume the prior evolution of such orders, which themselves emerge from the *in*articulate knowledge of individuals.

The rule of law cultivates order by allowing for creativity, complexity, and coordination. In leaving individuals free to use their knowledge and skills as they please, law opens the way for the creative exploitation of existing discoordination, leading to increased complexity and further attempts at coordination. The open-endedness of the law corresponds to the unknowable results of the creativity of human action and the unmasterable details of the complexity of the market order. Being unable to predict the course of the market, we are unable to mandate particular types of behavior. Creativity, complexity, and coordination are responses to the variety of specific historical contexts in which actors find themselves. The evolutionary process of the market is best served by allowing actors to use that contextual knowledge in their own attempts to find creative solutions to existing discoordination. The evolution of the law occurs in much the same way. As Benson (1990, p. 15) argues, "Both [markets and law] develop as they do because the actions they are intended to coordinate are performed more efficiently under one system or process than another. The more effective institutional arrangement replaces the less effective one." Legislation retards this process because the legislator presumes to know particulars that are beyond her knowledge. By mandating particulars, legislation limits the ability of social actors to adapt their expectation-formation processes to future events unforeseeable by both the legislator and the actors.

Law leads to order by protecting legitimate expectations, and the existing law determines the kind of expectations that will be considered legitimate. When judges render decisions and interpret the law, they fit their rulings into the existing framework of rules and expectations. The advantage of this process is that it causes the least amount of disruption to existing expectations and allows for plans to be better executed. Hayek (p. 97) says of these existing laws and customs that "they give rise to expectations that guide peoples' actions, and what will be regarded as binding will therefore be those practices that everybody counts on being observed and which thereby have become the condition for the success of most activities."

Like the price system, the law is a system of signs (Kevelson 1988). The expectations validated by the law provide knowledge to social actors that enables them to act with reasonable success within a complex and anonymous social order. As a social institution, the law is a crystallized network of ideal types codified in the written law which creates expectations. The analysis of social institutions as systems of signs has been undertaken using the method of inquiry known as "semiotics." As Kevelson (p. 4) describes it:

> All communication is a process of exchange of meaningful signs, and . . . all human societies have developed complex systems of both verbal and nonverbal sign systems which . . . evolve continuously to correspond with and to represent changing social norms and the evolving, growing social consciousness of a given community.

For Kevelson (p. 187), the evolutionary and semiotic aspects of the law are examples of broader communicative processes in the social world:

> Although the legal argument is the prototype of all ordinary arguments . . . the economic exchange is the prototypical model of semiotic transactions as a whole. The sense in which law is regarded as a

prototype is not as a historical Weberian ideal form, but rather as a model or representation of more general semiotic activity in society.

Despite Kevelson's claim for the theoretical priority of economic exchange, it must be remembered that *in practice,* economic exchange requires a legal order that defines notions of property, exchange, and contract and a monetary order that cultivates a stable medium of exchange that will facilitate monetary calculation. Nonetheless, it is a promising avenue of research to view both monetary exchange and the law as semiotic processes.

It is important to realize that Hayek's distinction between law and legislation is a theoretical one in that no real-world legal system behaves this way. Rather Hayek is spelling out an ideal that would lead to orderly economic processes. He wants to leave the law-making power to the judicial system and allow legislatures only to pass legislation that directs the organization called government (Hayek 1979, chap. 17).[50] The problem is that Western legislatures are involved with both making law and legislation. In particular they are trying to legislate not just the rules of government but spontaneous social orders as well. Judges also cross over from simply codifying expectations into the law to legislating outcomes. This latter phenomenon seems particularly true in the recent explosion of product liability cases. There appear to be *no* rules by which producers and lawyers can form reasonable expectations as to the potential liability they may have for even the most unintended uses of their products. Clearly this is not law in Hayek's sense of the term, and the actual rulings are attempts to legislate outcomes of market-ordering processes.

The evolution of the law is another example of an order-cultivating process. The existence of a case for adjudication indicates some legal discoordination as two parties are unable to agree on whose expectations are legitimate. The creativity element is the way in which individual judges interpret precedent and apply it to the case at hand. This creativity can be coordination-inducing, as the newly decided case clarifies which expectations will be viewed as legitimate. Legal clarification allows actors within the legal order to coordinate their actions that much better. The increased coordination of expectations leads to a more complex legal order because the new decision will further refine the structure of existing law. The evolution of law and market work hand in hand to bring about a creative, coordinating, and complex social order.

Our inherent inability to know exactly what each person's place in society is, and how people should go about what they do, requires that we develop some set of rules to guide our behavior. The law is exactly such a set. The kinds of institutions that evolve within a framework of Hayekian judge-made law (including the law itself) will be socially desirable because they cultivate the creativity, complexity, and coordination that lead to increasing economic and social order. Socially we are able to discover what we cannot know individually—namely, how to best use the dispersed and contextual knowledge possessed by actors within the social order. Legislation, by contrast, is an example of the *hubris* of modernity (Hayek 1952b, p. 185ff.). The legislator cannot know what she needs to know to successfully guide the particulars and will never achieve her desired ends.

When we ask what kind of economic system would be most likely to generate a high, and increasing, degree of order, the answer will be one that evolved within the rule of the Hayekian concept of law. Institutions that result from the interaction of social actors who are free to use their knowledge as they see fit, constrained only by the rule of law, will be the best we can do. Such institutions might pale compared to some constructed ideal, but one must ask if that ideal is even achievable. This is the fundamental point on which equilibrium approaches such as neoclassical economics and order approaches such as the Austrian-based one outlined here can be distinguished. For order analysis, the real question is not whether institutions that are the results of an undesigned evolutionary process are the *best* of all possible worlds, it is only whether they are *better* than ones that are constructivistically designed. In addition, truly being able to comprehend the evolution of social and economic institutions requires a theoretical framework appropriate to institutional analysis. As Hodgson (1989, p. 143) argues, "only by abandoning neoclassical theory can a tenable evolutionary analogy find in economics a proper place." The order-analysis approach outlined here provides an alternative to neoclassical economics and a remedy to its inability to render intelligible the evolution and operation of social and economic institutions such as money, markets, and the law.

Notes

1. An exhaustive list of references to works in Austrian economics, both past and present, is beyond the scope of one note. However, the following are works of general importance, rather than more applied or specialized studies. The interested reader should see Menger (1981, 1985), Mises (1966, 1976, 1980, 1981), Hayek (1948, 1973, 1977, 1978a, 1989), Lachmann (1956, 1986), Kirzner (1973, 1979, 1985a), O'Driscoll and Rizzo (1985), Lavoie (1985a, 1985b), High (1990) and the collections edited by Dolan (1976), Spadaro (1978), and Kirzner (1982, 1986). A more complete list of references can be found in Boettke, Horwitz and Prychitko (1986). In addition, an excellent, and recent, overview of the development of Austrian economics, focusing on many of the Mengerian strands discussed in this chapter can be found in Vaughn (1990).

2. This theme is most extensively developed in the work of the late Ludwig Lachmann. See his collection of essays (1977) and his last book, *The Market as an Economic Process* (1986).

3. In contrast to the plutological approach of classical economics, the Austrian variant of economics can be termed "catallactic" or exchanged-based. This distinction was introduced by Sir John Hicks and was used by Mises (1966, pp. 232-34).

4. The term *spontaneous order* itself is not Mengerian, though Menger (1985, pp. 129-59) did refer to "organic" social structures. The term *spontaneous order* is usually connected with Hayek, though was reportedly coined by Hayek's friend and fellow traveler Michael Polanyi.

5. The footnote attached to Hayek's (1952b, pp. 52-3, fn. 7) quote concerning subjectivism argues that all of Mises's theoretical advances and criticisms of neoclassicism flow directly from his subjectivism.

6. Mises's relationship to phenomenology and its modern descendant, hermeneutics, has been the subject of much recent research and controversy. Despite the attempts of some of his U.S. followers to disassociate Mises from hermeneutics because they fear its potential nihilism, one can marshal evidence of hermeneutical strands in Mises's work. For example, there are his numerous approving citations of authors considered to be forerunners of modern phenomenological hermeneutics. See the discussion and citations in Boettke, Horwitz, and Prychitko (1986).

Prendergast (1986), Ebeling (1987), and Boettke (1990b) address Mises's phenomenological roots, as does Schutz (1967, p. 197ff.) in his approving discussion of Mises's methodology. Lavoie (1986b) argues for a hermeneutical reading of Mises; Prychitko (1992, p. 23, n. 21), though sympathetic to hermeneutics and cognizant of its themes in Mises, sees Lavoie's reading as overstating the case and finds Mises's project to be ultimately a "grand Cartesian failure." Albert (1988) and B. Smith (1990) offer cogent arguments against any integration of hermeneutics and Austrian economics.

7. See also Vaughn (1990, p. 391): "All of Hayek's criticisms of market socialism center around two familiar Mengerian themes: the role of knowledge in society and the dynamic nature of market economies."

8. See also Hayek's (1945, pp. 85-86) famous example involving the price of tin.

9. Lavoie (1985a, pp. 65-76) draws an analogy from sociobiology. Although no individual termite is smart enough to accurately understand, monitor, and change the temperature of its colony, the colony as a whole is able to do so by a complex interchange of chemical signals—what is often called the principle of mass communication. For an enjoyable and enlightening discussion of the complexity of even the seemingly simplest human production process, see Leonard Read's (1975) "I, Pencil."

10. There is some debate over the lineage of evolutionary concepts. Hayek (1989, p. 24 and pp. 146-47) argues that Darwin appropriated the notion of social evolution from the Scottish moral philosophers. But, Darwin (1859, pp. 13, 53) himself explicitly refers only to Malthus's discussion of the struggle for survival as a starting point for his investigations of the results of competition in nature.

Nonetheless, in his essay "Darwin's Middle Road," (1980, p. 66) historian of science Stephen Jay Gould argues that although there were numerous influences on Darwin's thought, including Malthus, Adam Smith, and Auguste Comte, one can conclude that "the theory of natural selection should be viewed as an extended analogy . . . conscious or unconscious . . . to the laissez faire economics of Adam Smith." Silvan Schweber (1977) points out that Darwin had also read Dugald Stewart's *On the Life and Writing of Adam Smith* shortly before writing *The Origin of Species.* A more detailed examination of the parallels between evolutionary biology and economic evolution occurs further on in this chapter.

11. This is not to make a rational expectations type of assumption that expectations regarding the possible courses of future events will, on average, be correct. It is to say that the best we can do heading into an unknown, but not unimaginable, future is to project possible "skeins of time" and weight them as more or less likely. See Shackle (1986, p. 28ff.). Also see Polanyi and Prosch (1975, p. 97): "The imagination does not work like a computer, surveying millions of possibly useless alternatives; rather it works by producing ideas that are guided by a fine sense of their plausibility, ideas which contain aspects of the solution from the start."

12. One can see several variants on this basic point. Simmel (1908) asks "How is society possible?" given our uniqueness and mental isolation from each other. Simmel (1905, pp. 3-5) also asks "How is history possible?" and argues that Kant's fundamental question is How is nature possible? Gadamer (1985) asks How is understanding possible? given that we each begin inside our own mental universes. And the economist asks How is economic coordination possible? when value is a product of individual minds. The answers are ideal typification (for Simmel), the a priori and the categories (for Kant), language (for Gadamer), and a money-price system (for the economist). All of these serve as bridges between unique individual minds and complex, yet undesigned, social orders.

13. Hayek (1977, p. 5) gives the example of a man who takes a pocket knife with him when he walks, not for any particular purpose, "but in order to be equipped for various possible contingencies," as a type of rule of conduct. Rules are valuable because they make us able to overcome the uncertainty of the course of future events. Compare Hayek's argument with the point in Chapter 1 that the

holding of money provides the service of "availability" in that if one has money, one can cope with various unforeseen circumstances.

A deeper discussion of the interrelationship of rules and uncertainty is beyond the scope of this chapter. The following sections may render this discussion more intelligible. The interested reader should see Hayek (1952a, 1967c and 1978a).

14. Also see Schutz (1967, p. 149): "What makes my behavior social is the fact that its intentional object is the expected behavior of another person."

15. Also see Simmel (1908, pp. 9-10): "It seems, however, that every individual has in himself a core of individuality which cannot be recreated by anybody else whose core differs qualitatively from his own. . . . We cannot know completely the individuality of another."

16. On the concept of ideal types see the varied, and often conflicting, views of Simmel (1908), Mises (1966, 1976, 1985), Grathoff (1978), Stonier and Bode (1937), Weber (1968), Lachmann (1971), Ebeling (1987, 1988) and Langlois and Koppl (1991). The best description can be found in Schutz (1967, p. 184, emphasis in original): "Rather, the contemporary's unity is constituted in my own stream of consciousness, being built up out of a synthesis of my own interpretations of his experiences. This synthesis is a synthesis of recognition in which I monothetically bring within one view my own conscious experiences of someone else. Indeed, these experiences of mine may have been of more than one person. And they may have been of definite individuals or of anonymous 'people.' It is in this synthesis of recognition that the *personal ideal type* is constituted." Though he does not use the term "ideal type," Hayek (1967c, p. 48) does argue that "We generally act successfully on the basis of such 'understanding' of the conduct of others."

17. Compare Ebeling (1988, p. 15): "The *ideal type* is a composite image of an individual or group of individuals created in the mind of a person wishing to either understand their actions in the past or anticipate their actions or reactions to various circumstances in the future."

18. The Humean roots of these evolutionary-institutional explanations is apparent here as well. Hume (1961, p. 442) said of the institution of property rights: "Nor is the rule concerning the stability of possessions the less derived from human conventions, that it arises gradually, and acquires force by a slow progression and by our repeated experience of the inconveniences of transgressing it . . . this experience . . . gives us a confidence of the future regularity of [our fellows'] conduct."

19. Also see Hayek (1967a, p. 75) and Bernstein (1983, pp. 147-48). The relevance of this argument for constitutional disputes over the original intent of the framers should be clear. Literal intent becomes irrelevant with repeated applications. Instead, what matters is the meaning that has emerged from applications to particular situations. It still remains, however, that the guide for each application is some holistic understanding of the principles and ideas underlying previous interpretations of constitutionality.

20. See Lachmann's (1971, p. 79ff.) discussion of "flexibility vs. coherence." His distinction between "external" and "internal" (p. 81) institutions, where the former are less flexibile and create the framework for the evolution of the more

changeable internal ones, may also be relevant here. An external institution would be the legal order; the market institutions that operate within it would be internal institutions. Lachmann's distinction deserves more attention in the new institutionalism literature and is particularly susceptible to evolutionary explanations.

21. Or in the language of the economist-physicist, it deals with processes, not end states or equilibria. On this see also Nozick (1974, chap. 7).

22. As Hayek rightly notes (1977, pp. 124-25), any order must involve the fulfillment of some expectations at the cost of the disappointment of others. Futures markets, which are crucial to maintaining economic order through time, presuppose divergent, and therefore disappointed, expectations. This also provides an answer to those who are frustrated by the fact that economic growth necessarily involves some losers. Like biological evolution, where maintaining life requires that many species face biological death, it can be no other way in spontaneous social orders.

23. See, for instance, Rothbard (1956), Hayek (1978a), O'Driscoll and Rizzo (1985), Cordato (1986), and Kirzner (1989a).

24. O'Driscoll (1977) argues that Hayek's work in economic theory can fruitfully be seen as centering around the notion of coordination.

25. This has been Ludwig Lachmann's criticism of orthodox Austrian economics for many years. The debate sparked by Lachmann continues to the present day. Useful contributions of recent vintage include Fehl (1986), High (1986), O'Driscoll and Rizzo (1985), and Cowen and Fink (1985). For the views of two of the major participants see Lachmann (1985) and Kirzner (1985b). Overviews of the issues, and attempts at resolutions, can be found in Boettke, Horwitz, and Prychitko (1986) and Vaughn (1992).

26. As Cowen and Fink (1985, p. 867 emphasis in original) say of the attempt to show tendencies toward equilibrium, "[A] tendency towards equilibrium *in a world with frozen data* . . . implies little or nothing about whether there is a tendency toward equilibrium in a world where the data are not frozen."

27. This is precisely Kirzner's (1985b, pp. 2-3) worry about the implications of Lachmann's denial of the primacy of the market's coordinative tendencies: "It would be a bizarre irony indeed if the modern revival of the Austrian tradition . . . were to find its most sophisticated expression in the denial of any possibility for systematic market forces susceptible to general analysis." The order approach to be described in the following section can be seen as a response to Kirzner's concern.

28. Boettke, Horwitz, and Prychitko (1986, p. 22, fn. 12) distinguish between coordination and order as follows: "Though the notions of order and coordination are similar, they are also quite distinct. Both concepts concern themselves with ex ante expectations. While coordination emphasizes the limit where individual plans actually dovetail, order reflects the broader notion of internal predictability of the elements of an order to the individuals who are part of that order. . . . Coordination implies that the plan[s] and actions of different individuals are mutually compatible. The internal predictability necessary for social order, on the other hand, corresponds to the less limiting notion that individuals are capable of forming more or less correct expectations about the

actions of others. Order encompasses, but is not synonymous with, coordination. Thus spontaneous order explanations of market activity are not concerned solely with the coordination of economic phenomena."

29. Again, Hayek (1973, p. 106) argues: "Every change must disappoint some expectations, but that this very change which disappoints some expectations creates a situation in which again the chance to form concrete expectations is as great as possible."

30. See the discussion of novelty in Witt (1989) for a more in-depth treatment of some of the issues touched on here.

31. This argument is derived from Fehl (1986), who makes this point about market activities and institutions generally, rather than just about entrepreneurship.

32. This seems to be a version of Schumpeter's idea of "creative destruction." Kirzner's entrepreneur brings us closer to what people actually want, the Shackle-Schumpeter entrepreneur actually affects wants by offering new products or services not yet considered. See the discussion in Boudreaux (1988).

33. See Gadamer (1985), Bernstein (1983), and Polanyi (1958), among others.

34. This is based on High (1986, pp. 116-18).

35. Compare Menger (1985, p. 140, emphasis in original): "What remains for us now is to investigate how those problems for social research, *the solution of which is not attainable pragmatically according to the objective state of affairs* . . . can be answered in a way adequate to the nature of social phenomena as well as to the special goals of theoretical research in the realm of the latter."

36. The relationship between these open-ended processes and Hayek's (1967b) notion of "complex phenomena" is not entirely clear. Although *complex* in Hayek's sense is not the equivalent of open-ended, open-endedness might be one aspect of a Hayekian complex phenomena. Clearly certain processes, such as biological evolution or markets, are both complex, in Hayek's sense, and open-ended. Both also, as Hayek (1967b, p. 40) argues of complex phenomena, can be known only by their patterns: 'Though we may never know as much about certain complex phenomena as we can know about simple phenomena, we may partly pierce the boundary by deliberately cultivating a technique which aims at more limited objectives—the explanation not of individual events but merely of the appearance of certain patterns or orders."

37. Also see Polanyi and Prosch (1975, p. 204), who distinguish between "spontaneous" and "corporate" orders in much the same way.

38. See Rector (1987) for an example of this applied to the theory of the firm.

39. On the industrial organization aspect, see Rothbard's (1962b, pp. 585-86) discussion of why "one big cartel" is not a possible outcome of the market process. Implied in Rothbard's discussion and mine in the text is the argument against the possibility of rational calculation under socialism. See Hayek (1935) and Lavoie (1985b). It is the shift from complicated to open-ended that makes rational economic calculation problematic for the central planner but not for the entrepreneur.

40. There is a large debate among evolutionary biologists as to whether evolution occurs at the level of the gene, the individual, or the group. Much of this debate has come after the publication of Richard Dawkins's (1976) *The Selfish*

Gene, which argues for the first position. In an essay in his *Panda's Thumb,* Stephen Jay Gould (1980, p. 92) argues for the second position based on a kind of intelligibility criterion: Genes have to do their work in concert with other genes embodied in a physical organism, and it is that organism that must survive the biological imperative. This debate in biology may have useful lessons for debates over methodological individualism in the social sciences.

41. Giraffes have long necks not because they grew them in the process of stretching to feed on higher leaves. Rather those giraffes that were fortunate enough to be born with longer necks found it easier to survive and passed the trait of long neckedness on to their offspring. The former position is the one taken by earlier biologists such as Lamarck. Although Lamarckian evolution is not a valid theory of the natural world, it does have something to say about social evolutionary processes. See the discussion to follow.

42. It should be clear that I am not arguing that entrepreneurship is in any sense genetic, only that genetic mutations are to biological evolution as entrepreneurial acts are to socioeconomic evolution.

43. There are numerous other parallels between the two theories that space does not permit me to explore. The interested reader should closely examine *The Origin of Species,* a book that more economists and other social theorists should read.

44. Geoffrey Hodgson (1989, p. 143) also recognizes this point: "Thus the true analog to social and economic evolution in the science of biology is not the work of Charles Darwin, but the earlier notion of Jean Baptiste Lamarck."

45. See also Hayek (1989, p. 25): "Cultural evolution *simulates* Lamarckism . . . [making] cultural evolution incomparably faster than biological evolution."

46. The use of the word *fundamental* should not be construed to imply that the legal order must ontologically come first. It is clearly true historically, and theoretically, that markets and law have coevolved. The evolution of the law is an example of a creative response attempting to coordinate the increased complexity generated by concurrent evolution in the market itself. See Benson (1990) for a more detailed examination of these relationships.

47. This question, if one substitutes "efficient" for "orderly," is the foundation of the law and economics literature, begun by the work of Ronald Coase. One should note that my use of *orderly* rather than *efficient* points toward a more Austrian concept of the field of law and economics, based on the notion of order analysis outlined here rather than on the equilibrium analysis and Pareto criteria of neoclassical economics.

48. Compare Simmel (1908, p. 19): "Positions within society are not planned by a constructive will but can be grasped only through an analysis of the creativity and experience of the component individuals."

49. See Cordato (1989) for a parallel critical discussion of the Chicago school approach to the roles of the judge and of rules of property in the law and economics literature.

50. Benson (1990) argues that the division of powers *within* government may not be enough to ensure order-inducing judge-made law. He seems to suggest that it might take a First Amendment-style *separation* of law and state to do the job.

3

Money as the Language of the Market Process

Building on the previous chapter's discussion of the evolution of social institutions and economic order, I will in this chapter apply those ideas to the origin and function of money.[1] My main purpose will be to use order analysis to bolster the argument of the first chapter and to provide a framework for a different understanding of monetary institutions and their role in the cultivation of economic order. In particular, the work of the economist Carl Menger and the sociologist Georg Simmel will be given careful scrutiny.

The framework provided by Menger and Simmel will be extended by analogizing money's role in the communication of knowledge in the marketplace to language's role in the communication of knowledge in other social processes. Much in the same way that the spoken and written word make possible mutual understanding between individuals in society, so do money and money prices make possible orderly processes between economic actors in the market. In addition to performing this *analogous* communicative function, money, through its ability to make contextual knowledge socially usable, also *extends* the range of social communication beyond the limits of language and the physical senses.

Many other theorists of social order have noted the role that language plays in shaping our understanding of the world. In his last work, Hayek (1989) argues that[2] "we learn to classify objects chiefly through language, with which we not merely label known kinds of objects but specify what *we are to regard* as objects or events of the same or different kinds" (p. 15, emphasis in original). And, "More importantly, all usage of language is laden with interpretations or theories about our surroundings. As Goethe recognised, all that we imagine to be factual is already theory: what we 'know' of our surroundings is our interpretation of them" (p. 106). Polanyi (1958, p. 249ff.) develops his epistemology of personal knowledge by stressing the role of asserting a sentence as the conveyor of the personal aspect of knowledge:

> Only a speaker or listener can mean something by a word, and a word in itself can mean nothing. When the act of meaning is thus brought home to a person exercising his understanding of things by the use of words which describe them, the possibility of performing the act of meaning according to strict criteria appears logically meaningless. (p. 252)

And finally, Mises (1983, p. 13) notes the role of language as a preformer of, and a medium for, the exchange of thoughts:

> Community of language is at first the consequence of an ethnic or social community, independently of its origin, however, it itself now becomes a new bond that creates definite social relations. In learning the language, the child absorbs a way of thinking and expressing his thoughts that is pre-determined by the language, and so he receives a stamp that he can scarcely remove from his life. The language opens up the way for a person of exchanging thoughts with all those who use it; he can influence them and receive influence from them. . . . Consider what immense significance language has for thinking, and for the expression of thought, for social relations, and for all activities of life.

We have already pointed out the Continental heritage of the Austrian tradition in economics. Modern thought in Continental philosophy, especially the work of Gadamer, has developed this view of language into a whole approach to the relationship of thought and understanding. After examining how order analysis might view the origin of money, we will briefly explain the Continental approach to language and then attempt to weave these approaches to money and language together to find their similarities and differences. As we move back and forth between money and language, we will gain a better understanding of both.

Menger on the Spontaneous Evolution of Money

Discussions of money and monetary theory within the Austrian approach invariably turn to Carl Menger's (1892) theory of the origin of money. Many within the Austrian school point to Menger's monetary theory as the exemplary spontaneous order explanation of the evolution of a social institution and use it as a standard of comparison for similar theories.[3] Menger also saw that the origin of money was only one example of a number of social institutions whose origins and operation could be explained in this manner:

> I will first present the theory of the origin of social structures under discussion here by way of a few examples, that of the genesis of money, of states, of markets, etc., and thus by the genesis of social institutions which serve social interests to a high degree and the first origins of which in the great majority of cases can in no way be traced back to positive laws or other expressions of intentional common will. (1985, p. 152)

As in the rest of the Mengerian tradition, knowledge and evolution play large roles in the story of the origin of money.[4]

The main targets of Menger's argument are those who ascribe the origin and continuing existence of money to the force of authority or to a conscious explicit agreement. Menger counters that any theory that invokes explicit agreement or authority only pushes the question back one step further: Why should so many "agreements" and "authorities" all turn to a relatively small number of money commodities (i.e., the precious metals)? He (1892, p. 241) argues that explanation by authority "presupposes the pragmatic origin of money . . . [by not] explaining how it has come to pass that certain commodities . . . should be promoted amongst the mass of all other commodities, and accepted as the generally acknowledged media of exchange."

Menger argues that in order to better understand the origin of money, we must first recognize that one of money's most important, and most distinguishing, characteristics is that it is so easily salable. The problem in a barter economy, as noted in Chapter 1, is the absence of a double coincidence of wants. Fortunately,

> These difficulties would have proved absolutely insurmountable obstacles to the progress of traffic . . . had there not lain a remedy in the very nature of things, to wit, *the different degrees of saleableness of*

commodities. . . . The theory of money necessarily presupposes a theory of the saleableness of goods. (pp. 242-43, emphasis in original)

Immediately Menger's theory moves away from the context provided by the general equilibrium theories discussed in the first chapter. In GE, all goods are assumed to have equal liquidity (salability). In the real world, however, goods differ along this margin:

> Commerce and speculation would be the simplest things in the world, if the theory of the "objective equivalent in goods" were correct, if it were actually true, that in a given market and at a given moment commodities could be mutually converted at will in definite quantitative relations—could, in short, at a certain price be as easily disposed of as acquired. At any rate there is no such thing as a general saleableness of wares in this sense. . . . If we call any goods or wares *more or less salable*, according to the greater or less facility with which they can be disposed of . . . we can see by what has been said that an obvious difference exists in this connection between commodities. (pp. 243-44, emphasis in original)

From a Mengerian perspective, we can only explain the origin of money only if we drop any pretense of the equal liquidity of goods, thus implying the futility of a general equilibrium explanation of money. I t is interesting to note Menger's explanation of why the problem of salability has been ignored by economists: "The reason of this is in part the circumstance, that investigation into the phenomena of price has been directed almost exclusively to the *quantities* of commodities exchanged, and not as well to the greater or less *facility* with which wares may be disposed of at normal prices" (p. 244, emphasis in original). Ignoring salability is likely to continue as long as economists focus on quantities (as in GE theory) rather than on the intentions and plans of economic actors, which are the ultimate determinants of the salability of goods. Money's essence flows from its being more salable than other goods, and salability can make sense only when economic analysis begins with the subjective valuations of actors, for salable means that the good is desired by enough people to give the good a relatively small bid-ask spread. For Menger "desirability" has to originate in the minds of economic actors. The foundation of Menger's approach to money (i.e., salability) is a natural extension of his more general subjectivism.[5]

After explicating a number of factors that do and do not enhance the salability of goods, Menger proceeds to the heart of his theory. We can imagine a series of actors on their way to the market intent on executing exchanges in order to give up goods they have but do not want in order to obtain others that they do want but do not have. Such exchanges will be easier to execute if our actors bring to market goods that are more easily salable. It becomes much easier to trade for the things that others have when the good you are able to give them is something they desire in return. Even those who do not at first possess salable goods can always exchange what they do have for something somewhat more salable, which can later be exchanged for the ultimate desiderata. It may well be easier to acquire a certain good through a series of exchanges for goods of greater and greater salability, ultimately leading to the good in question, rather than by hoping for a double coincidence of wants with the originally possessed good and the desired good.

As Menger rightly notes, knowledge of which goods are more salable than others "never arises in every part of a nation at the same time" (1892, p. 249). As actors participate in markets, their success in using indirect exchange to acquire the goods they desire will indicate the relative salability of the intermediate good(s) they are using. Already, even before we have a money in any real sense, indirect exchange is generating knowledge for its participants. What is even more important for this process is that as we observed in our broader discussion of the evolution of social institutions, imitative behavior provides a built-in means of communicating this knowledge to other participants that does not involve language. As Menger (p. 249) puts it: "There is no better method of enlightening any one about his economic interests than that he perceive the economic successes of those who use the right means to secure their own."

Those who use more salable goods find it easier to obtain the things they want (i.e., increase their real income). This is the creativity aspect of the order-generating process of the evolution of money. The entrepreneurial decision to trade indirectly sets the process into motion. Seeing these gains, others imitate that behavior and use those same highly salable commodities in indirect exchange as well. In this way, knowledge of preferred goods is communicated, and this communication corresponds to the coordination element of the ordering process. As indirect exchange is used, more people are better able to coordinate their desires to buy with others' desires to sell. The complexity aspect arrives as these successful exchanges lead to further innovations and an increased extension of the use of indirect exchange.

The effect of the new demand for those objects is to increase their salability that much more. Now not only do the original users demand them as media of exchange but the imitators do as well. In addition to their original salability as objects of consumption, the intermediate goods of these indirect exchanges are that much more salable as a result of being used as media of exchange. The additional source of demand increases the complexity of the process, and we can then distinguish between the monetary and nonmonetary demand for the goods in question. Although the monetary demand for the goods may eventually completely eliminate the nonmonetary demand in that the goods might *only* be used as media of exchange and no longer as objects of consumption, Menger's theory makes it clear that any usable money, including fiat paper money, must have once been linked to some commodity with direct consumption value. It is the original nonmonetary use value that gives the good its original salability. Mises's (1980, p. 131) well-known "regression theorem," which argues that "the earliest value of money links up with the commodity value of the monetary material," can be seen as a natural outgrowth of the Mengerian theory of the origin of money, and, in particular, of its subjectivism.

As in the earlier analyses of order, the increased complexity of this multiplied salability can be coordinated, because the heightened salability of these goods makes it possible for more people to be successful in using them as media of exchange and because more imitators follow. This process continues until some very small (likely one) number of goods emerge as the most salable, and it is these that we designate as money or generally accepted media of exchange.[6] The existence of money is thus "the spontaneous outcome, the unpremeditated resultant, of particular, individual efforts of the members of a society, who have little by little worked their way to a discrimination of the different degrees of saleableness in commodities" (Menger 1892, p. 250).

Once such a medium of exchange has been arrived at, the vast majority of exchanges take place using it. Money touches all other commodities by virtue of the fact that it is being exchanged against them. To trade commodity for commodity becomes difficult without exchanging one for money first. As Menger (pp. 251-52) argues,

> What therefore constitutes the peculiarity of a commodity which has become money is, that the possession of it procures for us at any time, i.e. any moment we see fit, assured control over every commodity to be had on the market . . . the control on the other hand, conferrred by other

kinds of commodities over market goods, is . . . uncertain, relatively if not absolutely. . . . This difference in saleableness ceases to be altogether gradual, and must be regarded in a certain aspect as something absolute.

Thus every market is a market for the money commodity, as virtually every exchange is an exchange against money. As we shall see further on, this pervasiveness of money enables it to function as a means of social communication and dramatically to enhance the evolution of the market and society.[7] Again, the development of the social institution of a medium of exchange is an order-generating process embodying creativity, complexity, and coordination.

Advantages of an Order-Analysis Approach to Money

Menger's theory and its more recent extensions have a number of advantages over the general equilibrium approaches discussed in the first chapter. Most of these advantanges concern the roles of knowledge and evolution in understanding social institutions. Perhaps most important, Menger's theory is one in which the process of the evolution and use of a medium of exchange do not merely redistribute existing, objective knowledge from actor to actor but rather create knowledge that did not previously exist. A market characteristic of a good, such as salability or scarcity in comparison to wants, is not a piece of objective information according to Menger's theory. Rather such knowledge can be revealed or created only through the actual process of economic exchange.

According to Menger's theory, actors discover which goods are more or less salable—knowledge that was previously unknown, as in the earlier discussion of Kirzner's notion of discovery. Menger describes the process as a continual "discrimination of the different degrees of salableness." Not only is salability itself not inherent in goods, knowledge of such salability is not given to those who trade such goods. Salability is ultimately determined by the mental processes of market actors, and the discovery of degrees of salability is a process of recognizing, drawing out, and interpreting patterns in the behavior of other market actors rather than uncovering some objective (outside of the human mind) piece of information. Actions taken during the process of exchange that originates and extends the evolution of money bring knowledge from the personal to the social level. Knowledge about salability (and other subjective preferences and valuations) is generated by the process of exchange. To view the shift from direct exchange to monetary exchange as simply the redistribution of existing information, as do a number of general equilibrium approaches, is to miss the crucial point that such a shift *creates* what previously did not exist in any accessible form.

Perhaps the importance of these differing views of knowledge can be seen in what they imply about the efficacy of the knowledge-communication process happening during the evolution of money. Consider the following quote from Mises's (1966, p. 406, emphasis added) discussion of Menger's theory of money:

> The happy idea of [indirect exchange] could strike the shrewdest individuals, and the less resourceful could *imitate* the former's method. It is certainly more plausible to take for granted that the immediate advantages conferred by indirect exchange were recognized by the acting parties than to assume that the whole image of a society trading by means of money was conceived by a genius and, if we adopt the covenant doctrine, made obvious to the rest of the people by *persuasion*.

One way of looking at this passage is to note the alternative ways of communicating knowledge Mises demarcates. We can either observe the behavior of others, judge its success, and choose to imitate it, or we can enter a verbal or textual conversation with others and rely on the persuasive powers of their articulate thoughts to provide us with knowledge. Mises argues that imitation is, in general, a more plausible way by which particular types of behavior spread and evolve into a social institution than is articulate persuasion.

Mises's case for imitation is even stronger when we recognize that the actions involved in imitation and evolution can communicate the kinds of contextual knowledge that cannot be known through articulation.[8] Michael Polanyi (1958, p. 53, emphasis added) describes this process with the example of a master and a student:

> To learn by example is to submit to authority. You follow your master because you trust his manner of doing things even when you cannot analyse and account in detail for its effectiveness. By watching the master and emulating his efforts in the presence of his example, the apprentice unconsciously picks up the rules of the art, *including those which are not explicitly known to the master himself.*

Hayek (1989, p. 104, emphasis added) describes the function of money in a similar fashion: "Money is indispensible for extending reciprocal cooperation beyond the limits of human awareness—and therefore also *beyond the limits of what was explicable* and could be readily recognised as expanding opportunities." Despite the tacit nature of much of our knowledge, it can be made available to others through social action, such as exchange or exercising a skill, and communicated through a process of imitation.[9] To take advantage of this tacit knowledge we must recognize the importance of imitative learning in the extended social order. Relying solely on persuasion limits us to knowledge that can be communicated through speech and texts and chokes off other sources of knowledge.

Of course the contrast between imitative action and articulation is not a case of totally tacit versus totally articulate knowledge. Articulate conversations are a large constituent part of broader tacit processes, and even the most intimate conversation or text has tacit elements that constitute it. In the often anonymous and tacit world of the market, businesspeople do meet face-to-face to negotiate contracts, buyers and sellers haggle over prices and quantities, and the intersection of the economic and legal orders is the articulate world of the courtroom. But, even in an extremely articulate situation, such as a discussion between a husband and wife, there are dozens of unintended meanings and contexts as well as tacit visual and aural clues that provide meanings beyond the limits of the articulated words. The worlds of the tacit and the articulate comingle constantly.

What is crucial for social theory, however, is that articulation processes are never sufficient to describe the knowledge generated and communicated in spontaneous social orders. As argued in Chapter 2, knowledge of the details of a complex order is beyond the capability of any one individual or organization. The tacitness and contextuality of human knowledge and the limits of articulation are most obvious when communication has to take place between millions of actors, all situated in different contexts with differing information sets. The anonymity and complexity of the social world limits our ability to pass on knowledge in an articulate form. The use of money and the development of a money price system provide us with a means of communication that transcends what articulation can give us.[10] Articulation processes may be necessary to the evolution of social institutions, but they are not sufficient. If one ignores inarticulate knowledge, one has a hard time making sense of many articulate processes, not to mention broader social institutions.[11] Like M. C. Escher's famous drawing of two hands drawing each other, tacit and articulate processes coevolve and make each other, and socioeconomic order, possible.[12]

The use of money cannot be separated from the undesigned complexity of the social order, or from the tacit processes that underlie it. This poses the fundamental problem left unsolved by neoclassical models of monetary exchange: How is it possible to explain the origin and functions of money and monetary exchange while maintaining an objectivist view of knowledge? All of the authors[13] discussed in Chapter 1 are within the neoclassical tradition of utility maximization and equilibrium theory, which must hypothesize explicit and knowable utility functions based on given prices and knowledge of the market. It is precisely these atomistic maximization processes that have a great deal of trouble generating money as an outcome.

The closest approach to a Mengerian view was Jones's (1976). He dropped some of the atomism by integrating an explicit imitation process into his model. Others, such as Ostroy, Starr, Brunner and Meltzer, and Alchian had less explicit imitative processes as well. Their objectivism poses the paradox that they need to rely on some type of evolutionary-imitative process to generate money when the knowledge of money's benefits is objective and therefore communicable through more articulate means. If all of the relevant knowledge is objective, then why did we not simply do what Mises suggests is the other alternative: consciously foresee money's benefits and spread the word? One could counter that such an effort would be too costly in a large community, but this response confuses costly knowledge with not-yet-known (or undiscovered in Kirzner's sense) knowledge.[14] The relevant knowledge does not even exist in a ready form. The best, most sophisticated equipment in the world could not foresee the benefits of money. The benefit of allowing the evolution of social institutions through imitative processes is that these evolutionary processes communicate what would otherwise be largely unknown and discover what otherwise would not have come into existence. The whole raison d'être of evolution and imitation is negated by objectifying knowledge.

The tacit realm of knowing is a necessary partner to evolutionary theories and complex undesigned social orders.[15] General equilibrium theory cannot have both an objectivist view of knowledge and a sufficient explanation of complex social institutions. The advantage of Menger's theory of money is his recognition, at least implicitly, of the inseparability of the elements of knowledge, evolution, and order.

Georg Simmel's Sociology of Money

First published in 1900 and revised in 1907, Georg Simmel's *The Philosophy of Money* is an extensive treatment of the nature of money and its role in the extended social order of capitalist economies. Owing much to Menger and subjectivist thought, Simmel expands that perspective to a broader sociology of money, including some elements of Marxian social analysis.[16] Importantly, it is Simmel who makes explicit the analogy between money and language, which will be examined in more depth.

Like Menger and his followers in the Austrian tradition, Simmel (1978) recognizes the role of the individual as both the constructor of economic value and the fundamental unit of social analysis:[17] "At any moment when our mind is not simply a passive mirror of reality—which perhaps never happens, since even objective perception can arise only from valuation—we live in a world of values which arranges the contents of reality in an autonomous order" (p. 60). Also, "It is of great importance to reduce the economic process to what really happens in the mind of each economic subject" (pp. 83-84). Although this last statement might sound reductionistic, Simmel also recognized that individual action has patterns of unintended consequences that after a time would appear to be beyond the control of those individuals. Like Marx, Simmel felt that such spontaneous orders could and did turn back on their originators to exercise some kind of inescapable and undesirable influence on their thoughts and actions:

> Economic interactions take place with such admirable expediency, by subtly organized dovetailing of innumerable details, that it would be necessary to assume that they were integrated by a superior mind, operating with superhuman wisdom, if one did not fall back on the unconscious power of adaptation of the human species. The conscious intentions and foresight of individuals would not suffice to maintain the harmony that economic activity displays alongside its fearful discords and inadequacies. (p. 159)

From within this perspective, Simmel examines the ways in which money operates as an element of the broader processes of the market and society.

A crucial aspect of money's role in society is how it brings people into social processes by "facilitat[ing] the development of an ever widening circle of economic interdependence based on the dispersion of trust" (Frankel 1977, p. 14). In short, money socializes us by enabling us to utilize the contextual knowledge of others through the trust embodied in monetary exchange. Much as imitation provides the communication process necessary for advancing the complexity of the monetary order, trust serves that function in maintaining and extending the existing complexity of that order. For Simmel, virtually all social relationships involve trust due to the difficulty in acting "entirely on what is known with certainty about another person" (Simmel 1978, p. 179). He continues: "and very few relationships would endure if trust were not as strong as, or stronger than rational proof or personal observation. In the same way, money transactions would collapse without trust." The trust element here is the belief that others equally accept the money commodity as a medium of exchange.[18] Menger's explanation of money arising out of intersubjectively held values explains how this trust is generated. It is the evolutionary process by which the salability of money is continually heightened that creates the trust that we can exchange money for nonmoney goods whenever we please. The "absoluteness" of this salability permits the value of money to transcend the personal and achieve social acceptance and trust.

Frankel (1977, pp. 36-37) elaborates on how trust takes the place of detailed knowledge of others:

> When we trust a person, we are going beyond the mere assessment of probabilities. Indeed, trust or mistrust takes its place precisely because such an assessment cannot easily be made, or because it is too costly or time-consuming to do so. It enters where more exact knowledge is not available. . . . Individuals and societies are dependent on countless symbols, myths, beliefs, and institutions which function as indicators of trustworthiness or the opposite. That is why trust has been described as a means of reducing complexity and a form of social communication . . . [it] spans the problems of time and uncertainty.

Simmel (1978, p. 179, emphasis added) came to a similar conclusion: "To 'believe in someone,' without adding or even *conceiving what it is that one believes about him*, is to employ a very subtle and profound idiom." Trust then, is simply a type of rule-following behavior. We use trust to form expectations about individuals and institutions because we cannot have detailed knowledge of the people or institutions in question. Hayek (1989, p. 102) says of money that with it

> we reach the climax of the progressive replacement of the perceivable and concrete by abstract concepts shaping rules guiding activity: money and its institutions seem to lie beyond the boundary of the laudable and understandable physical efforts of creation, in a realm where the comprehension of the concrete ceases and incomprehensible abstractions rule.

When we are denied knowledge of the particulars, rules can serve as effective substitutes.

As with other rules, the knowledge involved in deploying trust is, to a great degree, tacit. The emphasis in the earlier quote from Simmel brings this out. The fact that the knowledge embodied in trust is tacit is what gives trust its power as a social communicator. When I say I "trust" someone, and you understand what I mean, I am making public a piece of contextual knowledge that otherwise would be unknown to you. You are able to utilize the knowledge of my context by choosing to rely, or not, on my trust. Again, like imitation for Menger, trust makes known effective patterns of behavior that would be difficult, if not impossible, to access otherwise. In so doing, trust also facilitates the evolution and use of social institutions formed from these behavioral patterns.[19]

The trust aspect of monetary exchange also expands the circle of social relationships beyond what can be achieved through face-to-face contact.[20] In Simmel's (1978, p. 182) words:

> Expanding economic relations eventually produce in the enlarged, and finally international, circle the same features that originally characterized only closed groups; economic and legal conditions overcome the spatial separation more and more, and they come to operate just as reliably, precisely, and predictably over a great distance as they did previously in local communities.

The fact that some anonymous "other" trades with money indicates that she shares the common trust in the social order that money embodies. In Schutzian terms, "moneyuser" becomes an ideal type at a very abstract level.[21] This ideal type gains us entry to the extended social order by providing knowledge to others without the need for direct face-to-face interaction. For Simmel, this aspect of money is the means by which monetary exchange expands the range of freedom available to the individual.

Money's salability means that it can be exchanged for anything with anyone. In insufficiently monetized economies, freedom is limited not only by the absence of a double coincidence of wants but also by the fact that it is frequently the case that certain exchanges can take place only if both parties meet certain narrowly defined social norms. For example, one might have to be a member of a specific occupation, social class, or family to engage in particular exchanges. In a monetary economy, the only requirement for exchange is that one be a money user. In many ways it was this aspect of money that was responsible for the market's ability to break down the barriers of social caste structures. The gold of the serf or the trader was just as salable as the gold of the lords and ladies.

For Simmel, the essence of money is that it is a tool. Rather than being an end in itself, money is a universal means to whatever ends are available in the market. As should be clear to this point, it is not a tool that humans have created but rather one we have stumbled across in our efforts to improve our place in the world. Simmel (p. 209) argues that social institutions in general fit this description: "The most typical instances of this kind of tool are perhaps social institutions, by means of which the individual can attain ends for which his personal abilities would never suffice." Simmel (pp. 210-11) then turns to money's role as such an institution:[22]

> Money is the purest form of the tool, in the category mentioned above; it is an institution through which the individual concentrates his activity and possessions in order to attain the goals he could not attain directly. The fact that everyone works with it makes its character as a tool more evident. . . . Money in its perfected forms is an absolute means . . . [and] is perhaps the clearest expression and demonstration of the fact that man is a "tool-making" animal, which, however, is itself connected with the fact that man is a "purposive" animal.

As we will see further on, the analogy of the tool is not quite right, mainly because we do not really "use" money (or language) in the same way we "use" other kinds of tools. Even so, Simmel has captured the extent to which money is a tool and shown how that role derives from our attempts to act purposively.

As Simmel notes, money, like other tools, allows us to achieve goals we could not attain directly. This happens through the transmission of tacit knowledge during individual acts of buying and selling and the resulting market phenomena. The economist's understanding of the market process can bring to Simmel's analysis an explanation of how money operates. More specifically, economic theory explains how money, by cultivating the process of specialization and exchange, enables us to exploit the efficiency gains of production by comparative advantage and to better satisfy human wants. It is surely important to recognize that money is a tool of some sort, but understanding precisely what it does and how it works (and why it frequently does not) is of great relevance for questions of economic theory and social policy.[23]

Simmel (p. 210) offers another social institution, language, as an analogy to money's role as a tool that allows us to access the more remote regions of social life:[24] "Just as my thoughts must take the form of a universally understood language so that I can attain my practical ends in this roundabout way, so must my activities and possessions take the form of money value in order to serve my more remote purposes." At another point (p. 120), he uses a similar analogy to compare the abstract nature of money's value as money to its value as a commodity:

> In this sense, money has been defined as "abstract value." As a visible object, money is the substance that embodies abstract economic value, in a similar fashion to the sound of words which is an acoustic-physiological occurrence but has significance for us only through the representation that it bears or symbolizes.

The analogy between money and language is a very strong one indeed, and this fact has not escaped others.[25] James Tobin (cited in Yeager 1982, p. 237), for one, notes that "both are means of communication. . . . Use of a particular language or a particular money by one individual increases its value to other actual or potential users." Though this correspondence has been noted, very little, if anything, has been done in extending and elaborating it. The remainder of this chapter will be just such an attempt. First we will briefly examine the characteristics of language as a social institution, utilizing Hans-Georg Gadamer's discussion of language and human understanding. Then we will compare and contrast language and money to fully elaborate money's role as the language of the market process.

The Language of the Market Process

To those within the spontaneous order tradition in political economy, the notion of language as a spontaneous order is a familiar one.[26] The details of just how language functions in this manner, and what that implies for human understanding and other issues in philosophy and the social sciences, have come from a parallel tradition—namely the modern descendents of the *verstehen* tradition in the social sciences. Of particular interest here is Hans-Georg Gadamer's (1985) theory of "language as the medium of experience."

As is frequently noted, the important aspect of a language is that it represents shared understandings (a coherence) among its users. The evolution of word usage and the rules of grammar are analogous to other evolutionary processes in other institutions. Gadamer (1985, p. 421) says that "the use and development of language is a process which has no single knowing and choosing consciousness standing over it." Like other social institutions, language extends the scope of our understanding beyond the limits of our senses. Language is one way in which we make our private knowledge available socially.

However, there is something more fundamental about language than about other institutions. As we noted in Chapter 2, language coevolves with other social institutions, and to the extent those institutions rely on articulation, they rely on language. Again, this is not to say that language is a sufficient condition for the evolution of other social institutions, but it is a necessary one. As Gadamer (p. 401, 407) argues, "Language is not just one of man's possessions in the world, but on it depends the fact that man has a world at all." And, "In language the reality beyond every individual consciousness becomes visible." For Gadamer there is no reality beyond our immediate physical senses except for that which is understood through language:

> Language is the universal medium in which understanding is itself realised . . . All understanding is interpretation, and all interpretation takes place in the medium of a language which would allow the object to come into words and yet is at the same time the interpreter's own language. (p. 350)
>
> The linguistic world in which we live is not a barrier that prevents knowledge of being in itself, but fundamentally embraces everything in which our insight can be enlarged and deepened. (p. 405)

The search for truth and understanding is a social process of communication, and that communication must take place in language. The implication is that we cannot distinguish what we call truth from the words and linguistic perspective in which we understand it.[27] What we will explore is whether, and how, this view might apply to monetary exchange as a social communication process.[28]

The point of departure for the analogy between money and language is to recognize that both mediate social processes; money is the "medium of exchange" for Menger and many others; language is the "medium of experience" for Gadamer and others in the Continental tradition. Just as language allows us to understand, through our own interpretive frameworks, the linguistically constituted thoughts of others, so does money allow us to elicit and interpret the tastes, preferences, and values of other economic actors. Both language and money are ways of extending our perceptual apparatuses beyond the immediate; the difference lies in to what each allows us access. The advantage of a monetarily extended language over language alone (and why the modern socioeconomic order is equally dependent on money, as it is on language, for its emergence and evolution) is that money allows us to utilize not only the articulate knowledge of others but, more important, their knowledge that cannot be put into language.

Both language and money allow us to make private knowledge socially available. However, this mediation process is not simply a copying (or mapping) of the mind onto words or prices that then are unambiguously received by others. Language and money do not *reveal* some preexisting mental constructs or preferences, rather they *constitute* the way in which we express those constructs and preferences.[29] Just as we cannot help but think in terms of the words that language provides us, we cannot help but act in the market in terms of the money prices of what we want to exchange.[30] As difficult as it is to communicate thoughts outside of language, so is it difficult to express market-relevant wants outside of monetary exchange.[31] Just as a thought that cannot be expressed in words is difficult to communicate in a conversation or text, so is an economic want not expressed in money difficult to communicate in the market process.[32]

It is here that we can appropriate Gadamer to advance on Menger and Simmel. For Gadamer (1966, pp. 62-63), language is not a tool:

Language is by no means simply an instrument, a tool. For it is in the nature of the tool that we master its use, which is to say we take it in hand and lay it aside when it has done its service. That is not the same as when we take the words of a language . . . such an analogy is false because we never find ourselves as consciousness over and against the world and, as it wore [sic], grasp after a tool of understanding in a wordless condition. . . . We are always encompassed by the language that is our own.

The view of language as a tool is a remnant of scientistic rationalism in that social institutions are seen as pure mirrors of subjective mental processes. For this rationalism, there is some ultimately knowable set of facts, values, tastes, and so on, that are hidden behind the veil of social institutions such as language or money.[33] The purpose of such institutions is to reveal the ultimate constituents of these mental processes.[34] In Gadamer's view, however, there are no such "ultimate constituents," rather language and thought coevolve in such a way that the idea of "thoughts without language" is a contradiction in terms. Communication in language is not a veil for reality, it *is* reality.

Humans have not made or chosen money and language like we make or choose a tool. Both are traditions, or institutions, that have been passed down to us through the cultural evolutionary process. Hayek and Gadamer both emphasize how institutions and traditions are neither rationally chosen nor instinctual but rather evolve during the development of social orders. Both also argue that those institutions and traditions preform the ways in which we act and understand in the world. For both, this is not a disadvantage of institutions and traditions, because there is nothing to compare them to that they fall short of. To the contrary, this is the great power of institutions and traditions; they make all other reason and knowledge possible.[35]

As with acknowledging the power of language, recognizing the force of tradition in determining money prices and economic outcomes does not mean we have to bow down to tradition and leave ourselves no way to change the course of events. As Gadamer, Polanyi, and Hayek have argued, we may examine bits and pieces of traditions, but not everything at once. When applied to money, this simply means that we are limited in our ability to rationally construct or alter a monetary order. We can certainly criticize individual elements and offer new rules or broad patterns of action, but we cannot redesign all of the details at once. We can also recognize that these limits to our reason imply that existing institutions based on an unreasonable conception of reason (i.e., those that are the undesirable unintended consequences of attempts at conscious design) may be causing more harm than good and may need to be changed or eliminated. To say that money carries the inertia of tradition is not to say that it is unalterable, only that there are limits to our ability to make changes.[36]

To stress the point that money and language both require real action to be meaningful, one might distinguish between a sign and a word. The usual notion of a sign is that it can be understood independently of the actions of those who use it. The meaning is in the sign itself rather than in how or when it is used. Words, however, require a user in order to have real meaning. We could conceivably construct an artificial system of signs (a mathematics, perhaps), but we could never construct an artificial system of words. Words require speakers and writers first, not after, the system is constructed. After arguing that the tacit nature of articulation involves confidence, Polanyi (1958, pp. 250-51) drives home the comparison of sign and word:

> Our confidence in the meaning of words is an act of social allegiance. . . . By contrasting the oblique use of words with their direct use, we can now show formally that these risks of confidence utterance are unavoidable. We may place a word in quotation marks, while using language confidently through the rest of a sentence. But the questioning of each word in turn would never question all at the same time. Accordingly, it would never reveal a comprehensive error which underlies our entire descriptive idiom. We can of course write down a text and withdraw our confidence from all its words simultaneously, by putting each descriptive word between quotation marks. But then none of the words would mean anything and the whole text would be meaningless.

Using quotation marks to hold a word's meaning in abeyance turns it from a word into a sign. Any individual word can be so changed only because it always has the contextual background of the other words that compose the unit of text in question.

However, we can never hold all meaning in suspension, because then we have no context left over to understand what we have done. We are always understanding *from* some shared context of meaning, some set of words that are actually used. The same is true in the market. We can understand one price only in relationship to other prices actually paid in markets. Prices that are arrived at outside of the market are more like signs, and only human usage can make them more like words.[37] To the extent those prices are prevented from changing via use, we restrict their value to market actors—much like freezing the meaning of a word renders it of little use to speakers of the language. Gadamer (1985, p. 404) emphasizes that "language has its true being only in conversation, in the exercise of understanding between people."[38] This is analogous to Mises's argument, noted earlier, that the evolution of money can be realized only by actual exchange. Constructed languages, and constructed price systems, contradict both the actual way in which both systems have developed and the ways in which they are best used.[39]

Money, Language, and Community

Inasmuch as the emphasis has been on money as an analog to language, it should also be pointed out that money also interacts *with* language during the course of social development. Just as tacit and articulate processes comingle in a broad way, money and language feed off of each other to make possible extended social orders.

It is crucial to remember that language evolves before money does, and it is language that first makes social organization possible. With the development of language comes the ability to communicate within small groups and organize productive activity. Joint production processes require the communicative agreement that language permits. Once production becomes possible, then trade and exchange evolve as producers realize they can trade their excesses for what others have produced. At this point comes the Mengerian evolution of money and the extended market order it makes possible.

The development of money extends the range of our social vision. As a full-fledged price system evolves, we now have access to the purposes, plans, and knowledge of the numerous other people who are participating in economic interaction. In turn, the increased efficiency that results from the superior knowledge-processing powers of the market makes it possible to sustain even more human lives and to extend the social order even further.[40] As we have seen, the coordinative powers of language are limited by our ability to articulate our thoughts. Much of our knowledge cannot be expressed well in language. Money extends language by giving us the ability to communicate and utilize this tacit component.

Given this, what role is there within the broader social order for the concept of community? Once we have developed money and a price system, are we all so dependent on it that we are totally unable to remove ourselves from its grasp? Is individual action for monetary gain the sole constituent component of social order? The answer is a conditional no. The concepts of community and solidarity as motivating forces still have vital roles to play *inside* the social order. We can link the role of community to Hayek's distinction between orders and organizations.

One can easily conceive of a small group of people, all of whom share a set of beliefs or desires on particular subjects. Within such a group, linguistic coordination may be sufficient, particularly because, as in Hayek's notion of organization, all agree on the importance of the ends to which the group aspires. Examples again could be families or firms, where keeping the family together or maximizing profits are the relevant goals. But more broadly, one could imagine somewhat larger social arrangements working the same way.

Consider something like a large condominium complex with a governing board elected by the lot owners. The complex may have certain shared goals it wants to maintain—no smoking, adults only, no pets. If all who buy lots there agree on the goals, then solidarity is possible among those actors. All agree on the goals, are willing to cooperate and sacrifice, and acknowledge the board's authority in order to achieve these goals. In addition, verbal communication may be sufficient to discover these goals and to reach consensus on how best to achieve them. People who have lived in small towns see elements of this in the way in which residents come to the aid of neighbors, pitch in to build a community project, or generally agree on what is needed to maintain the quality of life in the area. In all of these situations, the competitive market order can be overridden to the extent that there is agreement on the various ends and that the organization is not overly complex.

The limit to this concept of community arises when an attempt is made to extend it beyond its capabilities. Unlike Hayekian orders (such as the market), communities do not have the built-in coordinating devices that enable them to handle the increased complexity that extended socioeconomic orders require. As soon as disagreement emerges on the goals of the community, or more likely, when the number of people in the community becomes so large that there is no way to linguistically access knowledge about ends and means, the spirit of solidarity starts to break down. The more complex the organization, the less successful is the "town meeting" type of decision-making. As spontaneous order theory indicates, attempting to direct processes when the relevant knowledge is beyond our ability to access will prove to be fruitless.

A useful concept here might be the idea of governance. All types of organizations require rules of governance. A local club, a faculty senate, and a condo complex all need concrete rules by which they can direct their processes of resource allocation. The agreement on, and success of, those rules is contingent upon a unity of ends among the members. The more diverse the members and their goals, and the more complex the organization, the more abstract the governance system must be. Hayek's notion of law, as opposed to legislation, is itself an *order*-level governance system that evolves by resolving the conflicting expectations of individual *organizations*. The law's abstractness results from its being a set of rules for the entire extended social order, with all of the diverse and conflicting purposes of the organizations whose actions unintentionally create that order.

What we wind up with is the recognition that community and solidarity have a role to play within the organizations that constitute a social order. But when those individual communities desire to interact with other communities and make decisions that require access to the knowledge of countless anonymous others (such as those that require knowing the relative values of scarce resources), then the principles of governance appropriate to communities will not be sufficient. As constituent elements of the social order, communities must submit to the order's more abstract and unconsciously evolved rules—they must use money, markets, and prices to achieve their outside ends.[41] Community and solidarity can be powerful motivating and organizational forces, but they are checked by the inherent limits of articulate communicative processes. When successful action requires access to inarticulate knowledge, then money is necessary to extend language and become "the true *binding agent—the [universal] galvano-chemical* power of society" (Marx 1964, p. 167, emphasis in original).

The Market and the Model of the Text

In a fascinating paper in 1971, the philosopher Paul Ricoeur argued that the concept of a text could serve as a model for all human action and social institutions. Social actors, and social scientists, interpret the texts (visible traces) of society. When we act, we create a text from our actions, much like an author does when writing. Ricoeur (1971, p. 316) tries to show that "the human sciences may be said to display some of the features constitutive of a text and . . . their methodology develops the same kind of procedures as those of . . . text-interpretation."

For Ricoeur (p. 326, emphasis in original), "the meaning of human action is also something which is *addressed* to an indefinite range of possible 'readers.'" Much as exchange in a monetary economy is addressed to the ideal type of "money user," so is action in general open to those who can understand the language that such action becomes "textualized" in. The role of social communication for Ricoeur (p. 321) is that it "frees us from the visibility and limitation of situations by opening up a world for us, that is, new dimensions of our being-in-the-world." What language gives us is the ability to access the actions and thoughts of another in a form that transcends the individual subjectivity of those actions and thoughts. When we have a conversation or write a text, it is our way of aiming our thoughts at another and asserting their *inter*subjective (i.e., among others, rather than simply individually) validity by crystallizing them in words. Ricoeur (p. 327, emphasis in original) concludes:

> Like a text, human action is an open work, the meaning of which is "in suspense." It is because it "opens up" new references and receives fresh relevance from them, that human deeds are also waiting for fresh interpretations which decide their meaning. All significant events and deeds are, in this way, opened to this kind of practical interpretation through present *praxis*. Human action, too, is opened to anybody who *can read*. In the same way that the meaning of an event is the sense of its forthcoming interpretations, the interpretation by the contemporaries has no particular privilege in this process.

The text of human action is both the result of previous interpretations and the cause of future ones, and no existing view has automatic superiority over future ones.

The analogy to the market is that the market is a text too, but one developed from the language of money and monetary exchange rather than from only the spoken or written word. Membership in the market requires not necessarily the ability to read or speak a language but the possession of money.[42] The market process is a process of dialogue, and, it can be added, money is the language from which that dialogue is formed.[43] What happens day-to-day in the market is more like a spoken text; accountancy and other interpretations of the market are more like written text. Viewing money as a language reinforces the analogy of the market as a dialogic text.

This view has a number of implications for the methodology of economics.[44] In-depth discussion would be beyond the scope of this chapter, but one aspect of those implications should be pointed out. Foremost, the ideas of money as a language and the market as a text necessitate a recognition of the role of interpretation. What happens in the market is a constant process of interpretation and reinterpretation that acquires intersubjective validity through the social institutions of the market—money, prices, profits, and the like. As well, what happens during the economist's attempts to make sense of the market is a process of interpretation. The theorist is interpreting the texts of the market within the common framework of economic theory. Finally, what happens between economists as they engage in conflict over these interpretations of the market is itself an interpretive process. At all three levels, different types of language are crucial: money in the market, the vocabulary of economics in theory construction, and the language of social science between economists. And where there is language, there must be interpretation.

Approaches to economics that ignore or discount these interpretive dimensions (as does neoclassical economics) are unlikely to provide much help in rendering the institutions of the market process, and the scientific process, intelligible to any great degree. More specifically, dismissing these interpretive elements will make understanding the role of money extremely difficult indeed. How can we ever make sense of any kind of language without recourse to interpretive concepts?

Conclusion

Our journey this chapter has brought us full circle. We began by using an alternative approach to economics to help us make sense of the shortcomings of neoclassical models of monetary exchange. The ideas of

Menger and Simmel, combined with the order-analysis approach developed in Chapter 2, led us to view money as the language of the market process, and it is this analogy that itself further strengthens the advantages of an order approach to economics in general, and money in particular. However, this is in many ways only the beginning of the story. The existence of money leads to levels of economic complexity that cause the emergence of the various institutions of the money industry. Currency, checks, banks, credit, and other financial institutions play a crucial role in the further evolution of monetary order specifically, and economic order more broadly. The next chapter will extend this view of the evolution of money to the evolution of monetary institutions and monetary order.

Notes

1. Portions of this chapter use and revise some material previously published in Horwitz (1992), reprinted with permission of *Review of Social Economy.*
2. See also Hayek (1952b, p. 150).
3. The 1892 paper cited is Menger's *Economic Journal* article entitled "On the Origin of Money." Parallel discussions can be found in his *Principles of Economics* (1981, pp. 257-85) and his *Investigations* (1985, pp. 152-55) as well as in several as yet untranslated articles in German. The number of appearances this theory makes in his work is testimony to Menger's own perception of its importance to his vision of economic and social theory. Mises (1966, pp. 405-8) also saw this connection, titling a subsection of his chapter on money "The Epistemological Import of Carl Menger's Theory of the Origin of Money." He argued there that Menger "has also recognized the import of his theory for the elucidation of fundamental principles of praxeology and its methods of research" (p. 405).
4. A number of recent papers that emphasize or extend Menger's work can be found in Caldwell (1990).
5. See also O'Driscoll (1986, p. 611): "We can now assess the particular contributions of Menger to monetary economics. First, he solved the problem of the evolution of a common medium of exchange. He did so by applying his compositive method, which consisted of a thoroughgoing subjectivism."
6. This is not to imply that the process stops at some point. The evolution of money, like that of all social institutions, continues as long as there are actors utilizing it. See the discussion in Chapter 4 for more on the roles played by changes in legislation, human preferences, and so on, in the continuing evolution of financial institutions.
7. See also O'Driscoll (1986, p. 611): "Menger's money is much more than a numeraire or otherwise neutral economic institution. It is one of the driving forces of economic development, replete with real effects. The distinctive property of the money good is that, being the most marketable of all goods, it has

evolved into a common medium of exchange. Nearly all transactions are executed with the use of money, so money is the most liquid of all goods. It is 'for sale' in every market." See also Dyer (1989, p. 503, emphasis in original): "Contrary to the orthodox belief that money's medium of exchange function shows its *insignificance* in determining real economic outcomes, I will argue that it is precisely this function of money that gives it a major role to play in shaping life in a pecuniary culture."

8. Mises (1966, p. 407) does say that "only the conduct of exchanging people can create indirect exchange and money." Also see Polanyi's (1958, p. 54) discussion of the legal doctrine of precedence: "This procedure recognizes the principle of all traditionalism that practical wisdom is more truly embodied in action than expressed in rules of action." Both the economic and legal evolutionary orders embody and communicate inarticulate knowledge through the actions of their participants.

9. Social imitation is not, however, a mere copying of another; it is a genuine learning process of "constructive interpretation." This is one source of the creativity aspect of spontaneous orders. Polanyi (1958, p. 206) makes this point with respect to animal experiments and extends it to human learning: "It is no blind parrot-like imitation, but a genuine transmission of an intellectual performance from one animal to another: a real communication of knowledge on an inarticulate level. All arts are learned by intelligently imitating the way they are practiced by other persons in whom the learner places his confidence."

10. Also see Thomas Sowell's (1980, pp. 214-23) discussion of articulation and knowledge transfer in his critique of economic planning. Sowell (p. 35) also notes that the knowledge communicated in market exchanges "is not merely abstract knowledge, but knowledge conveyed in a monetary form, conveying persuasion as well as information."

11. Without going into a lengthy digression into the history of philosophy, one can note that the difficulties that philosophers have had in explaining even the most simple human actions may reflect a Cartesian preference for explicit, articulate knowledge and a dismissal of other ways of knowing. An obvious example here might be the way in which positivist and falsificationist versions of the scientific method bear little resemblance to the real activity of scientists. See Polanyi (1958) and Gadamer (1985) for complementary philosophical treatments of these issues. It seems very plausible that analogous failures by economists result from the same unexamined bias.

12. The metaphor of the Escher drawing was suggested by William Poteat's (1985) use of it on the cover of his book on Polanyi.

13. The exception is Shackle, who in other publications seems to recognize the existence of tacit knowledge yet does not draw many of the conclusions about money discussed here.

14. In fact, this would be the likely response of neoclassical economists to any argument concerning tacit knowledge. Such knowledge, they would argue, is not inaccessible, it is only very costly to acquire. Thus supposed arguments over tacit knowledge become another application of transaction costs-modified equilibrium theory discussed in Chapter 1.

15. See also Sowell (1980, p. 217): "However many limitations and distortions articulation may have as a means of communicating economic knowledge, its political appeal is as widespread as the belief that order requires design [and] that the alternative to chaos is explicit intention."

16. The link to Menger is never made explicitly by Simmel due to the absence of formal footnotes in his book. However, the striking similarity of their analyses could not be coincidental, especially given that both came from a German-language tradition. Secondhand references to the linkage are in Frisby (1978), Frankel (1977) and Laidler and Rowe (1980, pp. 100-101). Laidler and Rowe refer to personal communication with Fritz Machlup, who assured them that the Austrians of the 1930s and 1940s were aware of Simmel's work and considered it a parallel development to their ideas. Mises (1980) also refers to Simmel's book several times.

It is interesting to ask why there is so little conversation between modern Mengerians and modern Simmelians when they appear to share a common ancestry. The most likely explanation is that disciplinary and ideological barriers have falsely led both groups to conclude that there would be few gains from exchange. Perhaps those barriers can be overcome and the gains from exchange will be realized.

17. Also see Frisby (1978, p. 24): "In fact Simmel's own theory of value, with its subjective and relativist assumptions, has much in common with the subjectivist theory of value advanced by marginal utility theorists such as Menger and Bohm-Bawerk."

18. This trust element is relevant for any kind of money. It is most obvious in fractional reserve banking systems, where one must also trust that the issuer of money will not default. However, even base money still requires the trust embodied in the assumption that it is generally accepted.

19. It is interesting that Laidler and Rowe (1980, p. 99, fn. 4) argue that "Simmel's concept of 'trust' seems to bear a close relationship to that of 'the informational content of money' which is to be found in the work of Karl Brunner and Allan Meltzer (1971) and Armen Alchian (1977)." It is true that everyone is talking about money's ability to convey information, but everyone's conceptions of the nature of that information differ greatly. As argued previously, Brunner, Meltzer, and Alchian are in a world of objectivized knowledge, whereas Simmel is stressing money's role as a communicator of tacit knowledge.

20. Hayek (1977, p. 108) points out that the Greek word for "exchange" *(katallattein)* also meant "to admit into the community" and "to change from enemy into friend." Exchange then becomes a way to form social bonds among people who do not have face-to-face contact.

21. Aristotle defines man as a language user, which would make language use the next higher level of abstractness in ideal types. See the discussion in Gadamer (1966).

22. Also see Simmel (1978, p. 223): "Because money is the common point of intersection of the sequence of purposes that stretch from every point of the economic world to every other, it is accepted by everyone from everyone."

23. Laidler and Rowe (1980, p. 102) see the theoretical and policy implications of Simmel's approach to money: "If we take the view that money is best understood [as] one among a complex of social institutions, then we would expect the consequences of anticipated inflation to be not just an increase in the consumption of shoe leather, but an adaptation of the social order away from money and markets toward a greater reliance on one form or another of command organization . . . and hence a diminution of freedom. . . . In short, if monetary theory is best approached along Austrian lines, then we must conclude that mainstream monetary theory, for all its considerable accomplishments, not only trivializes the social consequences of inflation in particular . . . but that it grossly underestimates the destructiveness of monetary instability in general."

24. Almost all spontaneous social institutions allow us this access to others. Simmel (1978, p. 99) notes three others in addition to money and language: "Thus the need for the individual to transcend the self and so gain a more than personal support and stability becomes the power of tradition in law, in knowledge and in morality."

25. This similarity was also recognized by Hume (1961, p. 442) in his discussion of the evolution of rules of property, "In like manner are languages gradually established by human conventions. . . . In like manner do gold and silver become the common measures of exchange." See also Warneryd's (1990, pp. 94-95) discussion of the evolution of conventional behavior, where he notes the commonalities between money and language as coordinative institutions.

26. See, among others, Hayek (1973, 1977, 1979), Menger (1985), Mises (1983), and Lavoie (1987).

27. See also Polanyi (1969, p. 160), "All human thought comes into existence by grasping the meaning and mastering the use of language. Little of our mind lives in our natural body; a truly human intellect dwells in us only when our lips shape words and our eyes read print."

28. For a more extended discussion of Gadamer's theory of language and its relationship to monetary exchange, see Horwitz (1992).

29. The French philosopher Merleau-Ponty, in his *Phenomenology of Perception*, argues that "language does not express thought, it *is* the subject's taking up of a position in the world of his meanings" (cited in Polanyi 1969, p. 222).

30. See also Mises (1980, p. 62): "The whole structure of the calculations of the entrepreneur and the consumer rests on the process of valuing commodities in money. Money has thus become an aid that the human mind is no longer able to dispense with in making economic calculations."

31. See also Marx's (1964, p. 168, emphasis in original) discussion in the *1844 Manuscripts:* "No doubt *demand* also exists for him who has no money, but his demand is a mere thing of the imagination without effect or existence for me, for a third party, for the others, and which therefore remains for me *unreal* and *objectless.* The difference between effective demand based on money and ineffective demand based on my need, my passion, my wish, etc., is the difference between *being* and *thinking*, between that which *exists* merely within me as imagination and the imagined as it exists as a *real object* outside of me."

32. One can have nonmonetary wants just as one can have nonlinguistic mental phenomena. However, when we tackle questions of social interaction and coordination, our interest will be more with monetary wants and linguistically constituted thoughts because both involve social communication processes that evolve as sets of unintended consequences. To the extent that social theory attempts to explain the evolution and operation of social institutions and how they lead to social order, language and money and the phenomena they communicate will be of central importance.

33. An excellent example of the conventionalist view of language, and the problems with enlightenment philosophy in general, can be found in Thomas Hobbes's *Leviathan.* In his discussion of language, Hobbes (1968, part 1, chaps. 4-5) argues that what matters is the proper naming of things and not any process of evolution. This attitude corresponds to Hobbes's generally Cartesian view of knowledge, where the validity of tradition and authority are to be dismissed: "He that takes up conclusions on the trust of Authors, and doth not fetch them from the first Items in every Reckoning . . . loses his labour; and does not know any thing; but only beleeveth" (p. 112). He was also consistent on political theory, believing an external sovereign was needed to create and enforce the law, rather than allowing for an evolutionary process of precedence to generate good laws. One would expect that if Hobbes had written on money, he would likely have consistently rejected a spontaneous order view of money as well. Spontaneous order theory, though it derives from enlightenment thought, must eventually oppose its major conclusions. See Hayek (1952b) for an elaboration of this point. I would like to thank Karen Vaughn for calling this passage in Hobbes to my attention.

34. An example of this view in economics might be seen in the notion of an equilibrium price. Despite their talk of the importance of the relativity of prices, neoclassical economists cling to a notion of an equilibrium (objectively correct) price and use this as a standard of comparison for judging market outcomes. One particular example is antitrust. The idea that some freely determined market price is "too high" (i.e., a monopoly price) or "too low" (i.e., represents predatory pricing or "unfair" competition) is the basis for much antitrust activity. However, the judgment of "too high" or "too low" has to include an assumption that the right price is known without recourse to the knowledge generated in actual market exchanges. The argument of this chapter suggests that such knowledge is not obtainable. For a critical discussion of the idea of a monopoly price and its policy implications see Rothbard (1962b, p. 586ff.).

35. In a recent paper (Horwitz 1992), I extend the discussion of the analogy between money and language into a discussion of the analogy between philosophical concepts of truth and economic concepts of order.

36. As discussed in Chapter 2, our attempts to design are limited to the level of the basic rules of spontaneous social institutions. In Chapter 4 we will explore this point with respect to monetary orders in general and, in Chapter 5, to the history of the U.S. banking system in particular.

37. This observation may have important implications for the centrality of price reform in the economies of Eastern Europe and the former Soviet Union.

38. For more on this point see Ricoeur (1971, p. 317). Gadamer (1985, p. 375) also argues that "an ideal system of signs, the sole significance of which is the unambiguous coordination of all signs, makes the power of words, the range of variation of the contingent in the historical languages as they have actually developed, appear as a mere obscuring of their usefulness." Obviously, an attempt to view language as signs in this way would not correspond to Gadamer's view. This can be, and I would argue should be, read as an attack on Chomsky's theory of language. See also Gadamer (p. 366).

39. This view of money and language can also provide insights into the function of profit-and-loss accountancy. In a paper that inspired a number of the ideas expressed here, Lavoie (1987) argues that accounting is the "language of business." Accountants turn the events of the market into a text that can be used by entrepreneurs. My view here agrees with the substance of Lavoie's, but I do think his use of the term *language* to describe accountancy is too broad. As argued here, the better analog to language is money.

Accounting is more like storytelling than a language per se. Accountants and entrepreneurs have a subset of shared words and meanings that rely on both language and money. The accountant attempts to turn the language of money into the written word through a mutually accepted interpretive framework. Accountants are much more like creative writers, who pick and choose words from a particular vocabulary (a subset of the language of money) to try to tell a story for a particular audience. The closest word here might be *scribe*, especially in the sense of one who inscribes the actions of a historical process into a text that can be preserved and serve as a point of reference. Accountants speak the language of money, but their great skill is in selecting words and telling interpretive stories that entrepreneurs can understand and act upon.

40. See also Hayek (1989, p. 123): "Capitalism created the possibility of employment. It created the conditions wherein people who have not been endowed by their parents with the tools and land needed to maintain themselves and their offspring could be so equipped by others, and to their mutual benefit. For the process enabled people to live poorly, and to have children, who otherwise, without the opportunity for productive work, could hardly even have grown to maturity and multiplied: it brought into being and kept millions alive who otherwise would not have lived at all and who, if they had lived for a time, could not have afforded to procreate."

41. See also Hayek (1973, p. 46): "What in fact we find in all free societies is that, although groups of men will join in organizations for the achievement of some particular ends, the co-ordination of the activities of all of these separate organizations, as well as of the separate individuals, is brought about by the forces making for a spontaneous order. The family, the farm, the plant, the firm, the corporation and the various associations . . . are organizations which in turn are integrated into a more comprehensive spontaneous order."

42. Thus immigrants often find economic success long before they begin to climb the social ladder.

43. See Prychitko (1988, p. 137): "Spontaneously formed market institutions are *not* the result of atomistic individuals responding to a given array of prices, but the result of individuals already involved in a truly dialogical relationship."

44. Related contributions on this subject include McCloskey (1985), Lavoie (1987), Klamer, McCloskey, and Solow (1989), and Lavoie (1991), as well as the implicit message in Ricoeur (1971).

4

The Evolution of Monetary Order

Having seen the crucial communicative role that money plays in social and economic order, we need to examine in more detail the ways in which money is supplied to the market process and the kinds of institutions that are more likely to lead to monetary order, thus enhancing overall economic order. In particular, we can look at how monetary institutions evolve from the simple use of money, and how those institutions fit in to the broader evolution of the market process.

A monetary order will, as we have seen, be more than simply the emergence of a medium of exchange. The use of money opens up many new horizons within economic interaction. Money makes possible economic calculation and provides entrepreneurs with profit-and-loss signals that guide their production plans, leading to an increase in rationally allocated resources and the division of labor. These developments, along with double-entry bookkeeping and accounting skills in general, increase the complexity of the market process.

The evolution of simple monetary exchange and economic calculation stimulates and necessitates the increased use of money and provides incentives for the further evolution of monetary institutions. Banks, demand deposits, currency, clearinghouses, and other extensions of the financial industry come into being and evolve during this process of economic development. The increased complexity of the creative development of money requires coordination through more advanced monetary institutions. To be able to maintain a high degree of economic order, a properly functioning and sufficiently complex set of monetary institutions is necessary. Both the features of, and the interactions between, these advanced, complex monetary institutions constitute a monetary order. We can characterize the contents of this chapter in three questions: (1) how might these various monetary institutions freely evolve from the simple use of money? (2) Can these freely evolved institutions be fruitfully examined and judged by the approach of Chapter 2? and (3) Would freely evolved monetary institutions be more or less orderly than alternative institutional arrangements?

Free Banking as an Evolutionary Monetary Order

To discover what kinds of institutions constitute an orderly monetary system, we can trace the evolution of monetary institutions from the unhampered actions of individuals. The previous discussion of the evolution of a medium of exchange has given us a start, and George Selgin and Lawrence White (1987) have extended Menger's theory to describe the broader evolution of monetary institutions.[1] In this section I will reinterpret Selgin and White's evolutionary account with two purposes in mind. The first is to show that the unhampered evolution of a free banking system, as described by Selgin and White, meets our description of order from Chapter 2. As with Menger's story of the origin of money, their story is conjectural rather than an actual history of any particular monetary system. They are not arguing that any actual system has evolved the way they describe, though many systems have shared aspects of the system they elaborate. Rather they are attempting to show how an orderly, yet unregulated, system could logically arise as an unintended set of consequences of self-interested behavior. The second purpose is to argue that if we can show that such a free banking system meets our criteria of order, we can use it as a framework with which we can compare existing and potential monetary institutions and judge their orderliness.

Selgin and White start from the attempts by individuals to improve their well-being and then trace out the consequences of those actions. If we start from Menger's account of the origin of money, it can be shown how the emergence of a generally accepted medium of exchange would lead to further institutional advances such as coinage by weight and quality. Merchants attempting to minimize the costs of weighing and assessing commodity money are led to mark the commodity to indicate assessment. As other merchants do the same they begin to recognize each other's marks, saving them the cost of constant reassessment. It is a small step from this to coinage in its more modern form. Standardized markings and weights, as well as signals of trust (such as brand names or other recognized symbols), become more refined ways of indicating quality and value. There is also strong incentive for coins to be roughly the same size and shape, even if made by different minters. "Nonstandard coins must circulate at a discount because of the extra computational burden they impose, so that their production is unprofitable" (Selgin and White 1987, p. 442). Existing producers converge to a standard size, and new entrants either match it or bear the costs of differentiation.[2]

Even at this relatively early stage we see the three elements of order appearing—creativity in the form of merchants marking their money; coordination as others do the same to lower their own costs; and complexity as standard markings and coinage facilitate monetary exchange. These three elements allow for an increased amount of trade and specialization and enable the evolution of the more complex banking arrangements that follow.

The emergence of distinct banking firms is the next step (pp. 442-44). Traders may have two reasons to keep commodity money safely stored in locations other than their homes. First, coins may differ between localities, bringing forth the money changer, who mediates between the two areas for a small fee. Eventually, frequent traders find it easier to leave an account balance with the changer rather than constantly make trips back and forth. A second possibility is that commodity money might be left for safekeeping with a goldsmith or mintmaster. In either case, the receivers of such deposits are strictly "warehouse" bankers and not true financial intermediaries. They simply act as storage facilities.

The key to true financial intermediation is the recognition that deposited balances can be loaned out to others at a profit. Two factors make this possible (p. 443). First, money is fungible; that is, one need not withdraw the same coins one deposits. Second, deposits and withdrawals occur randomly; thus the law of large numbers makes fractional reserve banking possible. The probability of large withdrawals on any given day is so low as to decrease the risk of not holding significant redemption reserves. It is the bank's newfound ability to lend deposit balances that changes it from a warehouse to a financial intermediary. A further unintended consequence of this development is that it permits the paying of interest on deposits. Banks can attract more depositors by offering not only money-changing or security, but an interest payment as well. This, in turn, increases the use of the banking system, which increases the supply of loanable funds and spurs further economic growth.

These developments make "the effective money supply . . . greater than the existing stock of specie [the money commodity] alone," but it is the next series of steps that is crucial to the maturation of the banking system (p. 444). The problem facing banks at this point is that most transactions are made using actual commodity money, which increases the flow of funds in and out of the bank. The use of commodity money is also inconvenient for bank customers as it is both cumbersome to carry and more costly to store compared to paper money substitutes. Although commodity money transactions may "in the aggregate largely cancel out through the law of large numbers . . . they require the banks to hold greater precautionary commodity money reserves," which takes away a source of profit-earning loans (p. 444). The reason for the larger precautionary reserve balances is that the larger the number of transactions taking place, the higher the probability of a large amount being withdrawn on a given day (Selgin 1988b, p. 74ff.). The development of negotiable claims to commodity money that can pass between depositors themselves can remedy this situation. Negotiable claims would be desirable for bank customers (as they would make conducting transactions that much easier) and would reduce the number of clearing transactions at the bank. The use of negotiable paper claims leads to a decline in the need for precautionary reserves and to a corresponding increase in the banking system's ability to create credit, as well as draws in new deposits by making banking more convenient for potential depositors.

Selgin and White (1987, p. 444) describe one possible path to the use of negotiable claims. Transfers of deposited money at goldsmiths or money changers may require the presence of both the depositor and the recipient as well as the banker. Deposits may not be assignable without the approval of the banker. One could easily see an evolution toward the use of deposit receipts that are transferrable by endorsement, rather than toward witnessing in the strict sense. Although this might bring slightly more redemption risk to the bank, it would again attract business by making banking more convenient for depositors. The proper signature in a generally recognized place would suffice as consent to transfer. Such receipts could pass hand to hand through multiple endorsement. The next logical step would be bearer notes, not made out to any specific individual but redeemable by the holder. Once again, multiple endorsement involves transaction costs that bearer notes could reduce. Bearer notes not only eliminate the need to sign notes, they also eliminate the need to verify the various signatures. Although the move to bearer notes transfers the liability from the previous endorser to the bank itself, the new business made possible by the shift would likely be worth the additional risk.

These bearer paper notes are the equivalent of the modern bank note (p. 444).[3] Of course modern checking develops this way also, being a nonnegotiable claim payable to a specific party for a specified exact amount. Now banks have two procedures open to them. First, they can lend more reserve balances, and second and most important, they can give bank liabilities "not only to *depositors* of metal but also to *borrowers* of money," further increasing their credit making ability from a given stock of specie (p. 444).[4]

Again the three elements of order are present in the evolution from commodity money to bank money. The creative element is the lending out of depositor balances. This is an act of true entrepreneurship as the imaginative powers of individual bankers recognize the gains to be made through financial intermediation.[5] The use of fractional reserves increases the complexity of banking, as now banks must deal with reserve flows and the increased number of bad loans. At the same time, coordinative elements appear in the evolution of inside money (bank liabilities). Instead of using only commodity money and dealing with the difficulties of monitoring its unstable reserve flows, banks now use bank-created money and can thus reduce the precautionary demand for reserves and stabilize reserve flows. This eases the burden on bankers (inducing coordination) and also allows them to create even more credit based on a given stock of the money commodity (more complexity). All three elements intertwine in the Selgin and White account.

The evolution of the single bank involves an increasing substitution of bank money for commodity money, allowing the bank to economize on reserve holdings and increase its credit-creating power. As banks begin to interact, profit-seeking incentives lead to the same substitution process developing even further at the interbank level. The problem facing the individual bank is that its notes trade at par only in geographically limited areas because the costs of redemption (and ignorance of the soundness of the bank) rise with distance. Banks can partially overcome this problem by opening branch offices in distant areas. The degree of branching, however, is limited by transportation and communication costs throughout the economy (p. 445).[6]

The increased ignorance about the soundness of banks that comes with increased distance leads to the discounting of bank liabilities in rough proportion to that distance in order to compensate liability holders for the increased risk resulting from their ignorance. The disparity between note values across geographic regions gives rise to arbitrage opportunities for alert entrepreneurs. So-called "note brokers" develop specialized knowledge of distant banks and buy nonlocal notes at a discount, undertake the transportation expense and risk, and redeem or resell notes at par value in the issuing bank's area. Brokers charge a commission fee to cover their costs and earn a profit on the spread between the discounted price paid and the par value at which they redeem. Holders of nonlocal notes will pay the commission fee because note brokers can redeem notes at lower average cost by accumulating large enough stocks to offset the fixed cost of travel. In addition, "by accepting the notes of unfamiliar banks at minimal commission rates, brokers unintentionally increase the general acceptability of notes, and promote their use in place of commodity money" (p. 446). Merchants are more likely to accept nonlocal notes when brokers are in business than when they are not.

One assumption so far has been that banks would not wish to accept the notes of other banks. There might be good reasons this would be so, the main one being that refusal to accept limits the competition's market. However, profit incentives will lead to mutual acceptance through a variety of ways.[7] The best way to see this is that bank A has a profit-seeking reason to *accept but not hold* the notes of bank B. One reason for acceptance is that bank A can replace bank B's notes with its own. Rather than hold the notes of B, why not redeem them and use the commodity money to purchase an interest-earning asset? The demand for notes now met by bank B can be satisfied with bank A's own notes in the interim (p. 446). A second reason is that strategically, cooperation will win out in the long run in that bank A's acceptance of B's notes will lead to B's acceptance of A's notes. Mutual refusal to accept leads to losses for all parties concerned; reciprocal behavior benefits all parties. This, as Selgin and White note (p. 447), is an application of Axelrod's (1984) discussion of the benefits of "tit-for-tat" strategic behavior. Profit incentives lead to a widening of acceptance and promote organized means of note exchange.

One remaining problem for banks is that they still have to hold more reserves than they would prefer, or they would have to in a mature system. As the practice of banking spreads, and as banks begin to redeem each other's notes, they will be led to develop ways of dealing with the excess-reserves problem. In particular, they may wish to internalize the costs associated with note brokers by managing interbank redemption themselves. They might employ people to return notes to the issuing banks for redemption. This system of direct redemption means that banks have to settle their gross clearings in commodity money rather than their net clearings, as would occur if note exchange was conducted on a regular, organized basis, as in a clearinghouse (Selgin and White 1987, p. 448). Because each bank has to clear with each other bank individually, it must keep enough reserves to be able to meet the total reserve demand from all other banks. Under a clearinghouse system, the various credits and debits can be canceled on paper, and only the remaining net values determine the need for reserves.

The progression from direct redemption to clearinghouses is straightforward. Bank redemption agents frequently cross paths when making their various trips. In order to lower costs, they agree to meet at a certain place and time to physically exchange notes and then each head back to the appropriate bank. Eventually such behavior becomes institutionalized in an actual building called a clearinghouse (p. 449). The major advantage of the clearinghouse is that now exchanges can be made in terms of bookkeeping entries rather than by physical exchange of notes. Again, only net not gross clearings, need to be adjusted.

Banks deposit acceptable assets at the clearinghouse and are extended an appropriate account balance. As notes come in for clearing, a bank's net clearings (its returns of others' notes minus others' returns of its notes) is added or subtracted from its balance. Instead of having to have commodity money to meet the total amount of "others' returns of its notes" at any given time, it need only have on deposit the net amount. This reduces the need for reserve balances and expands the bank's credit-creating power. Of course, all of the banks benefit from clearinghouse arrangements, yet such arrangements do not result from collective decision or design; rather they are an unintended consequence of the profit-seeking behavior of the banks.[8]

The progression from the single bank to the clearinghouse system represents a move toward a higher degree of monetary order. The creative entrepreneurial activity of banks acting as note brokers makes possible interbank relationships that were previously difficult to execute. This leads to increased coordination as banks interact more efficiently and have a larger market for their notes. At the same time this process increases the system's complexity as bilateral note exchanges become easier and more frequent and as the clearinghouse reduces the associated transaction costs. The complexity can be coordinated, however, because the creative development of an institutionalized clearinghouse enables the system to cope with the new complexity while better coordinating interbank activities. The development of clearinghouses brings the system to a higher level of complexity, though not so high as to be beyond the coordinative powers of the other elements.

At this stage of complexity, banks serve as loanable funds intermediaries by holding assets such as commercial bills or government bonds and by issuing liabilities in the form of checkable deposits or paper bank notes. Such liabilities circulate at par through branching and clearinghouse arrangements and are distinguished by brand names and found in desired denominations. They are, in essence, financial supermarkets able to acquire assets and issue any kind of liabilities they wish within the limits of contract law.[9]

Importantly, very little commodity money circulates in this system. Banks always want to maximize the use of bank money because it increases their ability to create credit. Such increases are possible only to the extent that customers prefer bank money to commodity money. Selgin and White (p. 452) argue that monetary uses of the commodity money could conceivably be eliminated:

> In the limit, if inter-clearinghouse settlements were made entirely with other assets (perhaps claims on a super-clearinghouse which itself held negligible commodity money), and if the public were completely weaned from holding commodity money, the active demand for the old-fashioned money commodity would be wholly nonmonetary. . . . The problem of meeting any significant redemption request (e.g. a "run" on a bank) could be contractually handled, as it was historically during note-duelling episodes, by invoking an "option clause" that allows the bank a specified period of time to gather the necessary commodity money while compensating the redeeming party for the delay.

Of course, in such a situation, the value of bank money would still be tied to commodity money through the potential of redemption, though actual holdings of the money commodity by the general public would be zero. As long as holders of bank liabilities can eventually, if they so desire, redeem them for commodity money, the value of bank liabilities denominated in the unit of account is fixed by the value of the basic money commodity, and thus the price level is determinate.

Conspicuously missing from the system is any kind of central bank (p. 454). The logic of the evolutionary story shows no tendency toward the monopolization of either reserve or liability production. Historically, central banks have not been the result of any natural market evolution but rather the logical step for governments wishing to raise revenue (particularly for war) through monopolized note issue and inflation, and for bankers wishing to capture the profits from a government-protected cartel (V. Smith 1990, pp. 168-69; and Dowd 1989, p. 32).[10] These issues will be explored further in Chapter 5. For now, Selgin and White have described the path and properties of the evolution of an unhampered monetary system. Such a system exhibits the key features of the concept of an evolutionary order as developed earlier. We can now begin to examine how this system compares to alternative institutional arrangements.

Brand Names, Free Banking, and Monetary Order

The key to understanding how the orderliness of Selgin and White's free banking system compares to other arrangements is the informational content of bank brand names. With the so-called new learning in industrial organization, many practices that were previously thought to be monopolistic are now seen as the natural outgrowth of competitive market processes.[11] One of these practices is the use of a brand name. It was previously thought that brand names hurt consumers by raising the cost of entry into an industry. Not only did potential entrants have to come up with physical plant and labor, they also had to overcome the influence of the brand names of existing firms. The new learning has pointed out that brand names in fact help consumers; they reduce informational costs by providing knowledge about a firm in a short, condensed, readily available form. Consumers build up an expectation of future performance based on past successes or failures of projects associated with the particular brand name. Simply seeing the brand name connected with a project about which the consumer knows little will be an indicator of quality based on the consumer's past experience with the brand name.

The implication is that brand names are simply a form of ideal type. Like ideal types in general, brand names are used by consumers to form expectations and to build those expectations from past experience. The information embodied in brand names is expected rule-following behavior, with the rules being the quality and performance associated with the product in the past. The more the brand name comports with consumer expectations, the easier is plan execution. What should also be clear is that brand names have to have the same kind of flexibility-coherence mix as do ideal types generally. When products become more or less desirable over time, their brand names should change over time to reflect the new degree of desirability.[12] If such changes are not made, expectation-formation processes are less reliable and order is decreased. At the same time, a fair degree of continuity is needed in brand names. If they were constantly shifting and changing, they would lose their semiotic role as knowledge surrogates. As seems clear from the business world, it does take some time to both build and destroy a brand name.

The unhampered evolution of monetary institutions allows consumers and bankers to take full advantage of all of the benefits associated with brand names. Much of the literature discussing alternative monetary regimes has stressed that a desirable monetary system is one that removes its own influence as a source of entrepreneurial uncertainty (see Simons [1936], Buchanan [1962], and Friedman [1968]). Buchanan, for one, refers to this as the "predictability" norm: Social actors should be able to form accurate expectations of monetary policy in order to proceed with plans that require such information. He also argues (pp. 156-57) that it does not matter so much what particular monetary policy is chosen as long as it is predictable.[13] This meshes nicely with the previous ideal types-brand names discussion. The whole point of brand names is precisely to render economic interaction more predictable to market actors.

A freely evolved banking system brings these benefits to all forms of media of exchange. In general, the brand names that are most relevant to consumers in a complex free banking system are those that accrue to bank liabilities, not commodity money. Because the Mengerian account points to a small number (probably one) of commodity moneys in use at the same time, banks can really exploit their brand names only on forms of money that are their liabilities. Brand names in commodity money would at best refer to minting, stamping, and weighing procedures, but not to the commodity's acceptability *as money*. In modern U.S. banking, commercial banks can and do use their brand name capital to expand the market for their demand deposits and other liabilities.[14] The same, however, is not true of currency, because its production is monopolized by the Fed and it is therefore not a bank liability. Free banking, however, would permit banks to issue their own currency and would therefore allow them to exploit their brand name capital in the quality and acceptability of their currency.[15]

By monopolizing currency production, central banks overrigidify the informational properties of their "brand name." With consumers legally denied the possibility of choice, central banks can depreciate the value of their currency without feeling all of the effects that would accrue to a competitive firm who attempted the same. In a competitive market, consumers who lose confidence in a brand name will switch to a different brand or stop purchasing the product altogether. It is the possibility of this choice that gives brand names their informational content as reflectors of consumer confidence and satisfaction. With a monopolized product, this choice is denied, and changes in consumer knowledge cannot be communicated. The brand name loses its communicative value and therefore its value to expectation formation.

We see evidence of this process in the areas still open to bank choice. Commercial banks that overissue demand deposits will face adverse clearings either through the Fed or through a drain of currency and coin from their vaults. A failure to redeem (or a liquidity crisis in general) drastically affects the value of a bank's brand name.[16] Certainly the names Continental Illinois and Penn Square no longer carry the same positive informational content that they did before their troubles. The checks on the Fed's production of currency, however, are much weaker. The constant inflation since 1914 has made the dollar somewhat less acceptable, but legal-tender laws and the evolutionary forces of custom and habit make opting away from Federal Reserve notes more difficult.[17] With no effective domestic substitute available, people have to settle for a less-than-preferred state of affairs.[18]

However, there are substitutes for dollars if we expand the relevant market to a global scale. As David Glasner's (1989, p. 161ff.) discussion of the development of the Eurodollar market points out, the ability to hold a bank deposit denominated in a currency produced by a government other than the one with supervision over the bank in question forces some competition onto even domestically monopolized currencies. If, for example, residents of Great Britain are unhappy with the value of the pound, they can choose to hold deposits denominated in dollars created by British banks or by a U.S. bank subsidiary located there. It is also important to note that these deposits would not be subject to U.S. bank regulations, and banks that provide them may be better able to offer services or create credit that customers want. As Glasner (p. 161) concludes, the option of these so-called Eurodollar accounts is a way to avoid the inefficiencies of a monopolized currency.

Eurodollar accounts are also an indicator of the perception of a given currency's brand name. The original Eurodollar accounts during the 1970s reflected the perception that the dollar was preferred to other currencies. More recently, we have seen the development of similar accounts denominated in yen or marks. The relative growth of these accounts, particularly if they are at the expense of dollar-denominated ones, reflects a shift in the perception of currency brand names. Even given a monopoly, the spontaneous forces of the market will tend to emerge wherever they are able. To the extent that such competitive alternatives like Eurodollars exist, they offer money users a chance to affect and utilize the informational content of monopolized currencies.

To see how free banks can use their brand names effectively, we can argue that what free banks really produce is a bundled good of monetary services and trust. The trust relationship is inherent in the concept of fractional reserve banking, and it is even more important where banks are producing both deposits and notes. Ultimately what leads people to accept and hold the liabilities of a bank is trust that the bank will make good on its promises. A background condition for such trust is the legal environment that permits bank liabilities to be enforceable, but the law alone cannot explain trust differences *between* banks. Successful free banks will use their brand name capital to extend their trust to potential customers.[19] Advertising, reserve holdings, customer assistance, formal clothes, and physical features such as marble columns all add to the trust involved in a bank's brand name.[20] The more trusted the bank, the more acceptable will be its liabilities and the more profit-earning credit it can create. The informational content of free bank brand names will meet the predictability norm by becoming an ideal type that will allow expectation-formation processes to proceed as best they can, permitting the creativity, complexity, and coordination that can lead to a high degree of monetary order.

The False Dichotomy of Rules Versus Discretion

The neoclassical literature on monetary regimes generally portrays the path toward monetary order as a choice between giving a central bank the freedom to exercise discretion and binding it to preset or reactive rules.[21] The following sections are examinations of the cases for both discretion and rules and compare them with the free banking benchmark outlined previously. With the discussion of knowledge conveyance from Chapter 2 and the concept of monetary order from this chapter as a framework, it will be argued that a free banking regime can better achieve the macroeconomic effects (or lack thereof) desired from both rules and discretion and thus better preserve monetary order.

As Hayek (1945, p. 91) notes, the main question facing the social sciences is "the unavoidable imperfection of man's knowledge and the consequent need for a process by which knowledge is constantly communicated and acquired." For economists, the policy question becomes one of how to set "the rules of the game" in such a way as to make the best use of the price system's ability to process the necessary knowledge. The focus of policy-oriented debates then shifts to the constitutional and institutional level, where different regimes can be compared and analyzed in terms of their ability to deal with knowledge-related issues.

The debate on monetary order ought to be over the relative knowledge advantages and disadvantages of alternative regimes—in this case discretion, rules, and free banking—because epistemological issues ultimately determine the degree of order in a system. The earlier debate between rules and discretion, as represented by Henry Simons's (1936) classic defense of rules, was framed in terms of the uncertainty and distortions generated by differing degrees of political involvement in monetary affairs. As Simons argued then, the question was, How do we set up the rules of the game so that players within it can reach more desired states of affairs (Simons 1936, pp. 1-3)? The modern debate has shifted somewhat to cover the more complicated ground of expectations and reactions to announced and actual monetary policy. Most of the literature of the 1980s derives from Kydland and Prescott's (1977) argument that given rational expectations, consistent policy may not be optimal and vice versa. Within this rational expectations framework, rules and discretion can then be evaluated.[22]

Over the same time period, interest and literature concerning the possibility of competitively supplied currency has increased.[23] The theory of free banking argues that it could achieve many of the macro-economic goals sought by both discretion and rules. In the rest of this chapter, it will be argued that free banking can provide better solutions to the problems that both sides of the debate have with each other. In particular, we will focus on each regime's ability to allow the market to utilize knowledge and each one's resulting ability to cultivate and maintain monetary order.[24] When one adds the third option of free banking into the debate, rules versus discretion is revealed to be a false dichotomy.

The Case for Discretion

The basic argument for discretionary monetary policy is the one that underlies a great many arguments for government involvement in the economy, namely that in the absence of such intervention the voluntary actions of individuals could not supply the good or service to an optimal degree. In the case of money, an unmanaged supply would lead to either hyperinflation or the kinds of currency shortages and panics found in the pre-Federal Reserve Era. Interpreting pre-Fed crises as market failures is historically questionable,[25] but the argument still centers around the ability of market processes to match the money supply to money demand. Determining the correct supply of money forms the core of the problem.

Independent of the particular way in which a discretionary monetary authority proposes to measure and affect the money supply, one key determinant to its success will be its ability to know the magnitude of the demand for money.[26] Like any other good or service, the demand for money is constantly changing and is not easily calculated.[27] Knowledge of the state of current and future demand is the sine qua non of effective discretion. The standard approach taken by economists is to derive structural models of money demand and then attempt to measure all of the parameters and variables. Once estimated, the effects of different money supplies can be roughly forecasted. The accuracy of such models will depend on both the theoretical relationships postulated and on the quality of the policymaker's data. In his argument for discretionary policy, Tobin (1983, p. 516) warns that the Fed needs to be on guard as to data quality:

> Information [on] personal income, credit volume, prices, retail sales, production, employment, inventories and orders . . . should enable the Fed's experts to diagnose the shocks. . . . Central banks should ask their staffs to devote more effort to obtaining and utilizing alternative and supplementary information.

With all of this information necessary to success, the problem facing the discretionary monetary authority is a smaller, but no less intractable, version of the problem facing a comprehensive economic planner. There are two aspects to this problem. First, it will almost always be the case that acquired data are out-of-date by the time policy is implemented, and second, the necessary data may not exist in a form accessible by a central authority (Lavoie 1985a, p. 54ff.).

The difficulty with stale data is that they can lead to undesirable, unintended consequences. Many of these consequences are part of the standard discussion about policy lags. Normally policymakers face three types of lags. The first (the "recognition lag") involves the time it takes to recognize that a situation requires policy action. The second (the "implementation lag") concerns the time between recognition and policy action. The third lag (the "effectiveness lag") is the period between a policy action and its effects on the economy. The recognition lag also involves two steps. One is the time involved in actually collecting the data needed to determine if action is needed and the other is the time needed to examine the data to distinguish random changes from ones that require policy actions. These two aspects of the recognition lag can give rise to given changes in policy actions not taking effect until sometime after the relevant data have changed. So even if the *effects* of the action were immediate (i.e., if the implementation and effectiveness lags did not exist), the data informing the action may have changed between acquisition and implementation.

In the case of the demand for money, its ultimate determinants are the tastes, preferences, and judgments that lie deep in the human mind. As a result, the relevant data change as often as the human mind moves forward in time.[28] By the time any such data are collected, processed, and then acted upon, it may be too late. The monetary authority is constantly trying to catch up with the actors it is trying to counter. One possible result is exacerbation of the original discrepancy that called for action. Stale data may render countercyclical policy *procyclical*.[29]

The second difficulty with data acquisition is an even more complex one. The data needed to estimate accurate money demand equations may not exist in a form knowable to anyone but the decisionmaker at the moment of decision. As Thomas Sowell (1980, pp. 217-18, emphasis in original) argues,

> The knowledge needed is a knowledge of *subjective patterns of trade-off that are nowhere articulated.* Until . . . a moment [of decision] comes, I will never *know* even my own trade-offs, much less anybody else's. There is no way for such information to be fed into a computer, when no one has such information in the first place.

Simply asking what actors would do if faced with certain options, or surveying relevant factors affecting their decisions and computing a result, is not a suitable substitute for actual decision-making. What counts as options or relevant factors can only be known at the moment of actual choice, and not before. The problems in obtaining this tacit knowledge become sources of error for monetary authorities trying to act based on estimates of money demand. Structural models and statistical data may help, but perhaps not enough to be worthwhile. Frequently the costs involved with deriving models and attempting to acquire the relevant data may outweigh any marginal benefits that such models and data might provide to the policymaker.

The most recent knowledge-oriented criticism of discretion is rational expectations.[30] The thrust of the rational expectations criticism is to ask what happens if economic agents possess an information set identical to the monetary authority. If agents understand that increases in the money supply lead to proportionately higher prices, they will react to money supply announcements and central bank intentions in such a way as to prepare for the increase in prices.[31] If the intent of the monetary authority is to exploit the Phillips curve trade-off, it will be frustrated if agents have rational expectations. Agents will not be fooled by such attempts—they will have already accounted for them in wages and prices, having known that they were coming. As a result, the only way that inflation can have real effects is through random shocks; the Phillips curve is vertical in both the short and long run. By definition such random shocks have an expected value of zero, so rational agents will take no account of them in forming their expectations. Real effects will be generated to the extent that random shocks occur, but the apparent trade-off is not exploitable by the monetary authority. If the authority consciously attempts to exploit the trade-off, agents will systematically anticipate and neutralize the effects.

Kydland and Prescott (1977) extended this criticism of discretion into a stronger case for rules. ·They argued that period-by-period choice of optimal monetary policy may be inconsistent. For example, if actors expect 5 percent inflation, the monetary authority will need to generate inflation greater than 5 percent in order to reduce unemployment below the natural rate. However, if actors have rational expectations (i.e., they understand the relationship between the authority's actions and the rate of inflation) they will know not to expect 5 percent inflation because they know that the *monetary authority* knows that inflation has to be more than 5 percent in order to affect output.[32] As a result, actors will raise their expected rate of inflation until the monetary authority is no longer tempted to exceed it. In addition, the authority cannot run inflation *less than* actors' expectations without generating unemployment greater than the natural rate. The discretionary authority is trapped by high inflation and is unable to find the zero inflation-natural rate solution. Discretionary monetary policy brings high rates of inflation without a reduction of unemployment below the natural rate. Kydland and Prescott, and later extensions such as those by Barro and Gordon (1983a, 1983b), therefore argue that rules should be preferred to discretion.

In terms of our previous discussion of ideal types and order, discretion prevents the formation of accurate typifications because policy becomes excessively flexible. The past becomes less and less reliable as a predictor of future events. To form expectations humans need some continuity through time, and discretion does not provide it. The dynamic-inconsistency literature indicates that policymakers desiring macroeconomic effects will have to act in ways that are continually unpredictable. The more such inconsistent policy is pursued, the weaker the effects become, because actors are constantly trying to outguess the monetary authority. The result is a rather chaotic game of chicken. As a result, typifications become less reliable, and expectations and, eventually, plans are more difficult to execute. Though ideal types clearly need to adjust through time, some continuity is necessary for them to be useful. Discretion disintegrates monetary order by making our expectation-formation processes less reliable, because successful (from the monetary authority's perspective) policy-making may require inconsistency.

The Case for Rules

Most of the arguments for rules concern three issues—risk-minimization, price and output stability, and lack of room for political manipulation. The risk-minimization argument can also be viewed as an argument from ignorance. If discretion is impotent in controlling macroeconomic outcomes, why risk the potential negative effects discretion can cause? Standard models with shoe leather and menu costs that increase with inflation, or other arguments about the various costs of inflation, indicate possible reasons for avoiding even an impotent, but still inflationary, discretionary regime. High levels of inflation might even lead to an upward-sloping Phillips curve in the very long run (Friedman 1977). Instead, it is argued, we can minimize the risk of adverse effects by fixing some kind of growth rule, either a fixed percentage or an algorithmic reactive rule. Though such rules could be fully anticipated, as would any systematic discretion given rational expectations, they would not have the long-run consequences of even the fully anticipated higher levels of inflation expected under discretion.[33]

The argument that rules provide stability recognizes that discretion can lead to various sorts of instability. The most obvious possibility is that monetary policy could become unintentionally procyclical. Again, stale or inaccessible data may lead to policy actions that worsen the problem. As Keynes (1930, vol. 2, pp. 223-24) rather colorfully put it, the effects would be the equivalent of a doctor prescribing castor oil for diarrhea and bismuth for constipation. In addition, intervening relative price changes may make discretion's job even more difficult (Selgin 1988b, p. 106).

If we use a rule, cycles may not be eliminated, but their amplitude can be reduced. By eliminating discretionary power over changes in the supply of money, we remove much of the possibility of procyclical policy. Ideally, according to its supporters, a regime of rules could be used to achieve price-level stability. Given the validity of the quantity theory and the stability of velocity, growth in the money supply should have a predictable proportional impact on prices. If a growth-rate rule can be discovered that would be properly calibrated to changes in real income and the demand for money, then the price level could be stabilized. Discretion would tend toward wilder swings in prices, not only because of lag-related problems but also due to the possible unintended consequences of pursuing nonmonetary policy goals such as raising government revenue or monetizing debt. The inevitable political pressures faced by discretionary monetary authorities (whether they be government owned or directed) may lead to unintended increases in the price level. Tobin (1983, p. 516) argues, nonetheless, that better information will allow policymakers to observe "whether current instrument settings, targets and operating rules are having their expected and intended effects."[34] What Tobin is missing is the possible, and very likely, *unintended* effects of policy. A monetary growth rule might reduce these effects.

Both of the previous arguments recall Simons's (1936, p. 3) original call for rules as a means to reduce the general uncertainty facing economic agents: "We must avoid a situation where every business decision becomes largely a speculation on the future of monetary policy." Rules reduce the amount of uncertainty entrepreneurs face in planning for the future. Their decisions can now be made based on economic factors rather than on attempts to outguess a politicized monetary authority. Rules allow resources that would be diverted into ascertaining the latest and future policy direction of a discretionary monetary authority to flow back to other more highly valued uses. Instead of hiring two economists to monitor the Fed, firms can hire two (or more) employees geared toward the specific product being produced (Leijonhufvud 1981b, pp. 247-48).

Another important argument for rules comes from public choice economics. When examining the behavior of political actors, we can start from the same point that we do with economic actors. Political actors are motivated by the desire to improve themselves no more or less than are economic actors. For elected officials this means getting reelected, for appointed officials it means pleasing their oversight committees. For the Fed, it means responding to Congress and/or the president. In either case we have the possibility of politically generated macroeconomic fluctuations (Wagner 1977). Political actors may consciously use monetary policy to generate economic outcomes favorable to their constituents, their party, or the government as a whole. One can imagine politicians leveraging the Fed into generating short-term output increases to pump up the economy at election time, only to bear the inflationary consequences later. The ends of political actors are thus satisfied through this kind of political exchange.

Barro and Gordon (1983a and 1983b) combine the dynamic-inconsistency literature with public choice insights to argue that central banks may have incentives to constrain themselves. Even though policymakers have incentives to cheat on agreed-upon rules, they may not choose to do so. If they attempt to cheat, that is, take the optimal but inconsistent path, agents will begin to rationally expect systematic policy and neutralize it. This brings in the notion of reputation. The monetary authority does want to try to generate output effects. It wants to inflate, but it cannot allow itself to be anticipated. Even without a binding rule, the central bank will want to maintain its reputation as a low inflator so as not to induce offsetting expectations. As a result, the bank will sacrifice the gains from monetary shocks by holding to a low level of inflation. Any deviation from that level will cost the authority its reputation and its ability to generate output effects if and when it desires to do so (Barro and Gordon 1983a).[35] A central bank's concern for its reputation may serve as a proxy for a rule, though the welfare outcomes will lie in between those of the standard regimes of rules and discretion.

The crucial issue of Barro and Gordon's argument is the strength of a reputational equilibrium. If even small changes in the inflation rate cause significant changes in the public's perception of the central bank's intentions, then any given reputational equilibrium will be unstable. Such a scenario seems realistic, particularly in, or after, a period of relatively high inflation. It might take *several* years of very low inflation for a central bank to rebuild its reputation. Any slip during the buildup process will cause the next rebuilding process to be that much more of an uphill climb. It may be the case that these reputation equilibria are so unstable that any deviation by the central bank will induce forces that push the situation even farther from equilibrium. If these dis-equilibrating forces dominate any forces of self-correction, then reputation alone will likely not be sufficient to effectively constrain a central bank.

Cukierman and Meltzer (1986) extend Barro and Gordon's model to explain why governments prefer discretion over rules. They argue that constraining a central bank requires an effective enforcement mechanism but that such enforcement requires informational symmetries between central banks and voters that may not exist (p. 378). Since private agents are not fully informed about government behavior (often rationally so), the temptation is for the monetary authority to exploit that asymmetry by inflating and reducing social welfare. If agents are fully informed, the monetary authority will be forced to maximize social welfare (p. 378). The advantage of rules is that they greatly reduce the informational asymmetries through a publicly known policy. If asymmetries exist, central banks will maximize their welfare at the expense of the public. Without these asymmetries (under rules), the bank will (in its own interest as enforced by informed voters) be led to optimal outcomes.

All of these arguments suggest various dangers in giving the monetary authority discretion, yet the case for rules has one main problem. Although the major advantage of a regime of rules is that it binds the monetary authority, the constraint this regime imposes is also its greatest drawback. Rules prevent central banks from reacting appropriately to exogenous changes. By sticking to a rule, the bank may lose control over the price level and output if money demand fluctuates significantly. In quantity theoretic terms, the monetary authority should try to respond to changes in velocity by changing the nominal supply of money in the opposite direction so as to stabilize MV, or money supply times velocity, and implicitly stabilize PY, or the price level times real output (Selgin 1987b, p. 447). Rules generally preclude this kind of exact reaction, although more sophisticated rules do allow for feedback from changes in velocity *if* the rule (and the demand for money function) is correctly specified. The standard monetarist assumption of stable velocity must hold empirically true for more simple rules to be effective. If not, rules (or a fixed money supply as in Rothbard [1962a, p. 121]) will have to rely on price-level adjustments in the face of changes in velocity. Such price-level adjustments are problematic, whether inflationary or deflationary. Macroeconomic fluctuations can be caused by an overly passive authority that does not respond appropriately to exogenous changes in velocity.[36]

Going back to our discussion of the nature of order, we see that the problem with rules is that they are too inflexible. Whereas discretion was overly flexible and could provide little guidance, monetary rules are unable to react to external changes and reflect that information accurately to expectation formers. Monetary rules have to be rigid, that is their whole purpose, but extreme rigidity to counter extreme flexibility is no virtue. Can we develop an alternative regime that is both stable and flexible enough to effectively inform our expectation-formation processes? In terms of our furniture analogy (see this chapter, note 33), can we find what we are looking for without bumping into the furniture?

Flexibility and Knowledge Conveyance Under Free Banking

The major advantage of a free banking system such as the one outlined earlier would be that it would minimize the number and degree of deviations from the ideal of monetary equilibrium, defined as equating the real supply of money and the demand for real money balances without an intervening change in the price level.[37] The complaint against various versions of central banking is that they do not contain any kind of incentive structure to prevent deviations from monetary equilibrium. The value of achieving monetary equilibrium is that it removes any undesirable monetary influences from the determination of relative prices and allows the savings-investment nexus to be unhampered by such influences as well.[38] This allows actors to form reliable typifications in the all-important market for loanable funds. If monetary equilibrium is maintained, the monetary authority would not be the cause of any change in relative prices or in the price level. Monetary equilibrium would admittedly not stabilize the price level, as increased efficiency in production would cause it to fall slowly (Hayek 1928, p. 74).

One way to view this is that free banking changes the causality in the equation of exchange ($MV = PY$). The standard monetarist interpretation is that V is stable and Y is given, with M being exogenous and determining P. Under free banking, M is *endogenous* to changes in V (the inverse of money demand divided by income) if both M and V refer to bank-issued money and not base money. Y is determined by the real economy and P is determined inversely to changes in Y. An expanding economy (i.e., a rising Y), under free banking, will of necessity cause P to fall as the banking system holds MV constant. This can explain Hayek's argument that monetary equilibrium will involve slowly falling prices as production becomes more efficient.[39] Preventing a fall in the price level would require excess supplies of money and the inflationary consequences that would follow. These consequences would include distorted relative prices that otherwise would have fallen to scarcity-reflecting levels as well as inflation's social costs.[40] Though now taken to mean equiproportional effects on prices due to changes in the money supply, the term *neutrality* can and has been used to describe a money that will not distort the determination of relative prices when there are changes in its supply. Some (Lutz 1969 and Selgin 1988b, p. 56ff., for example) have argued that if the banking system is organized correctly, demand-driven changes in the supply of money will be neutral.

In monetary equilibrium, interest rates are allowed to reflect the true time preferences of savers and borrowers unaffected by distortions from the monetary sector. The argument here rests on the nature of the loanable funds market. Savers supply real loanable funds based on their endowments and intertemporal preferences. Banks serve as intermediaries to redirect savings to investors via money creation. Depositors give banks custody of their funds, and banks in turn create loans based on these deposits. The creation (supply) of money corresponds to a supply of funds for investment use by firms.

On the saving side, the key is recognizing that the act of holding a bank liability is an act of saving (Brown 1910). By holding a bank liability, either deposits or currency under free banking, the possessor refrains from redeeming it for outside money. To the extent such refraining occurs, the unclaimed reserves can be used as the basis for further loans. Looked at another way, the act of holding money is a refusal to consume and, by implication, and act of saving. If an actor sells her goods or services for money and holds that money as an addition to her real balances, she is saving in the sense that she is agreeing to postpone her consumption until the future. The bank borrower who spends his loan on goods and services is granted "credit" by the seller's acceptance and holding of the bank-created money offered in exchange. Bank loans enable borrowers to spend and buy goods and services through the willingness of the sellers to hold the lent liabilities and, therefore, refrain from redeeming them for current consumption.

Free banks are able to maintain this intermediation process by adjusting their reserve ratios in response to changes in the demand for their liabilities. Suppose, for example, that the demand to hold a bank's notes rises. The rise in savings would first cause an excess supply of loanable funds at the current market rate. However, the bank can now adjust its reserve ratio and pyramid more liabilities on its current level of reserves. If the bank is not a price-taker, increasing its supply of credit will force the bank to lower its market rate of interest in order to induce customers to borrow the newly acquired savings. The lower market rate will correspond to the new lower natural rate resulting from the hypothesized increase in the savings schedule. Free banks are thus pure intermediaries and prevent undesirable divergences between the market and the natural rate of interest. This also shows how free banks can prevent the Austrian story of a market rate too low (Mises 1980, chap. 19) and the Wicksellian story of a market rate too high.[41]

The key to this process is that market profit-and-loss signals generated through the clearing process guide bankers to take the appropriate actions. Banks that underissue liabilities discover that their reserves are going to waste. In letting unused reserves sit, the bank bears an opportunity cost of the forgone interest income from the further loans that could be created. Such an opportunity cost is the driving force behind the evolution toward fractional reserve banking from warehouse banking, as discussed in Selgin and White (1987), and continues to drive the process in more mature systems.

Modern central banks have been prone to inflate rather than to underissue. A free banking system can guard against this possibility through the same reserve-flow process. Imagine that a bank tries to issue more liabilities than its depositors wish to hold.[42] The bank may appear to be able to gain by doing so because it now has more purchasing power at the existing price level if it spends the new liabilities into the market, or because it earns interest by loaning the new liabilities. If the bank tries to overissue liabilities, however, it will find that the costs of redeeming them outweigh these potential benefits.

With the demand for money unchanged, overissue will cause holders of liabilities to find themselves with more than their desired level of real balances at the existing price level. Holders will shed the excess liabilities, through purchase, deposit, or direct redemption. Of course, notes used for purchase will wind up being deposited or redeemed eventually given the unchanged demand for money. The result will be a drain of the overissuing bank's reserves at the redemption desk and/or clearinghouse as more of the bank's liabilities are returned than it returns to its competitors. The bank now faces three costly options. First, it could live with its new lower reserve ratio and increased net clearings, but this risks a liquidity crisis that could destroy a free bank's all-important brand name capital, if not the bank itself. Second, it can shrink its liabilities or, third, discover or attract increased amounts of reserves.

The first option is probably the least likely, because the bank was in equilibrium prior to the overissue and there has not been a change in money demand. The costs of liquidity failure are too high a risk. The third option is also costly, as the bank must either bring forth new supplies of the outside money or convince liability holders at other banks to switch to its liabilities. Either would solve the problem with minimal macroeconomic consequences because the new reserves would be new savings to match the increased investment. Either strategy would force the competing banks to respond to a fall in the holdings of their liabilities, thus passing the first bank's "problem" on to others.

However, both of these options would require expenditures in order to increase the bank's market share or expenditures to obtain more commodity money. The most likely choice for the bank is to reduce its liabilities, bringing its reserve ratio back to the desired level. This is costly, too, in that it involves calling in loans and sacrificing the interest that could have been earned. The key point is that all the available options are costly enough to prevent overissue in the first place.

Crucial to this argument is that note holders discriminate between various brands of notes. If not, what is to ensure that holders shed the notes of the particular bank that overissues? If there is no brand discrimination, holders might shed any bank's notes rather than those of the inflator (Selgin 1988b, p. 42ff.), drastically lowering the cost to the overissuing bank by externalizing the costs of overissue to all of the relevant banks. Christ (1989) is unconvinced that such discrimination would occur (even though it does occur today with deposit liabilities) and uses it as a criticism of Selgin. One possible response to Christ is that discrimination is more likely in an advanced free banking system because the number of note producers with nationwide markets would probably be relatively small. Economies of scale and general competitive activity would lead to a small number of large, branched banks, not unlike the Canadian system today. Given the over 13,000 banks that populate the United States today, note discrimination would be unlikely, but if the choice was among only five or ten nationwide note brands, customers would likely be aware of the differences and have distinct preferences.[43]

Another criticism of free banking is the possibility that all banks might expand their liabilities simultaneously, therefore having the same effect as a central bank. If this occurs, no bank will experience any change in *net* clearings, apparently permitting them all to inflate successfully. However, as Selgin (1988b, p. 82) argues, the increase in *gross* clearings implies an increase in the variance of clearings, which implies an increased need for precautionary reserves. Although the long-run expected value of net clearings is zero, any *given* clearing session involves a 50 percent chance of being reserve deficient, and the expected size of a deficiency is larger given the larger value of gross clearings. This resulting increase in the precautionary demand for reserves provides a market check on the ability of free banks to expand in concert and further limits inflationary tendencies in a free banking system.

Another way to look at this is that free banking internalizes the cost of overissue. With a monopolized currency, note holders have no choice but to continue to spend excess real balances until the price level rises sufficiently to return the real money supply (M/P) back to its preexpansion level (Yeager 1968, pp. 50-51). Central banks externalize the cost of inflation on to the general public through the forced redistribution generated during the injection of the excess supply of money. The increased real supply of money is adjusted downward to the demand for real balances through movements in the price level, that is, movements in the prices of all of the goods that exchange against money. Under free banking, this adjustment is made through the nominal supply of money rather than the price level. In making such an adjustment, a free banking system mitigates, if not eliminates, the systemic effects of monetary disequilibria under central banking. The costs associated with relying on changes in relative prices in order to adjust the excess real money supply downward are spread out across the entire economy; the costs of adjusting the nominal supply of money are localized to the specific bank(s) involved.[44] In other words, free banking internalizes the costs of monetary disequilibria.

With exchangeable and enforceable property rights in currency, as under free banking, the current external costs of monetary disequilibria can be internalized to the offending bank (Kirchner 1988, pp. 232-34). As with many other issues, most economists see this point with other commodities, but not with money. The post-Coasean law and economics literature of the past twenty-five years is full of examples of internalization through appropriately defined property rights (i.e., pollution), but almost nothing has been done in applying it to money. In that light, one can see the argument for free banking as an application of property rights economics to the monetary sector, with the corresponding increase in the efficient use of resources and social order.[45]

The structure of property rights also affects the role that brand names play as ideal types. The fact that a free banking system includes property rights in currency enables note brands to more accurately reflect perceptions of bank quality. The reserve-flow process also plays a role here. As customers increase their trust in a bank and are willing to hold more of its liabilities, the bank can adjust its reserve ratio downward and issue more liabilities. In an important sense, sustainable reserve ratios are the visible indicators of the public's trust (and typification) of banks. As customers increase their trust, the banks respond appropriately by adjusting reserve ratios to reflect that trust.[46] The profit incentives that lead to appropriate changes in reserve ratios also allow the information contained in brand names and ideal types to be sufficiently flexible, yet still historically continuous, to serve as aids to expectation formation.

The knowledge aspect of this process is that free banks would not need to obtain data on aggregate money demand or other macroeconomic variables.[47]Although banks would want to try to forecast the ex ante demand for their liabilities, they would be able to rely on reserve levels and profits as ex post indicators of over- and underissue. Central banks have two shortcomings on this account. First, the ex ante forecasting problem is several times greater given the larger size of the relevant demand for money. Second, and more importantly, their only ex post indicators of success are changes in macroeconomic variables, such as the price level, that occur too late to react to. In addition, undertaking the appropriate policy reaction to this ex post data may not be in the bank's self-interest. Free banks with excess reserves would receive a condensed and interpretable indicator of the current state of demand for their liabilities. Banks who see their reserves draining away receive an indicator informing them of their mistakes.[48] In both the over- and underissue examples, the appropriate policy action for free banks lies in their self-interest to perform.

These knowledge questions are analogous to the knowledge-conveying aspect of prices stressed by Hayek (1945) and Lavoie (1986a).[49] The advantage of the price system is that prices indicate relative scarcity without market actors needing to know what caused the original scarcity. Price changes provide the information in a short and compact way. Banks do not need to know why, what, or who changed their demand for money, though such knowledge cannot hurt. All they need is information about changes in their reserve levels and profitability. Free banks can supply more appropriate amounts of liabilities without ever having to know the exact state of money demand or why it might be changing. Prices and profits make that knowledge available in a low-cost way.

Like discretion, free banking acknowledges the importance of responding to exogenous changes in the demand for money. But free banking provides the advantage that it does not face the knowledge problems that plague discretion. Free banks get around this by using profits and reserves as surrogates. Instead of having to rely on the intelligence of specific individuals to acquire all kinds of data in a central location, free banks receive the information in a compact and accessible form due to the polycentric interaction of multiple note issuers.[50] There is no need for free banks to estimate money demand equations; they need only to know the probability distribution over their net clearings and to observe their own reserve flows.

In addition, the expectational interactions should not be the same as under discretion. Because money supply decisions would be polycentric, it is not clear how agents could anticipate them. In addition, the whole justification for anticipating bank policy is to avoid the harmful effects of unanticipated inflation; but if banks have little incentive to inflate, why is there a need to spend time forming or modeling expectations? To the extent that overissue occurs, the normal reserve-flow process will stem it, even in the absence of rational expectations. Because agents do not bear the costs of inflation, there appears to be little incentive to try to anticipate bank behavior. To the extent such expectations are needed, the knowledge conveyed by brand names will suffice.

Free banking also removes the public choice concern over political manipulation. With a depoliticized money supply, political business cycles are not possible.

However, the whole case for rules derives from discretion's inability to achieve its stated goals. Because free banking can resolve many of the dilemmas of discretion, the case for rules is weakened because free banking can work without the drawbacks of rules. To the extent the case for rules is a second-best solution given the flaws of discretion, free banking allows us to achieve a first-best solution by going beyond the false dichotomy of rules versus discretion. It is the existence of central banking, and its monopoly over note issue, that forces us into the world of the second best. In that world, rules might well be preferred to discretion due to their ability to constrain political self-interest. However, if the first-best world is achievable, then the case for rules as a universal-best monetary regime disintegrates.

Again, the biggest problem with rules as compared to free banking is the inability of the central bank to respond when necessary.[51] Free banking overcomes flexibility problems by allowing individual banks to adjust the nominal money supply in the face of changes in the demand for their money. Most of those who favor rules agree that the problem with discretion is that it can play havoc with the price system; therefore, by turning to rules we can preserve the system's integrity. The irony of this is that rules force the banking system to ignore the very signals that the price system (under free banking) could provide so well.[52] The knowledge embodied in prices and profits in the money industry will do a better job preserving the price system's integrity than will excessively rigid rules. If the accuracy of price signals is the concern, why should the banking industry itself be prevented from supplying and utilizing such signals? The case for rules ignores price signals, and the case for discretion denies that price signals can coordinate bank behavior.[53]

Conclusion

Free banking permits the development of institutions that allow social actors to make use of the necessarily fragmented and uncertain knowledge of others. Within the broader concept of order discussed in Chapter 2, we saw how ideal types provide the needed "flexible continuity" to allow actors to form reliable expectations and lead to more orderly results. In the monetary realm specifically, free banking allows money itself to have this flexibility. Under free banking, the knowledge reflected by particular brand names of competitive money to serve as more accurate ideal types because more detailed information goes into them than would under a monopolized currency. Free banking thus leads to a higher degree of monetary order.

The ongoing evolutionary development of a free banking system exhibits the creativity, complexity, and coordination that are characteristic of economic order more broadly. Other monetary regimes fail to lead to order because they either cause monetary ideal types (i.e., brand names) to be unable to reflect any meaningful knowledge due to their overflexibility (as in discretion) or they prevent monetary ideal types from being flexible enough to adjust appropriately to changes in external factors (rules). In either case, the creative element of monetary order is limited or shunted into possibly second-best directions because actors are limited in their ability to respond with or initiate genuine novelty. These limits inhibit the development of further coordinated complexity and lower the overall orderliness of the system.

Only free banking can provide the mix of stability and flexibility that is needed to have accurate expectation formation processes and to permit the creativity, complexity, and coordination that are a part of any properly functioning monetary order. Evidence for this view will be examined in the next chapter as our evolutionary benchmark is used to analyze a historical episode of monetary disorder that resulted from the U.S. banking system's deviations from an unhampered evolutionary monetary order.

Notes

1. The reader might also want to see Glasner (1989, chap. 1), who offers a parallel and complementary account of the evolution of money and banking.

2. A modern example of this same problem would be the differences in IBM and Apple computer operating systems. An Apple user faces high costs in an office full of IBM users. The costs of differentiation are usually so high as to lead to standardization by the office.

3. Selgin and White cite English evidence to back up this conjectured evolution, but there is U.S. evidence as well, as the discussion in Chapter 5 will indicate.

4. It should be noted that one important subsidiary assumption here is that the legal system recognizes bank liabilities as legal contracts and penalizes failures to meet them. As Selgin and White (pp. 444-45) note, English common law recognized notes, albeit grudgingly, as enforceable contracts. This once again brings out the coevolution, and interdependence, of the monetary and legal orders.

5. This is an example of entrepreneurship in the technical sense of Kirzner (1973).

6. Branching can also be prohibited or limited by law, as was (and still largely is) the case in the United States. This type of intervention into the evolutionary process lessens the orderliness of the system by eliminating an application of creativity and removing the resulting coordination and complexity. See Chapter 5 for more on the specific case of the United States.

7. Selgin and White (1987, pp. 446-48) offer several related possibilities. For reasons of space and clarity, my account will combine aspects of all of those stories.

8. Clearinghouses serve other functions as well (Selgin and White 1987, pp. 449-51). They can and did serve as a financial overseer, a lender to banks in times of crisis, and often took on standard banking operations if need be. See the discussion about the U.S. clearinghouses in Chapter 5.

9. Note that this system provides no reason to expect the evolution of the kinds of limitations placed on U.S. banks today. There would be no Glass-Steagall separation of banking from securities, or any limits on the ability of nonbank firms to own banks. Deposit insurance is not a necessary development, and neither are the branch banking restrictions mentioned earlier. Most, if not all, of these deviations from the freely evolved benchmark have occurred as the result of special interest legislation designed to please the constituents of various

legislators rather than as a result of some market evolution. On the development of the Glass-Steagall Act and deposit insurance during the 1930s, see Glasner (1989, chap. 9). The politics of branching laws is summarized in Horwitz and Selgin (1987).

10. See also Glasner (1989, p. 30ff.) for an excellent discussion of this point: "Because the monopoly over coinage could be exploited quickly in an emergency, it was a welcome source of funds in wartime when other revenue sources could not generate funds as quickly. Providing the sovereign with security against both internal and external threats, the monopoly over coinage became the acknowledged prerogative of the sovereign." For a defense of central banks from an evolutionary perspective, see Goodhart (1988).

11. On the "new learning" see, among others, Bork (1978), Demsetz (1982), Kirzner (1973), and Williamson (1985).

12. An example here might be the rise in quality of Japanese brand names such as Toyota or Sony and the corresponding fall in U.S. brand names in automobiles and electronics.

13. Though this point may have some validity in times of relative monetary stability, certainly such a claim would be hard to justify under severe inflation or deflation. More important, no monetary policy can be completely predictable once one realizes that money is nonneutral in that it enters the market process not from a Chicago-based helicopter but at specific times and places. As a result, simply knowing the percentage growth rate in the money supply will not give actors enough information to predict the additional money's differential impact on their specific areas of economic intercourse. It is these relative price effects, not just the increase in the general price level that wreak havoc during inflation. See also Mises (1980, chap. 8) and the critical discussion in Humphrey (1984).

14. The use of brand names is substantially affected by legal restrictions, of course. One especially onerous set are the limits on interstate banking: Banks could clearly benefit consumers by being able to extend their brand name capital nationwide.

15. This is the crucial argument in Klein's (1974) pioneering contribution to the competitive-currency literature.

16. Again, it should be noted that current legal restrictions prevent this process from having full force today. In this case, the particular restriction is the provision of mandatory federal deposit insurance, which prevents brand names from being good knowledge conveyors by preventing them from accurately reflecting both failure and success. Bailouts, or their potential, prevent failed-bank brand names from conveying complete knowledge, as does the "tax" paid by good banks to finance a deposit insurance system they may never use. These good banks do not appear as profitable as they would be without deposit insurance.

17. One option open to unsatisfied consumers of Federal Reserve notes is to move to the underground economy and either engage in simple barter or use some other agreed upon medium of exchange, such as complex computerized barter networks. Though such activity may be illegal on several counts, recent evidence seems to indicate that it is booming. The primary motive is likely tax

evasion, but dissatisfaction with a continually depreciating monopoly currency might be one contributing explanation.

18. It seems reasonable to conclude that this argument would apply with equal force to any commodity monopolized through a government grant. Examples might include the brand name value of the U.S. Postal Service or Amtrak.

19. Haupert (1991) offers evidence from the U.S. free banking era to support the idea that banks will invest significant resources in their brand names in order to establish a good reputation with the public.

20. See Chapter 5 for some historical examples of this behavior and how it facilitated the use of bank-provided currency. It is also important to recognize that the particular activities that generate trust are greatly affected by the particular culture in question. What works for Americans may not work for the Chinese.

21. It should be noted that the word *rules* will be used here in a broader way than in previous chapters. The term *rule* should not be immediately interpreted, as before, as an ideal type. Unfortunately the word *rule* is the standard one in the literature and there is no easy way around the ambiguity. One question to be examined is just how well rules for monetary policy are capable of serving as ideal typical rules.

22. See also Barro and Gordon (1983a and 1983b), Fehtke and Jackman (1984), Barro (1986a and 1986b), and Cukierman and Meltzer (1986), among others.

23. See also Klein (1974), Hayek (1978c), White (1984), Selgin and White (1987), Selgin (1987b, 1988a, 1988b), Glasner (1989), and Dowd (1989). For an overview of the literature see Schuler (1988).

24. Selgin (1988b, chap. 7) does integrate the theory of free banking into the rules-versus-discretion debate and does (1987b, section 12) address some of the knowledge-related aspects of free banking, but he does not totally share the approach developed in the previous chapters and does not deal with some of the more recent literature.

25. On the 1837-1863 era see Rockoff (1974) and Rolnick and Weber (1983). See the discussion and references in Chapter 5 for more evidence on the National Banking (1863-1914) period.

26. Though monetary policymakers need to know other variables, I will use money demand as the primary example.

27. See Dowd (1989, p. 71): "That the central bank be able to predict the demand for money . . . requires not only that there be a stable demand-for-money function, but that the demand for money be predictable *ex ante* as well."

28. As Mises (1980, p. 153) argues at the opening of a section titled "The Stock of Money and the Demand for Money," "The process, by which supply and demand are accommodated to each other until a position of equilibrium is established and both are brought into quantitative and qualitative coincidence, is the higgling of the market. But supply and demand are only the links in a chain of phenomena, one end of which has this visible manifestation in the market, while the other is anchored deep in the human mind."

29. This, of course, has been Milton Friedman's continued contribution to the debate over the effectiveness of activist monetary policy. See Friedman (1968) for example.

30. On rational expectations see the pioneering contributions of Lucas (1976, 1977). For an overview of the literature, see Sheffrin (1983).

31. As strong as this assumption may sound, it is no stronger (in fact it is identical) to the perfect-knowledge assumptions made in general equilibrium theory. If there is a piece of information that agents can know that will make them better off (as would knowing the impending change in the money supply), then they will have incentive to acquire it and use it rationally.

32. A commonly used example of this phenomenon concerns patents. It makes sense for a policymaker to promise patent protection in order to stimulate innovation, but once such goods exist, the optimal policy is to revoke the patent and open the field to competition to avoid deadweight losses. However, once this is done, no promise of patent protection can be credible, and innovation in later periods will not be forthcoming. Much of the post-1977 literature has focused on the "reputation" effects of monetary policy choices.

33. One could draw an analogy to looking for a lost object in a dark room. Discretion says crawl around and feel for it. Rules recognize that the costs of bumping into the furniture may outweigh the expected benefit of finding the object. If so, the sensible course of action is to just stand still. Note that in neither case will you likely find the object.

34. Tobin's use of words like *instrument settings* and *operating rules* reveals a mechanistic understanding of the market process. As has been repeatedly stressed, markets are anything but mechanistic. They are expressions of the creative and imaginative elements of human behavior, and attempts to treat the market like a machine once again confuse order and organization. This attempt to ascribe mechanical qualities to the results of human action is referred to as "mechanomorphism" by Mittermaier (1986). The dangers of this view are not just theoretical but political as well; see also Hayek (1952b).

35. Glasner (1989, pp. 38-39) uses the reputation hypothesis along with the war finance motive to explain why many modern central banks have kept inflation relatively low: "[Inflation] can only be effective if it takes the public by surprise. . . . So to exploit its monopoly over money in an emergency, the state must avoid currency debasement or inflation at other times. Unfortunately, the better a government's reputation for monetary rectitude, the greater the payoff for springing a surprise inflation."

36. The preceding poses an interesting problem for rational expectations theory. The standard assumption is that agents use all the relevant information in forming expectations and in acting over time. However, by binding central banks to a rule, do we limit *their* ability to use potentially relevant information? A rule-bound bank would have to ignore changes in velocity that could conceivably be useful. If the central bank does not use this information, it appears to be acting irrationally. If one argues that such information is just not obtainable by the Fed, why isn't there information that is equally unavailable to agents in other models that assume rational expectations? The essence of rational expectations is that agents and policymakers supposedly have and can act on the

same information set. Does a monetary regime of rules prevent this assumption from being empirically true?

37. On the concept of monetary equilibrium, see Selgin (1988b, p. 56ff.) and the references there. It might seem strange to take recourse to an equilibrium concept after the discussions in Chapters 1 and 2. Unfortunately, the term *monetary equilibrium* carries with it the force of a tradition of use in monetary theory.

38. See also Mises (1990, p. 80) and V. Smith (1990, p. 194).

39. A more interesting point is that this interpretation indicates that the quantity theory of money (the idea that changes in the money supply cause proportionate changes in the price level), long held to be one of economic theory's sacred cows, is only *institutionally relevant*. Changes in M cause changes in P only under central banking. Under the institutional assumption of free banking, the much-debated and much-tested theory falls apart with respect to bank-issued money. The quantity theory would still apply to exogenous changes in the supply of base money under free banking. Aside from considering the practical and theoretical implications, one might ask what the nonuniversality of the quantity theory says about the methodology of positive economics and the universality of empirically tested hypotheses. For an overview of the history of the quantity theory and a more in-depth discussion of this entire argument, see the fine discussion in Glasner (1989, chaps. 3 and 4).

40. See the arguments in Leijonhufvud (1981b), Glasner (1989, pp. 209-13) and Horwitz (1991). Also see the sympathetic criticisms of Cowen (1991).

41. See also Wicksell (1950, chap. 4), Yeager (1973, 1986) and Leijonhufvud (1981a, 1981c).

42. It should be noted that an unmatched fall in the demand for money would have the same effects as an unwarranted increase in the supply.

43. An analogy might be found in credit cards. No more than half a dozen have nationwide acceptability. Clearly each offers different costs and benefits, and consumers and merchants appear to distinguish between different brands. Not all people carry the same cards, nor do all stores accept all cards.

One possible outcome under free banking is a small number of national currencies with local and regional banks picking up additional demand within their spheres of operation.

44. The costs of relative price changes are the usual ones associated with inflationary regimes. These costs are not just shoeleather and menu costs, because the effects of the excess supply of money do not affect all prices evenly. When changes in the money supply are nonneutral, the costs of inflation are that much greater. See the literature cited in note 40.

45. This argument is more fully discussed in Horwitz and Bodenhorn (1991).

46. Greenbaum and Thakor (1989) argue that reserve holdings act as a signal about the quality of bank assets. They add that reserve *requirements* impede that signaling process by forcing good banks to hold more reserves than they might otherwise, thus understating the quality of their assets. Under free banking, banks would be unencumbered by such requirements and reserve holdings would indeed fluctuate to reflect the trust that the public holds in a bank's liabilities and the confidence the bank has in its assets.

47. The following is an extension of Selgin (1987b, section 12).

48. Of course, price and profits are not "marching orders" (Garrison 1987, p. 339) but have to be interpreted by the agent. Such interpretations can be incorrect, and bankers who make such mistakes will not survive long in a competitive market.

49. See also Dowd's (1989, pp. 184-85) brief discussion of this point.

50. As Vera Smith (1990, p. 192) sees it: "To those who would prefer to place their trust in semi-automatic forces rather than in the wits of central bank managers and their advisers, free banking would appear to be by far the lesser evil. Banks which have not the possibility of abrogating their liability to pay their obligations in gold cannot go very far wide of the path following movements in their gold reserves."

51. See also Hayek (1978c, p. 77), who points out the shortcomings of this lack of flexibility: "As regards Professor Friedman's proposal of a legal limit on the rate at which a monopolistic issuer of money was to be allowed to increase the quantity in circulation, I can only say that I would not like to see what would happen if under such a provision it ever became known that the amount of cash in circulation was approaching the upper limit and that therefore a need for increased liquidity could not be met."

52. See also Glasner's (1989, p. 215, n. 7) related argument.

53. On this view it makes sense that many rule supporters also accept a rational expectations-general equilibrium view of the market. By assuming that all the relevant knowledge is known by the agent, those who hold such views ignore the market's ability to convey such knowledge. In parallel fashion it is also not a coincidence that Keynesians tend to support discretion. Keynesians have always doubted the price system's ability to coordinate and have simply applied this thinking to the money market.

5

Regulatory Chaos and Spontaneous Order Under the National Banking System

With the evolutionary framework developed in Chapters 3 and 4, we can now turn to a series of historical events and try to see if that framework can help us render the events intelligible.[1] This chapter is an attempt to compare the framework provided by free banking to the institutions of the United States National Banking System (1863-1914). In so doing we will offer an explanation for the financial panics that struck the system in 1893 and 1907 and make some observations concerning the succeeding reform debate and the origins of the Federal Reserve System.

One reason for examining these panics so closely is that the regulatory blind eye turned to activities of the private sector during the panics created a system of de facto free banking, and thus the panics provide an example to which a theoretical free banking system can be compared.[2] The panics provide an alternative to directly examining a free banking system by allowing us to examine instead the ways in which de facto unfettered private initiative responded to crisis situations. In this chapter I will argue that the actions of the banks, merchants, and public confirm many of the arguments of the previous chapters. Broadly speaking, it was the unplanned and only fragmentarily coordinated actions of these groups that restored some degree of monetary order to a system that had fallen victim to inappropriate attempts at conscious design. The themes that emerge in our historical investigation will echo many of our previous theoretical arguments concerning the ultimate sources of monetary order.

The key features of these panics were currency shortages, bank suspensions of payment, and the spontaneous reactions of banks to mitigate these situations. It will be argued that these shortages were caused by existing legal restrictions and that the crises were significantly alleviated by the banks, which came forth with a variety of currency substitutes. Though these substitutes were conscious attempts to skirt the legal restrictions, they were successful in filling the gaps left by the shortage of sanctioned currency and prevented the panics from worsening. We will examine in some detail the microeconomic aspects of the production and acceptance of these competitive currency substitutes, and we will see how they compare to our previously developed framework for monetary order.

Finally, it was these panics that led to the formation of the Federal Reserve System in 1914, and this chapter is also an attempt to make sense of the debate over the creation of the Fed and show how our evolutionary free banking system might have better solved the problems that concerned the monetary reform movement of the early twentieth century.

Provisions of the National Banking System

To understand why currency shortages and financial panics were recurring problems in the National Banking System, it is necessary to review the relevant legal restrictions it imposed and examine some of their unintended consequences. The system was created by Congress in a series of acts and amendments passed between 1863 and 1865. One of the main purposes of the National Banking System was to federalize the existing state banking systems. Prior to these acts, banks were chartered by state governments and were allowed to issue bank notes only if they bought certain approved assets as collateral. Frequently these assets were state government bonds, but some states allowed banks to use private-sector bonds, especially those of the railroads. Requiring state government bonds as collateral provided a convenient way for state governments to raise revenue. The problem with this system was that the differing state laws, along with prohibitions on interstate banking, prevented the development of a uniform (i.e., accepted at par) national currency. Creating such a currency became a major topic of mid-nineteenth-century debates over monetary reform.

As the Civil War continued, the federal (Union) government began to issue bonds to raise the money to pay for the war effort. Bond sales lagged early on, and various problems with the state banks and their currencies continued, so the idea of a national banking system was developed as a way to solve both problems. The federal government would begin to charter so-called national banks, which could issue currency only if they backed it with purchases of federal government bonds. The intent was to provide a captive market for the war bonds to provide the needed revenue and create the desired uniform national currency.[3] The legislation that formed the National Banking System included three broad categories of restrictions: bond-collateral requirements, reserve requirements, and limits on branching. The first of these was the proximate cause of the currency shortages, and the latter two contributed to their length and severity.

Under the provisions of the National Currency Act of 1863, nationally chartered banks were allowed to issue their own bank notes if they met certain conditions. Banks were required to purchase acceptable 2-percent United States government bonds in the open market and deposit them at the Treasury in exchange for notes in an amount equal to 90 percent of the lower of the par or market value of the deposited bonds. The deposited bonds were used as collateral for the redemption of notes of failed banks.

The bond-collateral requirements created a difficulty regarding the profit incentives facing national banks. When deciding whether to issue notes, the banks took into consideration two factors: the market price of approved bonds was the out-of-pocket cost of issue; the interest foregone on potentially higher-earning alternative assets indicated the opportunity cost.[4] As a result, the amount of notes circulated by national banks tended to correspond to variations in bond prices rather than to the demand for such notes. Higher bond prices, or higher rates of interest on alternative assets, meant that note issue was less profitable. There was no necessary connection between low bond prices and high currency demand,[5] so this system often led to currency shortages because it was unprofitable for banks to supply the demanded amount of currency to depositors and would-be borrowers.[6]

Other stipulations of the bond collateral requirements prevented the supply of currency from responding to changes in demand. There was also a significant time lapse before new notes could be issued by national banks, because the banks often had to wait for new bonds to be issued in order to have something to back the issue of the needed amount of notes. In addition the comptroller of the currency was responsible for physically printing the notes, so there was a time lapse between the acceptance of bonds and actual possession of new notes. State banks were unable to make up any deficiencies due to a prohibitive 10-percent tax placed on their issue by the National Currency Act.

In both 1893 and 1907, one primary catalyst for the panics was an increase in the public's currency-to-deposit ratio. This increase was mostly due to the need for cash during various parts of the harvest season. The seasonality of the relative demand for currency played a significant role throughout the period of the National Banking System (Andrew 1906). A rise in the relative demand for currency set the problems of the National Banking System into motion. Once the banks realized the need to issue more notes, they faced three related problems: (1) finding acceptable bonds, (2) buying them at a price that made note issue profitable, and (3) avoiding delays between purchasing bonds and getting notes in the public's hands. Concerning the first problem, a prominent national bank president in 1907 commented that "the real difficulty . . . has been to get acceptable securities. . . . One [New York] bank had to borrow from banks in California. This shows the effort the banks are making to take out circulation" (*NYT* November 12, 1907, p. 2).[7] During the panic of 1907, other bankers saw these problems as well. A. Barton Hepburn of Chase National Bank noted that "it is extremely difficult to secure the loan of government bonds which are necessary . . . to secure an increase in the circulation of any national bank" (p. 2).

When bonds could be purchased, the expense involved was often so much as to make further note issue unprofitable. Frank R. Vanderlip of National City Bank reported that "in order to get United States 2 percent bonds we have forced the price of them to the highest point on record" (p. 2). Hepburn indicated that in order "to purchase . . . 2 percent bonds, [banks] will have to pay $108 for them. By having to pay this price for these bonds to bring out circulation, the financial situation becomes aggravated rather than relieved" (p. 2). Hepburn recognized that further note issue was badly needed and that high bond prices were preventing banks from being able to buy the necessary bonds at a price that made note issue profitable. The bond-collateral requirement condensed the banks' buying power into a narrow bond market and raised prices in that market to unprofitable levels.

If the banks had been allowed to issue their notes backed by their general assets (as were their deposit credits), then the marginal costs of note issue would not have risen any faster than the marginal costs of deposit creation. In the absence of bond-collateral requirements, banks will be indifferent at the margin as to the form in which depositors choose to hold bank liabilities. It was assumed in Chapter 4 that banks were free to choose what assets they used to back their notes, and as a result, changes in the currency-to-deposit ratio were not a problem. However, under the legal restrictions of the alternative institutional arrangement of bond-collateral requirements, changes in the relative demand for currency could be problematic. In addition, if, under free banking, the need did arise to acquire significant amounts of new assets, the buying power of the banks would be spread across a whole range of possible assets rather than concentrated in one market for specific government bonds.

Selgin (1988a) illustrates this point by comparing free bank currency with Federal Reserve notes. Because free bank currency is bank-created money and central bank currency is not, shifts from deposits to currency in free banking systems do not mean balance sheet shrinkages. For example, Federal Reserve notes serve both as hand-to-hand currency and as bank reserves. When the public decides to increase its relative holdings of currency, it causes a drain on bank reserves, necessitating either a shrinkage of bank balance sheets or a countervailing injection of reserves from the Fed. Shifts in the currency-to-deposit ratio would have no effect on the reserves of a free bank, because neither currency nor deposits are counted as bank reserves.

Under the National Banking System, the bond-collateral requirements raised the cost of accommodating changes in the public's currency-to-deposit ratio, leading to currency shortages. Without such requirements banks would not have had to pay a premium for special assets (in this case bonds) to back their notes, because other, less expensive, assets (with higher risk-adjusted yields) were available.

In addition to the significant problems banks had in obtaining bonds at a profitable price, the procedure for approval specified by the bond-collateral requirements aggravated the currency shortages. Once bonds were acquired, actual shipment of notes from the Office of the Comptroller of the Currency could still involve a lengthy delay. During panic situations the Treasury was particularly burdened with various panic-related responsibilities. According to a banker quoted in the *New York Times*, currency shipments during the 1907 panic were delayed "owing to the great pressure of work being put upon . . . the Treasury staff" (November 12, 1907, p. 2). As a result, currency shipments took longest when they were needed the fastest. According to A. Barton Hepburn, banks (during a crisis) might have to wait thirty days or more after depositing required bonds before actually getting hold of new notes. So even if banks could find acceptable bonds at a reasonable price, any beneficial effects of their efforts might not be felt for a month, all due to the need for governmental approval. Add to this the usual bureaucratic delays in printing and transportation, and relief might be six to eight weeks away. These delays would not have occurred if there had been no bond-collateral requirements, as the banks's preferred-asset purchases would not have to be reported to, deposited at, or approved by the Treasury. Banks could have simply kept a stock of preprinted notes on hand for those who wanted notes for deposits and could have used the assets that backed their deposit liabilities to now back their currency.

Though the bond-collateral laws were the reason banks could not accommodate increases in the public's currency-to-deposit ratio, other legal restrictions of the National Banking System, in particular reserve requirements and branching prohibitions, exacerbated the currency shortages.

Reserve requirements involved a pyramiding of reserves among three different categories of banks. Banks were either rural banks, reserve city banks, or central reserve city banks. The rural banks were any bank located outside of specified reserve cities or central reserve cities. These banks had to hold 15-percent reserves against their deposits. They could keep up to three-fifths of this amount as deposits with approved reserve agents in the reserve cities. Banks in these reserve cities had to keep 25 percent as reserves, which could include up to one-half as deposits in the central reserve city banks. These latter banks (in New York, Chicago, and St. Louis) had to hold 25-percent reserves, all in some form of high-powered money such as gold, government legal tenders (greenbacks), or other government currency.

The major problem with this system was that when nonreserve banks faced reserve shortages they unintentionally initiated a domino effect throughout the banking system. For example, it was not unusual for rural banks to find their vault reserves depleting during the harvest season, which necessitated a withdrawal of deposits from the reserve city banks to replenish them. In turn, the reserve city banks would replace these reserves by drawing on their accounts at the central reserve city banks. These banks had to pay out in outside money, leading to an overall shrinkage of bank balance sheets. The ripple effect caused by these reserve arrangements played a significant role in worsening the currency crises. Between the demand for high-powered money coming from other banks and the increasing demand for it on the part of the currency-starved public, central reserve city banks faced severe drains on their reserve media.

Banks were also constrained by limits on their ability to open branch offices. Branching across state lines was prohibited nationwide, and it was up to the individual states whether they would permit branching within the state.[8] The unit banks of the period faced two problems common to nonbranched systems. First, they lacked diversification. Without the ability to branch, banks were tied to the fortunes of the local economy, which made them all the more susceptible to failure when local economic problems occurred. Banks that are more geographically diversified can increase the diversity of their asset portfolios, lowering their overall risk. If problems crop up in one location, funds can be moved from healthy branches to help ones in difficulty.

Second, the lack of branches prevented effective interbank funds movement.[9] If rural banks found themselves short on reserves, they either had to go to other rural banks (also probably short) or to the reserve city banks. Even if successful, these steps take time and trouble and involve interest payments. If the rural banks had been branches of larger banks, who had branches in other cities, the movement of funds would have been easier. Branched banks can help reserve-deficient branches by easily shifting funds from branches with excess reserves. Without branching, this movement of reserves is far more difficult. Both the lack of diversification and the costliness of interbank funds movement, like the reserve requirements, added to the problems set into motion by the bond collateral requirements.

The banking system's inability to react smoothly to changes in the currency-to-deposit ratio led to drains on bank reserves. Reserves could not be acquired from other branches due to legal restrictions on branching and had to be obtained through withdrawals of reserves from larger banks, leaving them short. All of these factors together contributed to the existence, and severity, of the recurring currency shortages under the National Banking System. In the panics of 1893 and 1907, the banks attempted to relieve the situation by issuing their own forms of currency substitutes. We can now look at the responses of the banks and see how these substitutes came into being and evolved into general use. After a review of the events of the panics, we can see how these currency substitutes might relate to our previous discussions of monetary order.

A Chronology of Events

In addition to the harvest season changes in the relative demand for currency, both the panics of 1893 and 1907 saw other exogenous factors that drove depositors to demand relatively more currency. If none of the aforementioned legal restrictions had been in place, none of these events by themselves would have been problematic. Unfortunately, the bond-collateral requirements prevented the banks from properly reacting, and the other restrictions constrained the types of actions the banks could take to solve the problem. Add to the legal restrictions certain exogenous factors affecting public confidence in banks, and the ingredients for a panic were present.

The stage was set for the panic of 1893 with the passage of the Sherman Silver Purchase Act in 1890. The act allowed the U.S. government to print and issue silver-backed notes for public use. The result was a dramatic increase in the stock of currency and heightened uncertainty about the financial system's future monetary standard. The correct perception of an inflated money supply, concerns over the health of a number of banks, and the agricultural demand for currency all led to an increase in the currency-to-deposit ratio.

According to Sprague (1977, pp. 162-63), the first sign of trouble in 1893 was the collapse of the Philadelphia and Reading Railroad on February 26. After the railroad was placed in the hands of receivers, doubts about other industrial stocks increased. The market slowed and bank balance sheets shrunk. This general economic downturn increased suspicions about many financial institutions. By the beginning of June, the New York banks were shipping currency and reserves to the South and West to handle a number of bank failures and suspensions there. This was a perfect example of the domino effect that the reserve pyramiding caused. The eventual drain on the New York banks spurred the New York Clearinghouse Association to issue clearinghouse loan certificates on June 15, which allowed the banks to clear among themselves without using up much needed high-powered money. The certificates were backed up by bank deposits of general securities at the clearinghouse.[10] The certificates had worked well in the past, and commentators such as Sprague agreed that they were issued early enough in the 1893 panic to head off worse trouble.

Problems seemed to have abated when a new wave of doubt about southern and western banks appeared toward the end of July. Again the

New York banks were drained of reserves as the rural banks began to call in reserves to be able to provide depositors with cash of any kind. In addition, the harvest season was at hand, and the relative demand for currency began to rise. By early August, banks in the East were forced to restrict or prohibit cash payments, and savings and loans began to enforce their time clauses on withdrawals. Around August 15, clearinghouse organizations all over the country, especially in the Southeast, began to issue the various currency substitutes that became the distinctive mark of this panic and the one in 1907. All kinds of items were used as hand-to-hand currency, including public versions of the clearinghouse certificates issued in small denominations. Banks also issued small round-denomination certified cashier's checks that circulated as currency by repeated endorsement. Firms used round-denomination bearer paychecks that worked the same way. In addition, it appears as though there were a few small-denomination bonds that were issued and circulated. These currency substitutes stayed in circulation for several months until all were deposited or cashed in. By that time other means were available to satisfy the demand for currency, and the height of the harvest season demand had passed.

The events of 1893 constituted the worst crisis (to that point) that the National Banking System had seen, and the voices of change were in the air. The severity of the crisis was difficult to measure, but Sprague (1977, p. 201) attempted to do so by comparing the change in gross earnings of the railroads between the same months in 1892 and 1893. During July through December of 1893, railroad gross earnings were down an average of 9.49 percent per month, compared to a 4.93 percent rise in earnings between March and June. Sprague also mentions numerous examples of factories closing after being unable to meet payrolls and a general slowdown in interstate commerce due to a lack of available credit. In the wake of these troubles, calls for monetary reform were inevitable.

Perhaps the most notable attempt to develop a reform proposal was the Indianapolis Monetary Convention of 1897. As stated in its report (Laughlin 1898, p. 3ff.), the convention was called jointly by businesspeople, bankers, and academics from a number of midwestern cities in order to develop some kind of proposal for the reform of the currency. They note in their original letter that "sentiment is abroad in the land, the business men are discussing and the press is urging currency reform" (p. 3). The commission met in January of 1897 and, after much discussion, drafted a plan of reform and a long report explaining the steps they were urging.

The author of the lengthy explanatory section was J. Laurence Laughlin, a University of Chicago economist. Laughlin correctly noted two of the major problems under the existing system and proposed positive steps to correct them. The first of these was the inelasticity of the note supply caused by the bond-collateral requirements (pp. 277-345). Laughlin saw that the requirements made the banks undertake more investment than they normally would, needlessly restricting the supply of currency and credit. He also noted that the bond requirements made note issue prohibitively costly, especially in rural areas where notes were needed far more than deposits. The commission's proposal included removal of the bond requirements, allowing banks to issue notes on the same basis as deposits.[11]

Laughlin also saw the prohibition on branching as a legal restriction that constrained the system's ability to respond to the needs of the public (pp. 376-86). Branches would have had great advantages for the increased circulation of currency in rural areas. They would have allowed an increased number of offices and increased competition between banks, both of which would have promoted the use (via easier redemption) of bank notes. With the removal of the bond-collateral and branching restrictions, note issue would have been increased in the rural areas, which was precisely where it was needed most. Laughlin (p. 384) also argues that branches would have made interbank funds movement easier, removing the domino effect of the existing reserve requirements. Branches would have also made out-of-town notes and checks easier to use, as the issuing bank would have been more likely to have a branch, or be known, in the new town.

This combination of asset currency and branch banking did not sell very well in Washington, as it did not please all of the various special interests involved. The effective result of the commission's reform proposal, combined with other lesser-known proposals, was only one very small change made by the Gold Standard Act of 1900. The change allowed banks to issue up to 100 percent, rather than 90 percent, of the lower of the par or market value of the required bonds, allowing the banks to issue roughly 11 percent more currency backed by the same dollar value of bonds. Obviously this was not a major structural reform of a poorly conceived banking system. Rather it was a bit of strikingly minor tinkering with a system in dire need of a major overhaul.

Concern remained high over the possibility of another panic, and these fears were realized in the fall of 1907 as a new set of factors combined with the usual harvest season problems to create another shortage and more bank runs. The exogenous factors here included questionable banking practices of members of the New York financial community. This began with the attempt of F. A. Heinze, a major financier and banker, to corner the copper market using depositor funds from his Mercantile National Bank in New York. His attempt failed and the bank became unable to meet its clearinghouse obligations in mid-October. One of Mercantile's directors, Charles F. Morse, was involved in other questionable activities, and when his connection with Mercantile became known, his banks were hit by runs. One of Morse's other connections was the Knickerbocker Trust company, which was hit by a run on October 21, which, in turn, led to runs on other banks in succeeding days. Aside from all of these specific causes, it was the height of harvest season, and country banks were drawing on city reserves as they were unable to meet the demand for currency with their own bank notes.

It is important to distinguish between two sets of problems that were occurring simultaneously. The first (what we might call a "currency run") is simply the result of a shift in the public's currency-to-deposit ratio. In this type of run, people do not want to stop holding bank liabilities, they simply want notes instead of deposits. During 1907, the currency run involved both the increase in harvest season demand and the use of notes as a way to transfer funds from distrusted banks to trusted ones. Many of those waiting to get notes for deposits from the Heinze-Morse banks simply intended to redeposit them at a different bank.[12]

Some of the runs on the Heinze-Morse banks were of a different character. A few people were requesting gold, or other outside money, for their bank liabilities. This type of activity (what we might call a "base money run") shows a greater lack of trust in the affected banks and in the banking system as a whole. Even though note demanders who intended to redeposit elsewhere wanted out of the Heinze-Morse banks, they at least were still willing to hold the banks' liabilities a little while. However, the direct-redemption demand of a base money run is a problem for any fractional reserve banking system. Although such runs can be an effective way for depositors to run an inefficient banking firm out of business, a complete lack of confidence can threaten the whole system. To the extent the Heinze-Morse liabilities were no longer desired at all, or that people wanted out of the banking system as a whole, a base money run might be a rational response. The problem is that these runs became intertwined with the currency runs, which aggravated the panic. Currency runs should not present a problem to a properly functioning banking system. Unfortunately the bond-collateral requirements prevented a smooth shift from deposits to currency, and combined with the outside money runs on the Heinze-Morse banks, the pressures on the banking system were more than it could handle.

After the run on Knickerbocker, various banks and other financial institutions, including the Treasury, moved to help the stricken banks. On Saturday, October 26, the New York Clearinghouse Association issued clearinghouse loan certificates, again allowing the banks to clear among themselves without recourse to much needed high-powered money. By November 6, the failed institutions were in new hands and were settling their obligations to former liability holders. The bank runs had ended and stock prices were recovering. There remained a premium on currency, however, with prices as high as $104 for $100 face value in currency (Sprague 1977, p. 281). Because so many non-New York banks had deposits in the city's banks, the shortage of currency there led to shortages across the country. By early November, these currency shortages were the only remnant of the panic. Due to the prohibitive cost of note issue, banks were unable to meet the increased demand for currency directly through increased note issue or reserve media. Instead the banking system and the nonbank public once again had to devise ingenious and sometimes amusing methods for evading the law and meeting the demand for currency. These currency substitutes, like those of 1893, circulated for a few months until finally being retired. Andrew (1908) estimated the total amount of such substitutes to be around $354 million during the 1907 panic.

By looking at the specifics of the currency substitutes that appeared during the two panics, and the other steps the banks took to restore monetary order, we can compare the evolution of the acceptance and use of these substitutes with our description of the nature of money and monetary order in the previous chapters. If the comparison is favorable, and if we can show that a free banking system might have solved many of the problems that led to the creation of the Fed, then we could legitimately cast doubt on many of the historical justifications for the Fed.

The Currency Substitutes

The first of the substitutes were the previously mentioned clearing-house loan certificates. These certificates represented "loans made to member banks by clearinghouse policy committees" (Timberlake 1984, p. 3). Normally banks cleared by using large-denomination certificates representing actual holdings of high-powered money. During panics, the clearinghouse created these new certificates for interbank clearing. Banks would deposit bundles of assets at the clearinghouse as backing for the certificates. By using these asset-backed certificates, banks were able to free up high-powered money in their vaults for depositor demands. These certificates had been used in previous panics (Sprague 1977, p. 47), but it was in the panics of 1893 and 1907 that they became accepted and habitual behavior for reserve-deficient banks.

Unique to these two panics was the issuing of such certificates for public use. The so-called clearinghouse certificates (no "loan") were notes issued by associations of banks backed by assets deposited with them (Warner 1895, p. 6, and Timberlake 1984, p. 5). These notes were issued in small denominations and intended for circulation and use by the public. The panic of 1893 marked their first appearance, and they were used again in 1907. The notes were marked "payable through the clearinghouse" and were accepted on deposit by member banks, though the clearinghouse itself held only a small percentage of the outstanding amount in cash reserves. One unusual factor was that many of these certificates appeared in cities previously having no clearinghouse. They were issued by temporary associations that used the term *clearinghouse* to gain brand name legitimacy in the eyes of the public, whose cooperation was needed for the success of the substitutes.

Gorton and Mullineaux (1987) refer to this subsuming of the banks under the umbrella of the clearinghouse as an example of hierarchical, as opposed to market, behavior. Gorton and Mullineaux (pp. 466-67) and Mullineaux (1987, p. 885) also argue that such hierarchical behavior casts doubt on the market's ability to regulate free banks. As Selgin and White (1988, p. 215) point out, this seems to indicate some confusion over what exactly constitutes "the market." Gorton and Mullineaux appear to view the market as simply a nexus of price signals and the rational responses of actors to such signals. Any resource allocation not done strictly via price coordination is therefore nonmarket behavior. However, one can also view the market more broadly as a nexus of voluntary exchange and contract. If so, then the hierarchical behavior of the clearinghouses is simply part of the contractual structure of this particular market.

As Mullineaux (1988, p. 221) admits, the question is not about market versus hierarchy, but about what types of hierarchy work and what the policy implications are for those that do not. If the question is one of hierarchy, the argument should simply be over the efficacy of particular contractual arrangements, whether price-coordinated or hierarchical. Price coordination and various types of nonprice coordination are all options open to firms in the market. The conscious coordination that takes place in the firm only indicates that *price* coordination is too costly, not that *market* coordination is.[13] It would therefore seem somewhat misleading to say that the collective behavior of the clearinghouse members casts doubt on the market's ability to produce monetary order. The contractual arrangements that constitute a clearinghouse *are* the market.

Another kind of currency substitute was the negotiable cashier's check. The banks would sell small-denomination bearer checks (in return for demand-deposit debits), written in round denominations of $5, $10, or $20, that were certified by banks and/or clearinghouses and drawn against the issuing bank. As Timberlake (1984, p. 5) points out, there were no special reserves held to back issues of such checks; they were general-asset currencies. Because they were checks, they had to be payable to some person or entity. They were frequently made out as "payable to bearer," though some used specific names or "John Smith." Some checks simply said "payable through the clearinghouse" or "in exchange." There were definite advantages to making the checks out to a particular person, because it made them look less like notes and more like checks.[14] If they were notes, they were either illegal because they were not bond-backed, or subject to the 10-percent state note tax if issued by state-chartered banks.

A fourth type of currency substitute, one not issued by banks at all, was the negotiable paycheck, or scrip. It was generally the case in this era for workers to be paid in notes and gold, not by check (Laughlin 1898, p. 311). Employees were reluctant to accept checks for wages, but during panics firms had realistically little choice. One way they reacted was to write round-denomination negotiable checks off a payroll account at a bank. For example, a worker might get paid $50 in four $10 checks and two $5 checks. These were passed hand to hand through repeated endorsement. Unlike the cashier's checks though, the scrip was not a direct liability of either a specific bank or the clearinghouse. Though it was drawn through the firm's bank in that it was written off the payroll account, the scrip was a *"liability of the firm that issued it"* (Andrew 1908, p. 512, emphasis in original). Scrip was accepted by the public as currency and was taken on deposit at banks. The receiving bank would send it through the clearing system like any other check, where it would be deducted from the firm's demand deposit account at its bank. When the need for substitutes passed, the scrip was either deposited or turned in for cash. Scrip was used in both panics and during the bank holidays of the 1930s.

Finally there were a number of miscellaneous ways in which banks and the public tried to cope with the shortage of currency. One was that much more use was made of demand deposits as a means of payment. In states bordering Canada, U.S. goods were sold at drastic discounts in order to get Canadian currency used in the states.[15] In 1907, a streetcar company in Omaha paid its employees in 600,000 nickels from its fareboxes (*NYT*, November 17, 1907, p. 1). The St. Louis streetcar company outdid the Omaha company by offering five-cent fare tickets to be used in exchange for checks or goods at local stores (*SGD*, October 31, 1907, p. 1). Evidently the fare tickets circulated fairly widely for several weeks. According to Warner (1895, p. 7), the panic of 1893 saw a long list of miscellaneous substitutes, including store orders and grain purchase notes. The question that all of the substitutes raise is: Why would anyone accept them? How did these contrivances become elevated to media of exchange? The answer is through a Mengerian evolutionary process.

Most of the currency substitutes were probably illegal, and the banks, public, and government knew it, yet no serious attempt was made to stop the activity. Nor did creditors take advantage of the law to pressure borrowers into paying in legal currency, which would have brought a premium profit. If bond-collateral requirements were in the "public interest," why didn't the Treasury step in and prohibit or tax the asset-backed currency substitutes? More fundamentally, why was the general public willing to accept such currency at the same value as national bank currency if bond collateral made the latter more secure? Currency in general sold at a premium during both panics, but there are no references to a differential premium on bond backed currency.[16]

The answers to these questions relate back to the previous discussions of the nature of money. Objects can become money only through use, and that usage has to evolve out of an intersubjective trust and understanding between members of a society. No outside force is needed, or is really able, to generate and maintain a monetary order. Instead it must emerge from the actions of those who participate in it. This was precisely the case during the two panics under discussion.

In Pittsburgh during the 1907 panic, newspaper reporters repeatedly noted that scrip was able to succeed because the public and merchants were willing to accept it in exchange for goods and services (*PP*, various reports, October-November 1907). In North Adams, Massachusetts, issuers of scrip during 1907 expressly sought the cooperation of, and explicitly addressed themselves to, the "Merchants and Tradesmen of North Adams," requesting them (on the note) to accept it and informing them of redemption procedures (*NYT*, November 4, 1907, p. 8).

One problem was how the public could know the quality of the substitutes they might want to use. A concern might be that note acceptance would be blind in that any currency substitute would be accepted by the public. This was not always the case. In Danville, Illinois, in 1907, workers threatened to strike unless they were paid in cash because an earlier firm had paid in checks and then skipped town. However, after meeting with local merchants and bankers, the workers agreed to accept scrip (*SGD*, November 6, 1907, p. 6). The public did exercise some brand name discrimination among notes and wanted at the least to be assured of quality. The local merchants frequently served as an information intermediary between the banks (or scrip-issuing firms) and the public.

In 1893, the Richmond, Virginia, banks met on August 10 to decide how to combat the currency shortage. After deciding to use certified checks, they called together top business leaders of the town and had a joint meeting (*RD*, August 11, 1893, p. 1). At the close of the meeting, the businesspeople endorsed the plan and announced they would accept the checks at par. The *Richmond Dispatch* endorsed the plan through its editorial voice (p. 3). Little Rock, Arkansas, saw a similar chain of events (*AG*, August 15, 1893, p. 1). Firms would also meet with employees to explain the check system before paying them in scrip (*RD*, August 13, 1893, p. 8). In both panics, stores competed vigorously to demonstrate their willingness to accept substitutes. Almost immediately, advertisements appeared in local newspapers that included the fact that the advertising store was accepting wage checks and cashier's checks. In 1907, a St. Louis jewelry store even offered a 10-percent premium on cashier's checks over alternative forms of payment, reversing the usual currency shortage condition (*SGD*, November 8, 1907, p. 18). A reporter in Pittsburgh noted "a strange desire among all of the storekeepers to be the first to let their customers know . . . the fact that wage checks would be as good as cash" (*PP*, November 3, 1907, p. 1).

This interlocking process of acceptance indicates the presence of the three elements of order. The creativity element is the initiative of the banks in issuing the currency substitutes and advertising their acceptability. These activities, in turn, made the merchants more willing to accept the substitutes, heightening their coordinative power. The willingness of the merchants, and the corresponding increase in the acceptability of the substitutes, convinced the public to use them, furthering coordination and increasing the complexity of the exchange process. Once this level of complexity was reached, the banks felt confident about the acceptability of the substitutes and were more willing to issue them in current and future crises. This snowballing of acceptability corresponds to the accounts of Menger (1892) and Jones (1976), and the whole development of a substitute-based monetary order displays many of the features discussed in Chapter 2.

Brand Names as Bank-Specific Information

One aspect of the success of the substitutes was the development of a trust between the banks, the merchants, and the public. The ways in which trust was earned also provide evidence for our conception of monetary order. As discussed in the previous chapter, monetary order rests on the existence of feedback processes for the formation of expectations concerning the behavior of money producers. It was argued there that bank brand names, in a competitive market, served as ideal types that could inform money users of the trust and reliability of various forms of bank money. If the market is sufficiently competitive, these brand names will have the flexibility to reflect public valuations of bank service and reliability. The attempt by banks during the two panics to earn the trust of depositors provides an example of how this process might work.

Using a brand name to promote trust was especially prevalent in 1907. In both Pittsburgh and St. Louis, scrip and cashier's checks were both endorsed by the clearinghouse. This endorsement was advertised both on the notes themselves and in public statements (*PP*, November 2, 1907, p. 1). In St. Louis the banks advertised their willingness to provide copies of their official signatures to local merchants in order to prevent fraud (*SGD*, October 30, 1907, p. 2). The Pittsburgh clearinghouse took out an advertisement announcing that it had hired Pinkerton security to guard against check fraud (*PP*, November 2, 1907, p. 1). A St. Louis bank director walked with a customer to a railway ticket office to personally endorse a check (*SGD*, October 29, 1907, p. 6). In Philadelphia, banks routinely certified the worthiness of paychecks at an employer's request (*NYT*, November 17, 1907, p. 1). Such procedures were aimed at promoting the acceptability of the various currency substitutes by showing that the banks stood behind them. Of course, wider acceptance of the substitutes meant the banks could more easily economize on their use of legal currency and reserves.

Closely connected were the ways in which banks tried to achieve mutual understandings with depositors. We already saw the way banks met with merchants in 1893 to inform them of their financial health and intended procedures. In 1907, Pittsburgh banks took out large newspaper advertisements explaining how paychecks worked and how they could be used to open a checking account for a depositor. The ads also pointed out the conveniences of using checks and the safety measures taken (*PP*, November 6, 1907, p. 6). In St. Louis, a cashier explained to a recalcitrant customer how he could pay his employees in cashier's checks: "Give the men checks . . . they're good at the butcher's and baker's" (*SGD*, October 29, 1907, p. 6). Another educational device was the explicit printing of instructions and conditions on backs of checks (*PP*, November 5, 1907, p. 5).

These informational issues are evidence of the importance of the informational content of money. As noted in Chapter 1, Brunner and Meltzer (1971), Ostroy and Starr (1974), and Alchian (1977), among others, all stress the informational properties of goods that vie for the status of a medium of exchange. Brunner and Meltzer and Alchian explicitly argue that the lower the cost of recognizing the quality of a good, the more likely it will become a medium of exchange. The attempts of the banks and merchants to provide this type of information can be viewed as lowering the cost of using substitutes and as making them more acceptable as media of exchange.[17]

One other means of restoring order was the use of bank-specific information to internalize the costs of confidence deterioration. The long-recognized problem with bank failures (as opposed to other businesses) is that one failure can very easily spill over to other banks because the public is unable to distinguish between good banks and bad banks and will run on any bank once failures start.[18] The inherent interconnectedness of financial institutions makes it possible for panics to spread quite easily. One way out of this contagion problem is for banks to provide bank-specific information to depositors. This allows depositors to distinguish between the problems of individual banks and problems common to the whole system.[19]

One way banks provided bank-specific information during the panics was to advertise it. It was common during this period for banks to advertise the soundness and trustworthiness of their institution. In an era before federal deposit insurance, trust and confidence were the sine qua non of banking. During panics trust was all the more important, and banks resorted to stronger and more innovative ways of emphasizing their soundness.

The 1907 panic is particularly instructive here. After the panic first began in New York, banks began to shift the emphasis in their newspaper advertisements. It was standard for banks to indicate both balance sheet and management information as well as more sales-oriented pitches. During the panic, the emphasis on balance sheets and directorates became relatively stronger (*NYT*, October-November 1907). In the *New York Times* of October 25, 1907, at the height of the bank runs, there was a full page of advertisements compared to the usual quarter- or half-page. The advertisements included short versions of balance sheets and long, detailed lists of bank personnel, including specific information on other business connections of the board members and directors. The banks, like the public, were sensitive to the existence of interlocking directorates, and any connection with anyone of shady dealings was bad for business.

This type of bank-specific information provides support for Gorton's (1985) view that the cost to banks of providing such information was a cause of the clearinghouse's increased importance during panics. By "hiding behind the skirts" of the clearinghouse, bad banks received a kind of brand name capital transfer from good banks because they all became part of one "firm." This transfer also gave the clearinghouse incentive to police the behavior of its members. Goodhart (1988) argues in several places that a profit-seeking "private central bank," like a clearinghouse, will find that its own interests conflict with those of the system as a whole and will be unable to act appropriately during panics. He also claims (p. 54) that clearinghouse interventions might create a moral hazard problem whereby member banks will be less cautious in the future because they will come to expect clearinghouse assistance. The evidence from 1907 appears to contradict both arguments. Not only were the clearinghouses crucial in restoring monetary order, they did so by monitoring member banks' behavior in precisely the ways Goodhart claims would not occur (see the discussion that follows). Whether the moral hazard problem existed cannot really be known due to the creation of the Fed. However, the crucial question is not whether clearinghouses created moral hazard problems but rather whether a central bank would avoid similar ones and not create new ones. The issue is what clearing-houses did compared to what central banks do.

Although banks did hide behind the clearinghouses, it also appears that banks had other ways of attempting to solve the problem without transferring their brand name capital by turning to the clearinghouse. One way banks internalized the costs of confidence deterioration was to refuse to accept deposits from customers who had drawn the funds from sound banks. Winmill and Fish Bankers advertised that it would not accept deposits from "reputable banks and trust companies to their unnecessary embarrassment" (*NYT*, October 25, 1907, p. 15). As Gorton (1985, p. 280) points out, information externalities gave banks incentive to prevent competitors from failing. These ads were a way to inform depositors of a bank's financial health and to indicate the nonsystemic nature of the base money runs.

Another unusual move was made by the New York Clearinghouse Association, which made available for public scrutiny balance sheets of member banks that had suspended payments. The clearinghouse also made public a list of all member bank directors and their various business connections. The *Wall Street Journal* made it standard practice to publish this clearinghouse information as soon as it was released (*WSJ*, October-November, 1907). This was another way in which banks' brand name capital could provide bank-specific information. It also points out the role of the clearinghouse as a monitor of bank behavior.

A discussion of the informational content of brand names should also address J. P. Morgan's role in resolving the panic of 1907. His major contribution was as a liaison between the New York banks and the Treasury. He earned this role through both the extent of his involvement in the New York financial industry and his connections in U.S. government and European financial circles. Though Morgan was an expert banker and a talented lobbyist for government favors, the crux of his role in the panic was that he was the biggest brand name of all. Despite his occasionally questionable business practices, people trusted him and believed his banks would not fail. When his involvement became public, people seemed to breathe a sigh of relief. As the *Wall Street Journal* bluntly put it, "Mr. Morgan represented confidence" (*WSJ*, October 24, 1907, p. 1). A cartoon in a New York paper showed Morgan as a stork delivering a baby labeled "confidence" down a chimney labeled "Wall Street" (Corey 1930, p. 344). The *New York Times* devoted a special Sunday feature to hailing Morgan's role in resolving the panic (*NYT*, November 10, 1907). Morgan's involvement and his ability to project the needed trust and confidence point out the positive role that trusted brand names can play in providing sound banking and a viable medium of exchange.

The question remains, however, What was responsible for the confidence the public showed in Morgan? Was it due to his banking skill, or was it due to the feeling that where Morgan went the government would not be far behind? And are these two factors hopelessly intertwined (i.e., was he successful as a banker because of his connections)? If the answer is that governmental involvement meant confidence, then the case for free banking is perhaps weakened.

One could offer the following explanation: People wanted some trusted institution to enter in and provide the confidence that was needed. In this case it happened to be the private-public mix that Morgan represented. Historically, trusted (private) Scottish banks performed analogous roles by taking over the liabilities of failed banks (L. White 1984, p. 32). The difference between public or private intervention concerns the *unintended* consequences of the particular institution's actions. In the Scottish case, the system survived with only very minor disruption. In the Morgan case, he received a $42-million interest-free loan. Not only was this loan inflationary and a transfer of wealth to Morgan, it also set up potentially dangerous incentives for corporate-government partnerships in both future panics and other economic crises whether real or imagined.

The importance of all of this historical evidence is that it provides support for the theory of money put forth earlier. Money is a product of individual voluntary action; no act of state intervention can "create" a money. Money is what people decide to use, and this use rests on trust and knowledge. The basis of a sound monetary order is ultimately the behavior of the individuals and organizations in the market and how they interact to form social institutions and practices. In two situations where state action had caused a significant degree of monetary disorder, we have seen how the undesigned responses of the public, banks, and merchants were able to restore order in a way consistent with our previous discussions of monetary order. Although far from conclusive, these cases do seem to be good evidence for many of the views argued previously.

Order, Politics, and the Origins of the Fed

After the panic of 1907, calls for currency reform arose again. This time the plans were numerous and diverse. Many of the proposals that arose out of independent conventions or from Congress called for the elimination of the bond-collateral requirements and some kind of asset-backed currency. Some New York bankers and many rural bankers leaned more toward central bank issue of such currency, mostly as a means of solving the reserve-flow problem.[20] The midwestern bankers also sought some kind of asset currency (many of them felt it should be competitively issued), but they were the only ones supporting any liberalization of the branching laws.

Out of all this came the Aldrich-Vreeland plan in 1908. Its main provision allowed asset currency during specified emergency situations combined with a high tax on issues exceeding specified limits. Again, this was not a major reform. The adoption of the Federal Reserve Act in 1913 was the final result of the reform movement, but it too did not address the major problems of the National Banking System. One piece of evidence for this argument is the name of the act. The legislation was more concerned with reserves than with notes. If the bond-collateral requirements were the main problem before the Fed, then legislation to correct it should have focused on note-related reforms. Reserves were a problem mainly because of the domino effect initiated as a result of banks' inability to profitably supply sufficient currency. If the bond-collateral requirements had not existed, there would have been significantly fewer major reserve problems. The Fed did not remove the bond-collateral requirements; it was and is a patchwork central banking system that proved over twenty years to be ineffective in preventing further major failures in the U.S. banking system.[21]

What lessons can we learn from the creation of the Federal Reserve System? Clearly it is at odds with our previous notions of monetary order. Most observers argue that the Fed was a classic example of a political compromise designed to meet the interests of all of the parties involved. However, that compromise is usually viewed as concerning the particular organizational details, not the question of a central bank or no central bank. It is often argued (e.g., Parthemos 1988) that the regional nature of the system (which is different from most central banks) resulted from the particular political forces in the early twentieth-century United States. Although this is likely true, the following argument is stronger: The *entire idea* of a central bank was a compromise; the particular details were secondary.

Perhaps the best way to frame this discussion is with James Buchanan's (1986) distinction between preconstitutional and postconstitutional economics. Preconstitutional questions are concerned with "the rules of the game" or with what constitutes a "good game." Postconstitutional economics attempts to analyze the social outcomes that will emerge under whatever set of rules is adopted.[22] For the example at hand, the preconstitutional question was whether to leave the determination of a monetary order to market processes or to the political process. Postconstitutional economics can explain the likely outcomes given the choice that was made. I argue that the mistake made during the debate over the Fed is that virtually all of the participants were concerned with the *post*constitutional question of how a politicized banking system would be organized, rather than with the more fundamental *pre*constitutional question of whether politics should play a role at all.

The lack of attention to the preconstitutional question likely resulted from a confusion over the nature of social institutions and order. Calls to make a system more orderly usually develop due to disorder in the current system. This was certainly true under the National Banking System, as has been documented here. The question for reformers concerns the cause of current problems and the implied solution(s). Most academic observers, both present and past, generally recognized that the existing regulations were responsible for the problems of pre-Fed banking.[23] The two main targets were the bond-collateral requirements and the pyramiding of reserves among the three levels of banks.

Even when the causes were correctly diagnosed, however, there was no guarantee of the appropriate cure. How such causes were interpreted through the ideological mindset of the period, and how various historical actors perceived their best interests in the political process were to determine the final outcome. The irony of the National Banking System (as with many cases of government action) was that the very regulations this system created caused the problems leading to its abolition in favor of more comprehensive government intervention. Once one intervenes in the order of the market to correct supposed market failures, one risks the possibility of creating additional failures, thus creating the apparent need for further intervention.[24] Faced with disorder in monetary affairs, and steeped in the momentum of the Progressive Era, the public naturally expected the government to "do something" to organize things more "rationally."[25] Along with the banks' recognition that their rent-seeking interests were at stake in any reform, these ideological forces generated a tacit understanding that the solution had to be a political one.

Given that there was a desire for a more orderly monetary system, people perceived that the only order that could come about was one consciously constructed by human actors. If order was desired, it had to be designed. However, as we have argued repeatedly, there are also undesigned, or spontaneous, orders. Both money itself and the institutions that provide it are examples of such orders. One cause of the confusion was that era's faith in the powers of science and reason, what Hayek (1952b) refers to as "scientism," to solve social problems. A great deal of the Progressive Era's social reforms derived from a belief that only rationally designed plans for institutions and regulations could lead to social order.[26] These ideas were widespread among the early twentieth-century intelligentsia and had certainly begun to work their way into the consciousness of the population at large.[27]

The irony of the debate over the Fed was that even though many recognized that the National Banking System's attempts to design order were the proximate causes of the problem, most concluded that the specific design was flawed and that a better system could be constructed. Opposed to this is the view we have discussed here. If money and monetary institutions are undesigned orders, then removing the relevant restrictions of the National Banking System would have led to a more orderly banking system. Further regulation and supervision is not the means to more order; in fact, pre-Fed banking indicates that regulatory intervention led to a diminution of order. Order emerges as part of an undesigned process of evolution.[28]

To allow for the evolution of an undesigned banking system, reform would have had to include removal of prohibitions against nationwide branching, removal of the bond-collateral requirements (permitting open issue of asset-backed currency), and removal of mandatory reserve requirements. None of the participants in the political debate over reform took this radical a position, but the one group who came closest got trounced in the debate. We can examine the probable results of these alternative reforms and see how they mesh with our understanding of monetary order.

All three areas were discussed in the previous chapter. Branch banking would have been able to spread the trust embodied both in money itself and in the brand names of good banks. Simmel (1978, p. 183) argues that only government, with its geographical reach, can effectively spread money's trust. Branch banking, however, is a viable alternative. In particular, branching would have allowed for par redemption of notes across the country. Though this may not seem to be a problem with modern transportation and communication, at the time, it was difficult to get par redemption at any distance because little was known about the issuing bank. Permitting branching would have spread the bank's brand name and thus spread the trust involved in its notes. Allowing nationwide branching would have allowed the monetary order to evolve more quickly and more efficiently by spreading the trust inherent in that order more effectively.

Unrestricted asset currency could have also made the system more orderly. Allowing banks to freely issue notes based on their general assets would have permitted them to differentiate their notes from the competition's. When all notes are backed by the same bonds, there is no way to distinguish the notes of quality banks from those of inferior ones, thus making the formation of ideal types through brand names that much more difficult. Removing the bond requirements would have opened up the choice of assets to rivalry among the banks. Such rivalry would have allowed banks to exploit their individual knowledge about financial markets in order to purchase quality assets instead of binding them to a preselected set. In addition, asset currency would have solved the elasticity problem created by the bond-collateral requirements. Banks could have easily reacted to changes in the currency-deposit ratio and avoided future occurrences of the very shortages that precipitated the panics and the resulting calls for reform.

Two recent articles on the origins of the Fed (Miron 1986 and Holland and Toma 1991) point out the need to minimize the seasonal fluctuations of interest rates during the National Banking System period as a rationale for creating the Fed. Both articles argue that changes in the relative demand for currency associated with seasonal crop movements led to significant seasonal variation in bank loans and nominal interest rates.[29] Miron argues that Federal Reserve open-market operations were effective in smoothing nominal interest rates; Holland and Toma view the Fed's lender-of-last-resort function as crucial to smoothing. Implicit in both views is that no alternative policy could have done the job as well.

The problem with both versions of this argument is that they ignore the role played by the bond-collateral requirements. In Miron's review of the National Banking System's laws, the bond-collateral requirements are not even mentioned, and Holland and Toma make the same omission. The seasonal variation in bank assets, in particular the banks' need to call in loans when the currency-to-deposit ratio rose, can be traced directly to the difficulty in supplying additional currency due to the bond-collateral requirements. Because of the time and expense involved in acquiring the needed bonds, the national banks were frequently unable to meet depositor withdrawals with their own notes and had to use reserve media instead. By drawing down their reserves this way, banks were forced to call in loans (or simply hold excess reserves every fall) to maintain their required level of reserves. Not surprisingly, these changes in reserve levels were likely a strong cause of interest-rate seasonality. If so, then removing the bond-collateral requirements and allowing true asset currency would have enabled the banks to meet the seasonal fluctuations in the relative demand for currency without reducing reserves and/or calling in loans, thus minimizing fluctuations in interest rates. By ignoring the role of the bond-collateral requirements, Miron and Holland and Toma see seasonality as a problem requiring a solution of conscious policy-making by a central bank rather than an unintended consequence of legal restrictions. Although the Fed may have been able to smooth seasonality, it may also have brought with it additional costs, such as the risk of inflation, which a free(r) banking system with asset currency might have avoided.

The additional step of removing reserve requirements would have allowed the banks to adjust their reserve ratios to compensate for changes in the demand for money. With prescribed ratios, banks can meet increases in the demand for inside money only by attracting new reserve media. Without such requirements, demands for inside money can be met by issuing more liabilities from existing reserve stocks, that is, by lowering desired reserve ratios as a response to more public confidence in the bank's liabilities.

All three of these reforms would have allowed the market process to discover the kinds of arrangements most preferred by banks and the public. The perceived need for government action appears to have been based on the idea that expert politicians and/or academics knew best how the monetary order should look, thus they should construct the reforms necessary to make it happen. The Hayekian notion of spontaneous order argues the exact opposite. The whole justification for removing regulations is that we do not know what the details of the resulting order will be. The process of competition allows individuals to discover the desired arrangements and provides them with a feedback mechanism (profits and losses) to indicate the correctness of their behavior. Governmental institutions do not have the needed incentives, nor can they obtain the knowledge necessary to discern the details of a monetary order.[30]

Unfortunately, once the preconstitutional question was decided, namely that some form of government involvement would be the result, the debate became one over which interest groups would benefit the most under the new system. As public choice economics points out, once one chooses the political process as the method for solving the problem, political competition will determine the exact solution. The result was that the preconstitutional discussion over monetary reform turned into a postconstitutional political battle between several interest groups over who would gain or lose from whatever reforms were adopted. Such political competition cannot be squelched by well-intended discussions of the "general interest" and by idealized reform solutions. Once the political process is chosen, the competition of special interests will determine the result, and there is no guarantee that any agreed upon notion of the general interest or of economic order will emerge.

The three major interest groups involved in this debate were the rural bankers, the midwestern city bankers, and the New York bankers. Of these, only the second were interested in anything close to the reforms outlined here. This was due to both their better understanding of the relevant economic theory and their seeing these reforms as a way for them to compete more effectively with the New York banks.[31] The New York banks were interested only in maintaining their fading hegemony by blocking any reform that gave any competitive edge to either of the other two groups. Playing to the scientism of the day, they often argued that expert control was needed, and that they were the only ones who could provide it. The rural banks were passionately afraid of the New York banks and would oppose any legislation that risked allowing the New York banks to compete directly with them. The rural banks therefore strongly opposed liberalizing branching limitations and were concerned that central banking proposals not give too much power to New York banks. It was precisely "expert control" that the rural banks feared: Too much power to the New York banks would give them a monopoly that could eliminate the rural bankers.

The rural banks had the political advantage in terms of sheer numbers. This was particularly true in the Senate, as farm states far outnumbered urban states at this time. With two votes per state, there were more votes for rural bankers. In particular, the rural bankers were able to lobby for defeat of any and all branch banking proposals. Asset-currency proposals could not make any headway because most were connected with branch banking. Many people also feared that asset-currency proposals would be inflationary. In fact, the rural banks might have supported competitive asset currency if branching had not been attached. The irony is that competitive asset currency is likely to be inflationary when there is no branch banking.[32]

The result of the reform debate was that once asset currency and branch banking were determined to be politically unpalatable, some form of central banking was inevitable. The regional nature of the Fed reflects the rural bankers' fear of concentrating central bank power in any one place. The double irony of this result was that the rural banks and the New York banks wound up on the same side of the issue by opposing branch banking and that, as it turned out, the New York banks did wind up with disproportionate influence in the Fed because all open-market operations are conducted through the New York Fed in the New York financial markets. The combination of special interests and the general desire for some form of government action, derived from a faulty view of the basis of monetary order, led to the creation of the Fed and the particular form it took.[33]

Conclusion

This historical investigation makes it clear that private note issue and a freely evolved monetary order were not tried, debated, and found wanting. We have argued that the crises that characterized pre-Fed banking resulted instead from the legal restrictions imposed by the National Banking System. Indeed, during these crises, order was restored precisely through the kind of undesigned Mengerian process that we have described in previous chapters. Thus it was private initiative that was able to combat the disorder caused by inappropriate legal restrictions, which provides further support for the idea that monetary order results from the unplanned, spontaneous social interaction of the individuals who participate in monetary exchange.

We have also argued that the adoption of the Federal Reserve System as a solution to these crises resulted from a misunderstanding of the nature of monetary order and from the perceived need to satisfy various political interest groups. The decision to increase governmental involvement in the monetary order would prove to be a crucial one, because the worst crisis of all, the Great Depression, can be attributed to the actions of the Fed.[34]

The decision to further politicize banking had more important unintended consequences. With the apparent failure of capitalism in Western economies during the 1930s, many looked toward other economic systems, such as socialism and fascism, to solve the problems that capitalism seemed to be unable to handle. Thus there is a strong relationship between an economy's ability to maintain monetary order and its ability to maintain order as a whole. When monetary systems fail, economies go down as well and people demand alternatives. As we try to make sense of alternative economic systems, we cannot afford to ignore the role money plays in each and how government policy helps or hinders the evolution of monetary order. It is the efficiency and viability of a monetary order that is crucial to cultivating the broader economic and social order that good economic systems induce. Ultimately the debate over the origins and functions of various monetary orders is a necessary complement to debates over alternative economic systems.

Notes

1. Parts of this chapter use and expand on some material from Horwitz (1990a), reprinted with permission of *Southern Economic Journal*.

2. See also the following for histories of the partial or complete free banking systems of Scotland (L. White 1984), China (Selgin 1992), Sweden (Jonung 1985), eighteenth-century France (E. White 1990) as well as others in the collection edited by Dowd (1992). Schuler (1992) has collected evidence showing that dozens of countries on almost every continent had some partial form of free banking at one time or another.

3. Both current and contemporary observers noted that the bond-collateral requirements appeared to be a scheme to finance the war debt. A contemporary account can be found in Laughlin (1898, p. 207ff.); a modern one is in E. White (1983, p. 11). To finance an unpopular war one can simply print the money needed to fight it (e.g., the inflation of the Vietnam War era) or force note-issuing banks to buy up war bonds as collateral. Thus the much-criticized relationship between international finance and foreign military intervention is not endemic to market economies but is rather a product of government intervention in financial markets.

4. Observers during that era indicated that the 2-percent return on the required bonds was below the average return on investments. An average investment would earn a risk-adjusted return of about 5 to 6 percent. See the figures in Laughlin (1898, p. 224ff.).

5. In fact, low bond prices would mean high interest rates, which would tend to lower the demand for noninterest-bearing currency. For empirical evidence on the interest rate-demand for money relationship see the survey by Laidler (1985, chap. 10).

6. It is beyond the scope of this chapter to give a detailed treatment of the exact cost of note issue. However, it does appear that Friedman as well as Schwartz and Cagan are mistaken in concluding that the proper supply of private bank notes is inconsistent with profit-maximizing behavior. Rather, the specific legal restrictions of the National Banking System set up incentives that made underissue the profit-maximizing choice. In the absence of these constraints, profit-maximizing behavior would tend to produce the correct supply of notes, as outlined in Chapter 4 and in L. White (1984) and Selgin (1988b). For a more detailed treatment of these issues, see the controversy among Bell (1912), Cagan (1965), Goodhart (1965), Friedman and Schwartz (1970), James (1976), L. White (1986), Cagan and Schwartz (1991), and Champ, Wallace, and Weber (1992). For a surprisingly perceptive contemporary view see Laughlin (1898).

7. The following are abbreviations used for newspapers cited in this chapter:

AG — Arkansas Gazette	*SGD — St. Louis Globe-Democrat*
RD — Richmond Dispatch	*PP — Pittsburgh Post*
NYT — New York Times	*WSJ — Wall Street Journal*

The focus on these cities is due to the proliferation of currency substitutes in those areas. Warner (1895) notes Little Rock and Richmond; Andrew (1908) notes New York, Pittsburgh, and St. Louis.

8. For a survey of branching restrictions at the time, see Cooke (1903). He argues that states that permitted branching, especially those in the South and West, generally had stronger economies and fewer and less severe financial crises than those that did not.

9. See the discussion in Horwitz and Selgin (1987). Those who argue that the type of wildcat banking found in the 1837-1863 period could only be prevented by bond (or other) collateral requirements seem to forget that one reason banks could overissue notes and close up before redemption is that the lack of branching prevented quick and easy reflux of excess supplies of notes. Had banks been allowed to branch in that period, wildcat banking would have been a far less serious problem because notes would have been presented for redemption much quicker and the development of a nationwide clearinghouse system would have been that much more likely.

10. Timberlake (1984) provides a discussion of the role of clearinghouse associations during panic situations. He also describes the clearinghouse certificates in more detail. Recent articles by Gorton (1985) and Gorton and Mullineaux (1987) explore many of these issues in more detail as well.

11. The proposal did not remove all of the relevant legal restrictions. It had a number of provisions designed to prevent overissue and abuse by banks. Though some of these lingering legal restrictions could have become problematic, the net effect of the Indianapolis proposal would have been unambiguously preferable to the then-existing system.

12. A *New York Times* reporter asked a man from Rahway, New Jersey, why he was waiting in a bank line. His response was that he wanted to move his funds to a bank nearer his home where he felt more comfortable with the management (*NYT*, October 26, 1907, p. 1).

13. This confusion may be due to some ambiguity in Coase's (1937) well-known essay on the nature of the firm and general equilibrium theory's sole emphasis on the role of price adjustment for market clearing.

14. Once again the legal and monetary orders intersect, as these bearer, or "John Smith," notes had to be recognized as payable to the holder by the legal institutions of the time.

15. In this regard it should be noted that the Canadian banks had neither bond-collateral requirements nor limits on branch banking. The Canadian system was much less affected by any of the pre-Fed panics despite its close economic ties to the United States. Even after the Fed was established, Canada saw only one bank failure between 1921 and 1929; the United States lost over 5,700 (Ely 1988, pp. 52, 55).

16. I would like to thank George Selgin for bringing this point to my attention.

17. It should also be noted that the means employed by banks and merchants were not simply acts of "data-supply" but attempts to reach some kind of mutual understanding. The public had to "see where the banks and merchants were coming from," in colloquial terms. This requires more than mere data concerning balance sheets and reserve levels. The advertising and instructions were all attempts to put the substitutes in terms that the public could relate to. This relates back to the discussion of language in Chapter 3. The dialogic process

of information dispersion and advertising made possible the types of mutual understanding that gave rise to the success of the substitutes. Just as language allows a fusion of horizons in verbal communication, so do the institutions of the market make possible fusions of economic horizons.

18. This is one of Goodhart's (1988) main objections to free banking and underlies his case for the necessity of a central bank.

19. As is noted, the bond-collateral requirements limited competition in the choice of assets for backing notes, thus preventing the dissemination of bank-specific information about currency and limiting the flexibility of the brand names of notes. If banks had been allowed to choose their own assets, then note brand names could reflect the differing assets that backed them.

20. The thinking here was that centralization of reserves would allow for faster movement to needed areas through the discounting process and end the ripple-effect flow out of the cities. As noted earlier, nationwide branching would have provided similar benefits, but at a much lower economic cost.

21. As economic historian Robert Higgs (1987, p. 108) accurately notes, the Fed "was an anomalous, yet characteristically American institution: a decentralized central bank."

22. An example of a preconstitutional question would be whether to have a constitutional amendment to balance the budget. The corresponding postconstitutional analysis would chart the effects of both choices.

23. Modern accounts include Friedman and Schwartz (1963, pp. 168-69), E. White (1983), Livingston (1986), Wells (1987), and Parthemos (1988). Contemporary criticism came from Laughlin (1898), Andrew (1908), and Sprague (1977) as well as the well-known Marxist Rudolf Hilferding (1981, p. 275).

24. See Mises's (1966, pp. 858-61) diagnosis of the instability of interventionism.

25. Higgs (1987) looks at U.S. history since 1896 from this angle. In times of crisis, government is expected to "do something." If the crisis is then solved, people assume post hoc, ergo propter hoc that the government solved it. This process then justifies further intervention in future crises.

26. See the excellent studies of the Progressive Era by Wiebe (1962), Kolko (1963), and Weinstein (1968). On the Fed more specifically, see Livingston (1986).

27. The seductiveness of scientism is so strong that even fifty years after the end of the Progressive Era, intellectuals like Erich Fromm (1960), in his foreword to Edward Bellamy's utopian novel *Looking Backward*, could still say: "Contemporary man is fascinated by technical visions of travel to the moon and to the planets. It seems that this kind of scientific utopia is a poor substitute for the humanist utopia . . . the vision of the 'good society' in which man makes his world a truly human home. Yet it is certainly no more difficult to devise plans for a rationally organized and truly human society than it is to construct atomic bombs, intercontinental missiles, and travels to the moon." There is no doubt that such "rational" plans can be devised, but putting them into practice, especially when the results have been Lenin, Stalin, Hitler, Mao, and Pol Pot, seems more problematic.

28. Some might object that removing such restrictions (and implicitly the system outlined in the previous chapter) is an attempt to design an order. However, this argument confuses pre- and postconstitutional theory. The argument for free banking is one about the rules of the game, not the particular outcomes. The whole justification for rules (such as the legal rules that frame free banking) is that we cannot know what particulars the future will bring (see Chapter 2). Rules allow for the open-endedness that characterizes evolutionary processes like markets. As we have stressed, we do, to some extent, have the ability to talk about and implement different sets of rules. The discussion of free banking versus central banking is one about monetary regimes, which are amenable to some scope for design; discussions about specific reserve requirements or alternative limits on branching are about the particulars, which are not capable of being designed.

Analogous arguments can be made about personal behavior. Because no one can know exactly what is the "best life" for another, we simply set up the rule of law (and do not plan the particulars) and thus allow ourselves the liberty to become "the person we want to become" (Buchanan 1979, p. 112).

29. See also Calomiris and Hubbard (1989, pp. 431-32, fn. 5), who endorse this view.

30. Any discussion of the knowledge arguments touched on here and explored earlier in Chapter 4 is curiously absent from Goodhart's (1988) critical assessment of free banking.

31. In a sense this is a rent-seeking interest as well. Certainly some groups receive differential gains when regulations are removed, not just when they are passed. If the unintended consequences of deregulation lead to increases in economic order, then this "rent seeking" should not be seen as problematic. If the unintended consequences of government regulation lead to a diminution of economic order (as indicated by a decrease in creativity, complexity and coordination), then rent seeking for that regulation is problematic. The economist's job is to trace out as well as possible the nature of these unintended consequences and help to determine if they increase or decrease social and economic order.

32. The reason is, as was noted earlier, that a lack of branching prevents quick and efficient redemption procedures from developing. The longer it takes to clear notes, the more that banks can get away with overissuing, because the effects would not be felt immediately.

33. Rothbard (1984) argues that the Fed was simply a result of the New York bankers' attempts to effect cartels in the banking industry much as was done in other industries during the Progressive Era. There may be a kernel of truth in this point, but it is not enough to explain the establishment of the Fed. The Fed has the form it does because few understood the undesigned alternative and because the rural banks' fear of the New York banks helped defeat the proposal that could have prevented the possibility of a cartel: branch banking.

34. See Friedman and Schwartz (1963) and Rothbard (1963), among others. Though economists do not agree on the precise causes and cures for depressions like that of the 1930s, almost all economists of every political persuasion find at

least some fault with the Fed's handling of the Great Depression. Friedman and Schwartz, and most others, see the blame lying with the Fed permitting the money stock to drop 30 percent during the early 1930s. Austrian economists such as Rothbard add that it was the Fed's expansionary policies during the 1920s that precipitated the crisis, which was exacerbated by the Fed's later inaction.

6

Conclusion: Money in a Nonrationalist Approach to Economic Systems

The Importance of Money in Theory and Society

The unifying theme of this study has been the absolutely central role that money plays in forming economic and social orders. As we have seen, language is the only other social institution that is more central. Unfortunately, the importance of money in social practice is not mirrored in social theory. In the course of one of the key debates in the history of political economy, the debate over the possibility of rational economic calculation under socialism, very little was written of money and its role in understanding and comparing the institutions of alternative economic systems.

This is particularly ironic when one considers that when Ludwig von Mises launched the socialist calculation debate in 1920, it was also the war communism period of the early Soviet Union. During this period, the Bolsheviks were attempting to eliminate money in practice as part of their interpretation of Marx's socialism. The disastrous effect the policies of war communism had on the Soviet economy should have spoken louder than any text about the importance of reuniting the theory and practice of money.[1] The failure of war communism's attempt at complete central planning and the elimination of money should have forced a drastic revision, if not abandonment, of Marx's proclamations on the subject. What does not work in practice is likely the result of bad theory. To this day, the message goes unheeded.

Neoclassical economists are no less guilty. They are constantly frustrated by the fact that money in the real world does not behave the way their theoretical models say it should. This is particularly true of neutrality doctrines. Money should not matter as much as it does if neoclassical economics is right. Here again, the very fact that money in practice is far more important than their theory says should make neoclassical economists think twice about their theory.

Thinkers within the broad "interpretive turn" that has been the backdrop for much of this study have generally agreed that there is a split over practice and theory that plagues the social sciences and real-world political action. Money stands as an excellent example of the misunderstandings, and undesirable unintended political consequences, that can arise from such splits. Neither of the two aforementioned theories of money can adequately account for the way money works in practice. One of the goals of this study has been to reunite real-world monetary practice with a better theory that recognizes real human actions and interpretations and begins to understand money as the ultimately human institution that it is.

Reuniting the theory and practice of money is only one step on the road to an effective social-theoretic conversation. Once we begin to understand money, we have to bring our understanding to bear on the important questions in the social sciences. For example, no debate over the merits of capitalism and socialism can afford to ignore the role that money has historically played in each, and the role that it will (or will not) play in the liberated future that each promises. Although an understanding of money itself cannot settle such debates, we should be that much more skeptical of social theories that cannot come to grips with the way money works.

Monetary Order and the Theory of Economic Systems

Any examination of the theory of economic systems has to begin with Marx. Though Marx was reticent to write recipes for the cookshops of the future, his critical analysis of capitalism seems to have implications for the organization of economic activities in the socialist future. The problems of alienation, exploitation, and economic crises under capitalism all find their source in capitalism's relations of production, that is, the production of commodities.[2] Whatever socialism is, it must involve the absence of commodity production and all that it implies. Assuming that noncommodity production implies no production for the purpose of exchange, then production will have to be organized by some sort of social plan. As Marx (1906, p. 92) argues in *Capital:* "The life-process of society, which is based on the process of material production, does not strip off its mystical veil until it is treated as production by freely associated men, and is consciously regulated by them in accordance with a settled plan." Planning would presumably be more rational than the blind forces of the market and would lead to a world with enough material goods to allow the flourishing of the human spirit.

Mises (1920) responded to this line of argument by claiming that socialist planners would be unable to determine whether they were using resources efficiently in the absence of market prices.[3] He argued that economic calculation required some standard of comparative value, which labor power could not provide but money prices could. However, money prices required markets, and markets required the ability to exchange. If goods were to be exchangeable, particularly capital goods, then there had to be private property in those goods. Thus, Mises concluded, rational economic calculation required private property in the means of production, and economic planning could not give results superior to the market.

Oscar Lange (1936) and other neoclassical economists were not convinced by Mises's critique.[4] Lange, for one, argued that the problem facing planners was no different than the "problem" that markets solved every day. If one interpreted prices to mean "the terms on which alternatives are offered," rather than money prices actually paid in a market, then planners could find equilibrium prices and rationally allocate resources. Lange proposed a central planning board that would have all the same information required to reach equilibrium in a competitive market (i.e., the terms on which alternatives are offered, utility functions, and cost functions). The board would then declare a set of prices (as the Walrasian auctioneer does in general equilibrium theory), look for excess demands or supplies, and adjust prices accordingly. Like the trial-and-error process of the market, Lange's "market socialism" would grope its way toward the equilibrium price vector.

Although this solution satisfied much of the economics profession, some, such as Hayek, were unconvinced. In a series of papers in the 1930s and 1940s, Hayek argued that Lange's formulation missed the fundamental point that market discovery processes create and utilize knowledge that is inaccessible to planners. Lange assumed away the whole problem by positing that the central planning board could know the cost-and-demand information he assumed it could. The whole rationale for markets, Hayek argued, is that this information could be known no other way. The problem facing all forms of planning is ultimately epistemological; there are types of knowledge (i.e., tacit forms) that can be revealed only through market activities and that would be unavailable in their absence. Hayek's critique of planning is consistent with the view of knowledge and money put forward in this study.

To see more completely why proposals for planning (both Marxist and market socialist) run into difficulties, we need to recall the discussion of money as language from Chapter 3. Both Marx and market socialism are looking for some kind of Archimedean point from which to assess value without recourse to monetary calculation. However, as was pointed out, money, like language, does not permit such a point. Economic behavior is constituted in money, just as our thought processes are constituted in language. We cannot reach a nonmonetary Archimedean point of value any more than we can reach knowledge outside of that which is expressed in language. The communication of economic knowledge (i.e., knowing what projects are rational from an economic standpoint) requires a language, and that is what money and money prices provide.

Marx (1971, p. 71) recognized the potential analogy of money and language but dismissed it:

> It is no less false to compare money with language. It is not the case that ideas are transmuted in language in such a way that their particular nature disappears and their social character exists alongside them in language, as price exist alongside goods. Ideas do not exist apart from language.

Marx correctly saw the relationship between language and ideas but did not see the same connection between economic knowledge and money. Indeed, as he argued, ideas do not exist extralinguistically, but he did not see is that neither does economic value exist extramonetarily. Marx wanted to argue that the commodity mode of production masks the true value of economic goods by endowing them with an ultimately false monetary exchange value. By moving to a social order without monetary exchange, we could accurately assess the true value (based on socially necessary labor time) of human creations. There is a "real" value lying behind the veil of monetary expressions in the marketplace.[5]

It would seem as though Marx's view of value without money is predicated on the feasibility of the socialist future. A true value exists because we can imagine a workable world where we could organize society around those values. Perhaps if Marx could have been convinced that a future telepathic world was possible, one where we could access "true" meanings without the mediation of language, then he would also have argued that language masks those true meanings.[6] Because such a telepathic world is apparently not feasible any time soon, we have to accept and appreciate the linguistically constituted world in which we live. When viewed from the ideal perspective of a completely telepathic world, the misunderstandings inherent to linguistic communication do seem to be wasteful and frustrating, much in the same way that real-world competition seems wasteful when viewed from the perspective of Marxist socialism (or neoclassical perfect competition). However, this is not the right perspective for judgment if the future telepathic world is not achievable. The proper comparison is between a world with language and a world without it, that is, between a world where communication takes place frequently though imperfectly versus one where communication is much more the exception than the rule.

What eliminates the possibility of Marx's Archimedean point is the recognition of the subjective nature of economic value. By still adhering to a labor theory of value, Marx believed he had a point of view outside of the human mind and the market by which to assess value. However, once we admit that economic value, as a form of meaning, is a product of the human mind, then the futility of looking for a measure of value outside the mind becomes apparent. Marx wants a correspondence theory of value: a correspondence between goods and the objective amount of labor power socially necessary for their production. But value is nothing more than the amount of money that people subjectively choose to part with to obtain the expected subjective utility from what they purchase. Value can be assessed only in terms of money and money prices, as Mises pointed out in 1920, just as meaning and truth can be expressed only with language and words. If we are to determine relative values and make rational economic calculations, we cannot dispense with money.

The thrust of Mises's original argument is assisted by this view of money. Marx does not recognize the knowledge problem faced by planners because the knowledge his planners would need concerns the socially necessary labor time for useful goods. However, as the Mises-

Hayek critique of planning makes clear, it is the subjective knowledge of valuing human actors that is relevant for determining value, and *that* knowledge cannot be objectivistically accessed, as labor time might be. Tacit knowledge has to be socially revealed through actions that use the language of money and money prices. Money is the means by which the knowledge needed for economic calculation becomes socially usable, because that knowledge (including relative labor costs) becomes embedded in the price system through actual acts of monetary exchange. There is no way outside of the process of monetary exchange to assess value, and as a result, there is no way for a central planner to accurately determine the economic viability of various production processes.

This is the sense in which money prices, like words, are "aids to the mind" (Mises 1920, p. 102). As bewildering as the forest of economic possibilities is, so is the complex of possible thoughts of the human mind. In the same way that money prices aid us in forming reliable interpretations of which economic possibilities are more viable, words allow us to form interpretations of others' meanings.

Money becomes the language of the dialogic process of the formation of capital and capital values, and of the determination of which processes of production should be applied to which consumer goods. The constant flux of the capital structure is the result of the continuing dialogue of monetary exchange in the market process. The advantage of markets is that they incorporate the interpretations of a larger number of participants than does planning and therefore expand the ability of the process to generate results that satisfy more people. As with other dialogic processes, meaning cannot be defined before the process itself, rather meaning emerges as a social resultant of the pushes and pulls of persuasion and interpretation. The value of capital goods, and their appropriateness in various processes of production, can be known only through an actual competitive process of monetary exchange.[7] This requires private property in the means of production and an open market for exchanging that property against a generally accepted (and competitively supplied) medium of exchange.

In addition to strengthening Mises's objection to the supposed economic rationality of central planning, viewing money as a language can also help in further dissecting the flaws in Lange-type market socialism. The key to Lange's criticism of Mises was the notion of prices as "terms on which alternatives are offered." Once the central planning board sets a price, under this definition, it is demarcating such terms and thus, according to Lange, calculation is possible. Like Marx, Lange is in search of an Archimidean point from which his board can adjudicate value. Rather than opting for the labor theory of value, the bedrock of classical economics, Lange opts for general equilibrium theory, the bedrock of *neo*classical economics. Lange's theory is, in broad terms, formally similar to Marx's in its attempt to go outside of subjectively formed evaluations and monetarily constituted market prices to get to value.

The problem with Lange's "terms" is that although they do indicate trade-offs potentially available, they do not provide a context through which those trade-offs can be meaningfully interpreted. A planning board can declare the price of a good to be anything it wants, but that act does not endow the price with the social meaning necessary for it to serve its purpose as a communicator of knowledge. I might define a new word, say "gorkle," as "a dark shade of red," but unless others have some context with which to understand my word, or some set of words or meanings through which "gorkle" can be understood, the word is meaningless. Words require a linguistic history and context in order to be rendered intelligible.

Consider Polanyi's example about enclosing words in quotation marks. We can hold the meaning of individual words in doubt by doing so, but we cannot do that for every word (or even some large number of words) in a sentence. If we do, we have eliminated the necessary context for understanding any of the quoted words. If only one such word is quoted then we can form interpretations of its meaning through the context provided by the rest of the sentence. The more words we enclose, the more context we lose and the less meaning we can attach to the highlighted words.

Lange's "terms" are like words in quotation marks. However, Lange wants all prices, or at least the prices of all-important capital goods, to be this way. In doing so, these prices become meaningless to entrepreneurs and consumers. There is no economic equivalent of "the rest of the sentence" (such as the market prices of other capital goods) from which we can form a context of meaning. Lange (1936, p. 80) recognizes the need for an "objective price structure" but argues that socialism can provide one if "the parametric function of prices is retained." If the planning board treats prices as given, then those prices will form the structure necessary for it to calculate. The problem is that this structure is meaningless unless it somehow reflects the subjective valuations of consumers and changes as their preferences and interpretations change. As Lavoie (1985a, p. 80) argues, "Neither articulated statements nor posted prices have any meaning when divorced from their inarticulate foundations."

The formation of prices through acts of true market entrepreneurship is a dialogic process from which meaning emerges. To deny entrepreneurs the possibility of dialogue by assuming that prices have to be taken as parameters eliminates the very process by which prices become meaningful and removes the context necessary for others to make sense of individual prices. Lange's insistence on parametric prices is a direct result of the general equilibrium foundation of his version of market socialism. The criticisms that economists such as Kirzner have made of general equilibrium's inability to explain how real-world prices change can be modified to apply to Lange. Price formation requires a context of meaning that can emerge only from some kind of participatory dialogue. For Kirzner (1973), the alertness of entrepreneurs to discrepancies in the price structure, that is, the possibility of pure arbitrage profits, drives the movement of prices. This theory of price movement involves a continual interplay between taking prices as momentary givens and the active effects that market actors have on those prices through the resulting acts of entrepreneurship.

Prices are the words of the text of the market process, and that text is continually being reinterpreted through acts of entrepreneurship by all of those who act within it. This is how prices change and provide meaning to market actors. Kirzner's theory of entrepreneurship is an example of a dialogic conception of price formation that can be used against the monological (and therefore meaningless) conceptions of general equilibrium theory and Lange's market socialism. By holding the meaning of prices in doubt via the enforcement of parametric pricing, Lange's scheme prevents the entrepreneurial activity necessary for the dialogic development of a context of meaning out of which the intelligibility of any particular price can be determined.[8]

The Lange-type schemes fail because they ignore the fact that the effective use of prices for calculation requires a context of meaning. The semiotic function of prices can arise only out of social acts of monetary exchange by economic actors. The same is true of words in a language. The multitude of other words and meanings in a language create the context of understanding for any individual word. English words are defined only in terms of other English words, themselves defined by yet other English words. Lange wants to perform the equivalent of defining a new word in terms of words that no one else has ever used.

Prices conceived only as the "terms on which alternatives are offered" are most likely going to be irrelevant for rational economic calculation because they lack a context of interpretation. The market is a meaningful dialogue requiring that those who use its meanings also participate in the process of meaning formation and be to some extent aware of the contexts in which those meanings are formed and interpreted. Just as words require actual human speech acts (or in Polanyi's [1958] terms "acts of assertion") to be meaningful, so do prices require actual human offers of money. Only monetary exchange can suffice to provide the intersubjective context necessary to imbue prices with meaning and allow the interpretive process of economic calculation to take place.

The concern with parametric prices and equation solving reveals the equilibrium thrust of Lange's approach. This brings us back to where our study began—Chapter 1's discussion of the disadvantages of equilibrium approaches to the study of monetary phenomena. As we have stressed throughout, such approaches are likely to overlook the crucial contributions that money brings to economic calculation and order. The debate has to be over real-world, monetary economies, which drastically limits discussions of equilibrium. Money's role in making economic communication and calculation possible cannot be understood in equilibrium terms—an alternative approach is necessary. Marx understood the dynamics of monetary exchange, but he thought he could transcend it. As a result Mises was led to respond to Marx in terms of monetary exchange and the importance of money. However, when Marxism is replaced by watered-down static-equilibrium socialism, any discussion of money is left behind. However, as Lavoie (1985b) has forcefully argued, dynamic questions were the relevant ones.

To the extent that general equilibrium does not tackle the questions that matter in the real world, it cannot be used as a defense against Mises's objections. The economics profession's acceptance of Lange's argument reveals the shortcomings of its own methodological approach to the role that money, prices, and economic calculation play in the real world. Questions of methodology, method, and the philosophy of science are not mere abstract ruminations over metaphysics; they matter for the most important questions of political economy.[9] The inability of neoclassical economics to answer the question of the merits of capitalism and socialism is due to an outdated methodology and an outdated method of analysis. Equilibrium theory, and Marxist value theory, belong with the modernism of the Enlightenment. Recent developments in the philosophy of science and in the theory of knowledge, as discussed in Chapters 2 and 3, point toward a new direction for economics and the way in which it should grapple with the big questions in political economy.[10]

One of the first tasks in attaining a more philosophically sophisticated understanding of money and economic systems should be to make the argument against central planning complete by fitting the last piece to the puzzle. We have also noted, in Chapters 2 and 3, the crucial role that money plays in allowing the benefits of the market order to make their presence felt. Yet those who pointed out the difficulties of economic calculation under socialism accepted some role for planning *in the money market.* Mises and Hayek both gave government scope to, at the very least, set the standards of weight and measure, and perhaps to exercise some control over the production of money and money substitutes.

This seems to be a glaring anomaly in the case against planning. If a properly functioning money is necessary for the market to best utilize the contextual and tacit knowledge of its participants, then we should take great care in entrusting the provision of money to a set of institutions that can best anticipate its demand and regulate the behavior of its suppliers. The very case against socialism shows that markets are superior in precisely these respects, yet very few defenders of the market have insisted that the market should therefore supply money. Selgin (1988b, p. 96) asks the fundamental question: "Is the price system, which is supposed to be superior to central planning as a means for administering resources, itself dependent upon the centralized administration of money?" The case against planning has to be completed by questioning planning in the very market that makes all other markets possible—the money market. Without this last link, the theory of the market rests on a foundation of planning. A more sophisticated understanding of the market process must reject an approach arguing that the market requires some extramarket foundation in order to operate properly. Instead, we must recognize that money and markets coevolve and that they are mutually supportive of each other. Centrally supplied money is neither needed nor able to provide a foundation for market processes and economic and social order. A more interpretive theory of the market process helps us to understand why foundational approaches are neither necessary nor correct.

The arguments of Chapters 4 and 5 show how a freely evolved monetary order can function smoothly and avoid the kinds of crises that have plagued generally market-based economies. We can now put the argument of those chapters in a somewhat different light. The argument for free banking is simply an application of the nonrationalistic epistemological argument against planning, which itself utilizes a nonrationalistic conception of money. If markets are better at conveying and utilizing contextual knowledge, and if decentralized control over resources leads to more orderly patterns of resource allocation, then money should be no exception. This is even more important when we realize that the failure to apply this argument to monetary institutions has led to the exact kinds of real-world crises that fuel the arguments of those who desire some form of planning. It is events like the Great Depression, the income redistribution that takes place during times of inflation, or the wars financed by central banks that can shift ideologies toward planning. Because of its importance to the proper functioning of all other markets, money should be the first good allocated by the market, not the last. The critics of planning have weakened their own argument by not fully extending the argument to the monetary order.[11]

Reason, Tradition, and Economic Order

Emerging from this nonrationalistic view of money and its institutions are new conceptions of the ideas of reason and tradition. Enlightenment philosophy has always opposed tradition in favor of reason. In this view, the function of reason is to strip away the prejudices of tradition and render all human behavior explainable by some method that is guaranteed to reach objective certainty. Tradition in itself cannot communicate truth, only reason can.

The germ of this idea has fueled radical movements from the liberalism of the seventeenth, eighteenth and early nineteenth centuries to Marxism and the scientism of the early twentieth century. From Hobbes's conception of the sovereign as the reason-driven creator and enforcer of the law to Rousseau's demand for freeing the general will from the chains of social traditions and practices to Marxism's case for the superior rationality of economic planning, radical meant using reason to abolish the false pretenses of traditional political and economic institutions, whether those institutions were feudal manors or capitalist factories. With the advance of reason and certainty would come the perfection of social organization. Radical political movements since the Enlightenment have been wrapped up in its notions of reason and tradition.

This way of thinking is slowly changing. In both of their writings, Gadamer and Hayek want to rehabilitate the truth claims of traditions and critically examine Enlightenment claims about the power and scope of reason. For both, unlimited faith in reason is ultimately connected with the desire to scientifically control and manipulate human social processes. As Gadamer (1967, p. 40) puts it:

> These [social] sciences increasingly see themselves as marked out for the purpose of scientific ordering and control of society. They have to do with "scientific" and "methodical" planning, direction, organization, development—in short, with an infinity of functions that, so to speak, determine from the outside the whole of the life of each individual and each group. Yet this social engineer, the scientist who undertakes to look after the functioning of the machine of society, appears himself to be methodically alienated and split off from the society to which, at the same time, he belongs. . . . It is the function of hermeneutical reflection, in this connection, to preserve us from naive surrender to the experts of social technology.

Hayek (1978d, p. 34) echoes this line of thought: "The recognition of the insuperable limits to his knowledge ought indeed to teach the student of society a lesson in humility which should guard him against becoming an accomplice in men's fatal striving to control society." Although neither Gadamer nor Hayek deny that reason has a place in understanding the world, and in finding truth, both want to show that there are definite limits to what reason can do.

Instead, both emphasize the way in which knowledge can be conveyed and socially utilized by traditions and institutions. For both, much that we know as a society cannot be articulated by individuals but is wrapped up in social processes such as art, literature, science, and the market. Both Gadamer and Hayek also agree that we need not accept tradition blindly. Rather the authority of tradition is granted in our process of appropriating it. Their accounts of reason do permit us to examine individual aspects of our traditions and to see how well they fit in with the rest, and in that way we grant tradition its authority. What we cannot do is to completely step outside our traditions to examine them in the light of pure Cartesian reason.   Warnke (1987, p. 123) paraphrases Gadamer's argument that

> human beings are and always will be conditioned by prejudices and elements of their tradition over which they have no control. This is not to say that individuals will be unable to see through any of their prejudices;   still it is to say that every dissolution of one prejudice depends on a conscious or unconscious reliance on a myriad of other prejudices.

Hayek (1978a, pp. 19-20) also contends that:

> the proper conclusion . . . is by no means that we may confidently accept all the old and traditional values. Nor even that there are *any* values or moral principles, which science may not occasionally question. The social scientist who endeavours to understand how society functions, and to discover where it can be improved, must claim the right to critically examine, and even to judge, every *single* value of our society . . . [but] never at one and the same time question *all* its values. . . . This is the discipline of reason . . . itself a part of civilisation. All we can ever do is to confront one part with the other parts. Even this process leads to incessant movement, which may in the very long course of time change the whole.[12]

Perhaps the most important point to realize is that both orthodox Marxism's central planning and general equilibrium market socialism are products of Enlightenment views of knowledge and science. For both groups, what is not rationally constructed or explainable from rational choice is to be transcended in the name of rationality. The Marxist desire to remove the "anarchy" of capitalist production that takes place "behind the backs" of workers and capitalists reflects this Enlightenment rationality.   Marx's explicit attempts to build upon the work of the French rationalist socialists such as St. Simon and Fourier, and the desire of Marxists that Marxism become a social version of Newtonian physics or Darwinian biology, are more evidence supporting this point (Hayek 1952b). General equilibrium's focus on utility maximization and rational choice under complete certainty also reflects an Enlightenment view of rationality and knowledge. The work of Polanyi, Gadamer, and others on the nature of knowledge, rationality, and science have given us powerful reasons to suppose that both versions of the Enlightenment view are outdated.

In the philosophical world of Polanyi and Gadamer, there is room for institutions that are not the product of rational deliberation and construction, or the result of blind instinct. For Hayek (1989, p. 23) too, much of human culture is "between instinct and reason":

> Just as instinct is older than custom or tradition, so then are the latter older than reason: custom and tradition stand *between* instinct and reason—logically, psychologically, temporally. They are due neither to what is sometimes called the unconscious, nor to intuition, nor to rational understanding. Though in a sense based on human experience in that they were shaped in the course of cultural evolution, they were not formed by drawing reasoned conclusions from certain facts or from an awareness that things behaved in a particular way.

The rehabilitation of the ideas of custom, tradition, and authority that is evident in these thinkers' works is key to a more philosophically sophisticated understanding of the market process. The market is a tradition that embodies a great deal of social knowledge about the "right" things to do. In particular, capital goods and successful production processes in competitive markets are embodiments of our evolving knowledge of these "right things." For Gadamer, the tradition of a language and the authority we grant those who have given us the classics of our culture embody the same sense of social knowledge. For Polanyi, the skills and judgment of the scientist are embodied in the traditions of the scientific process and the norms of its operation. For Hayek, Gadamer, and Polanyi, no explicit list of instructions is available, or needed, for the operation of society. We already know what to do; only the pretense of those who think they know better (the economic planner, the historicist social scientist, or the objectivist philosopher) stands in the way. As Hayek wrote in 1944 (p. 166, emphasis added),[13]

> It may indeed be said that it is the paradox of all collectivist doctrine and its demand for "conscious" control or "conscious" planning that they necessarily lead to the demand that the mind of some individual should rule supreme—while only the individualist approach to social phenomena makes us recognize *the superindividual forces which guide the growth of reason*. Individualism is thus an attitude of humility before the social process and of tolerance to other opinions and is the exact opposite of that intellectual hubris which is at the root of the demand for comprehensive direction of the social process.

The specific subjects of this study, money and its institutions, are further examples of such superindividual forces. The development and use of money guide the growth of human reason and forever change us in ways that cannot be reversed. Money and money prices embody a great deal of historical knowledge, and like the classics of culture, those monetary institutions that have worked deserve authority and those that have not need to be rethought. When we realize that we cannot completely escape from a monetary tradition, we can then start to think in further detail about the kinds of things we can do within its bounds.

Recognition of the truth claims of tradition or authority does not imply blind submission to whatever it is or says. Rather true authority is always granted by acts of acknowledgment. Gadamer (1985, p. 248) elaborates this point:

> On the basis of [the Enlightenment's] concept of reason and freedom, the concept of authority could be seen as diametrically opposed to reason and freedom: to be, in fact, blind obedience. . . . But . . . authority . . . is based ultimately, not on the subjection and abdication of reason, but on recognition and knowledge . . . and hence on an act of reason itself which, aware of its own limitations, accepts that others have better understanding.

Authority does not apply only to people, it can apply to social institutions as well. We grant authority to money and monetary institutions through our acknowledgment that they embody socially usable knowledge, though we do not know what specific knowledge may come our way. Like other traditions, and authority, money is continually reaffirmed by our using it and taking advantage of the things it makes possible and by thinking about how it can be cultivated and refined.

To try to explain money's origin from some extratraditional standpoint is to want the unattainable. No rational deliberation, no utility-maximization experiment can adequately explain the use of money. For Hayek (1989, p. 68, emphasis in original) it is a tradition like language, law, and morality:

> All this begins to become evident when it is realized that *nothing* is justifiable in the way demanded [by Enlightenment rationalism]. Not only is this so of morals, but also of language and law and even science itself. . . . No matter what rules we follow, we will not be able to justify them as demanded. . . . If we stopped doing everything for which we do

not know the reason, or for which we cannot provide a justification in
the sense demanded, we would probably very soon be dead.

The power money has over us is also something we can never totally
explain or justify. It is a tradition that forms the backdrop for all of our
thought and action in the marketplace.

Of course money is only one among many similar social institutions.
Law, morality, religion, etiquette, and other practices and institutions are
also important parts of the broader social order. Money is not *sufficient*
to constitute a society in any meaningful sense, but the argument we
have made is that money is *necessary* for any advanced, complex, and
prosperous social order.

Socialism's defenders have tried to transcend the necessity of money
and monetary calculation by attempting to guide or replace the apparent
anarchy of the market with "rationally" organized, planned production.
Socialism's critics have explained why planning cannot work, and why
society can neither dispense with nor improve upon money and
monetary exchange. It is only through money that we come to know the
world of value, just as it is only through language that we come to know
the world of human thought, expression, and action. What Gadamer
(1967, p. 35, emphasis in original) says about the linguistically constituted
nature of reality also applies to those who have claimed access to
economic value and calculation outside of how it is monetarily constituted:

> It only suggests that there is no societal reality, with all its concrete
> forces, that does not bring itself to representation in a consciousness that
> is linguistically articulated. Reality does not happen "behind the back"
> of language; it happens rather behind the backs of those who live in the
> subjective opinion that they have understood "the world" (or can no
> longer understand it); that is, reality happens precisely *within* language.

In the same way, economic reality does not happen "behind the back" of
money but within it. This serves as both an explanation for, and a
warning about, the failure of Marxism and neoclassical economics to
understand the nature of money and monetary order and the roles they
play in judging the relative merits of capitalism and socialism. If society
is to come to a self-understanding about the momentous issues in
political economy (particularly those concerning explanations of the
collapse of the so-called planned economies of Eastern Europe and the

former Soviet Union) and develop an effective praxis with which to solve the world's problems, we must recognize the truth claims inherent in human traditions such as language and money. We need not choose between the false dichotomy of an antiscientific humanism and an antihumanistic scientism.[14]

What results from this view of reason and tradition is a new conception of what it means to be a radical. The Enlightenment concept of reason winds up depositing us in a world ruled by experts—those who have acquired supposedly certain knowledge via method. This world is ultimately a conservative one where political decisions are made not through the consultation or actions of the governed but by the demands of supposed reason. In practice, such reason comes down to the reasons of those who rule. A true radicalism must throw off the Enlightenment concept of reason and begin to appropriate traditions in light of the reasons of all, not just those who rule. As Polanyi and Prosch (1975, p. 108) argue, the modernist demand for a complete, explicit, rational account of human actions and institutions, and its dismissal of tradition, is absurd: "We cannot start discussing new ideas, even in science, without first adopting a whole framework of ideas which others have had before us. Indeed the very idea of demanding absolute autonomy for our thoughts is itself a traditional doctrine." The rationalism that was, and often still is, seen as the "radicalism" of the Enlightenment has itself become a piece of blind tradition that cannot be defended against a now more reasonable post-Enlightenment concept of reason.

Gadamer's emphasis on conversation, which has its economic analog in the dialogic movements of monetary exchange in the market, is the basis for a new radicalism. This radicalism is one that recognizes the limits of human reason and acknowledges the fact that all members of the human community are involved in the process of discovering truth and coming to understandings. The ongoing conversations in both science and everyday life are after the same thing—understanding the world around us and understanding how it can be improved. This new radicalism can be described by the term *openness*. The true radical is open to better explanations, to other ways of life and other interpretations of culture and tradition, and to the continuing conversations about those same subjects. Being open does not mean assuming that one's conversational partners *have* superior knowledge, only that they *might*, and that no person or group has privileged access to truth. The economic analog of this openness is the freedom of voluntary contract and exchange available in an unhampered market process.

In fact, the whole point of conversation is this continual groping toward truths. We talk and we communicate in order to understand. Again, this is not to deny the role of reason, only to understand its limits and proper function. Warnke (1987, p. 173) offers this understanding of reason and rationality:

> Gadamer define[s] rationality, then, as a willingness to admit the existence of better options. The awareness that one's knowledge is always open to refutation or modification from the vantage point of another perspective is not a basis for suspending confidence in the idea of reason but rather represents the very possibility of rational progress.

To be radical is not to sweep away the traditions and institutions of existing society in the name of reason. The real radical is one who is capable of examining and cultivating the interconnected structure of traditions and institutions that make up society while still recognizing the pressing truth claims they contain and maintaining the openness to alternatives that critical thought demands. The critical appropriation of tradition and its knowledge is a surprisingly radical idea against the Enlightenment's tradition-bound faith in reason and method.

In light of this concept of reason and the limits to what it can consciously create, what Hayek (1989, p. 76) says of economics in general is particularly applicable to the study of money: "The curious task of economics is to demonstrate to men how little they really know about what they imagine they can design." Money, like other spontaneously ordered social institutions, is a tradition to be kept and cherished and to be continually cultivated. And, like these other institutions, money in some way reflects both our essence and our limits as human beings. Michael Polanyi's (1958, pp. 377, 380) warning about the attempt to design other human traditions contains the essence of money's role as a social institution and its importance to a free society. It also demarcates the limits to our ability to consciously construct a monetary order:

> It is indeed only by the lives of ordinary men within a free society that the principles to which it is dedicated acquire their effective meaning. The superior knowledge guiding a free society is . . . embodied in its tradition[s]. . . . And we can establish it now as a matter of logic that man has no other power than this. He is strong, noble and wonderful so long as he fears the voices of this firmament; but he dissolves their

power over himself and his own powers gained through obeying them, if he turns his back and examines what he respects in a detached manner. Then law is no more than what the courts will decide, art but an emollient of nerves, morality but a convention, tradition but an inertia. . . . Then man dominates a world in which he himself does not exist. For with his obligations he has lost his voice and his hope, and been left behind meaningless to himself.

Indeed, to "know thyself" and to attempt to understand the meaning of the social institutions that surround us is to recognize that we *are* humans and not gods, and to recognize both the limits and opportunities this implies. The lesson of the twentieth century is that this self-knowledge will not come from rationalistic modes of thought such as orthodox Marxism and general equilibrium theory, which arrogantly dismiss our attempts to recognize the authority of irreplaceable human traditions as unscientific metaphysics.

Notes

1. On this interpretation of war communism see Yugoff (1929), Brutzkus (1935), Roberts (1971), and Boettke (1990a).

2. See Roberts and Stephenson (1973).

3. The debate this article launched has recently been revived and extended. The best overview is Lavoie (1985b). See also Mises (1966 and 1981), Hayek (1935a, 1935b, and 1940), Hoff (1981), Vaughn (1980), Murrell (1983), and Boettke (1990a, chap. 1).

4. For a complete discussion of the neoclassical response see the discussion in Lavoie (1985b).

5. It is strange that this quote appears in *The Grundrisse*, because many years later, in *Capital*, Marx seems to contradict this point: "Value, therefore, does not stalk about with a label describing what it is. It is value, rather that converts every product into a social hieroglyphic. Later on, we try to decipher the hieroglyphic, to get behind the secret of our own social products; *for to stamp an object of utility as value, is just as much a social product as language*" (1906, p. 85, emphasis added). Is language a social process that masks true ideas, or do such ideas not exist outside language? It has been argued throughout this work that ideas, in fact, cannot exist outside language. Whatever Marx's view of language, his view of money and value can be criticized for implying that value can exist outside of its monetary form.

6. Marx's theory of false-consciousness is not an answer to this point. False-consciousness is a result of historical materialism and is thus a result of the social relations of production. False-consciousness argues that we have the thoughts we do because we live in a particular historical epoch with specific relations of production. The point in the text is epistemological, dealing with how we know

anything rather than with why we know (or believe) the particular things we do at any time.

7. See Buchanan (1982) for a broad statement of the idea of order being defined only in the process of its emergence.

8. See also Kirzner (1985a, pp. 126-29) for more on the role of entrepreneurship in the context of the calculation debate.

9. See also Mises (1976, p. xxvi): "Abstract problems of logic and methodology have a close bearing on the life of every individual and on the fate of our entire culture . . . [and] no problem of economics or sociology . . . can be fully mastered without reverting to the logical foundations of the science of human action."

10. For an overview of the relationship between this new view of science and many of the ideas presented here, see Lavoie (1989).

11. Hayek (1978c, p. 14, emphasis added) would later see the flaws in his earlier position and provide a path-breaking idea toward its solution: "The chief blemish of the market order which has been the cause of *well-justified reproaches*, its susceptibility to recurrent periods of depression and unemployment, is a consequence of the age-old government monopoly of the issue of money. . . . Private enterprise . . . would long ago have provided the public with a choice of currencies . . . and would have prevented both excessive stimulation of investment and the consequent periods of contraction."

12. Polanyi (1958, p. 294) also gets in on this act: "Though every element of our belief can conceivably be confronted in its turn with all the rest, it is inconceivable that all should be subjected simultaneously to this operation."

13. See also Hayek (1952b, p. 152) for a similar argument.

14. See also Lavoie (1989, p. 633): "The choice between being pro-science and pro-human is a false one, a legacy of modernist thinking that is being overcome in the new view of science. There is a third alternative that is at once humanistic and scientific. Similarly the choice between socialism and conservatism is a false one. . . . There is a third alternative, namely, a truly free society that minimizes the overall role of government and allows the spontaneous forces of the competitive market process to produce social and economic order."

References

Albert, Hans. 1988. "Hermeneutics and Economics: A Criticism of Hermeneutical Thinking in the Social Sciences," *Kyklos*, 41.

Alchian, Armen A. 1977. "Why Money?" *Journal of Money, Credit and Banking*, 9 (1), February.

Alchian, Armen A., and Harold Demsetz. 1972. "Production, Information Costs and Economic Organization," *American Economic Review*, 62 (5), December.

Andrew, A. Piatt. 1906. "The Influence of the Crops upon Business in America," *Quarterly Journal of Economics*, 20 (2), May.

——. 1908. "Substitutes for Cash in the Panic of 1907," *Quarterly Journal of Economics*, 22 (3), August.

Arnold, N. Scott. 1990. *Marx's Radical Critique of Capitalist Society*, New York: Oxford University Press.

Axelrod, Robert. 1984. *The Evolution of Cooperation*, New York: Basic Books.

Barro, Robert J.. 1986a. "Recent Developments in the Theory of Rules versus Discretion," *Economic Journal*, 96 (384), September.

——. 1986b. "Reputation in a Model of Monetary Policy with Incomplete Information," *Journal of Monetary Economics*, 17 (1), January.

Barro, Robert J. and David B. Gordon. 1983a. "Rules, Discretion, and Reputation in a Model of Monetary Policy," *Journal of Monetary Economics*, 12 (1), July.

——. 1983b. "A Positive Theory of Monetary Policy in a Natural Rate Model," *Journal of Political Economy*, 91 (4), August.

Bell, Spurgeon. 1912. "Profit on National Bank Notes," *American Economic Review*, 2 (1), March.

Benson, Bruce. 1990. *The Enterprise of Law*, San Francisco: Pacific Research Institute for Public Policy.

Bergson, Henri. 1960. *Time and Free Will*, New York: Harper Torchbooks.

Bernstein, Richard J. 1983. *Beyond Objectivism and Relativism*, Chicago: The University of Chicago Press.

Boettke, Peter J. 1990a. *The Political Economy of Soviet Socialism: The Formative Years, 1918-1928*, Boston: Kluwer Academic Press.

——. 1990b. "Interpretive Reasoning and the Study of Social Life," *Methodus*, 2 (2), December.

Boettke, Peter, Steven Horwitz, and David L. Prychitko. 1986. "Beyond Equilibrium Economics: Reflections on the Uniqueness of the Austrian Tradition," *Market Process*, 4 (2), Fall.

Bork, Robert H. 1978. *The Antitrust Paradox*, New York: Basic Books.

Boudreaux, Donald J. 1988. "Schumpeter and Kirzner on Competition and Equilibrium," *Market Process*, 6 (2), Fall.

Brown, Harry G. 1910. "Commercial Banking and the Rate of Interest," *Quarterly Journal of Economics*, (24).

Brunner, Karl, and Allan H. Meltzer. 1971. "The Uses of Money: Money in the Theory of an Exchange Economy," *American Economic Review*, 61 (5), December.

Brutzkus, Boris. 1935. *Economic Planning in Soviet Russia*, London: Routledge.

Bryson, Gladys. 1968. *Man and Society: The Scottish Inquiry of the Eighteenth Century*, New York: Augustus M. Kelley.

Buchanan, James M. 1962. "Predictability: The Criterion of Monetary Constitutions," in Yeager, ed. (1962).

———. 1969. *Cost and Choice*, Chicago: The University of Chicago Press.

———. 1979. "Natural and Artifactual Man," in *What Should Economists Do?* Indianapolis, Ind.: Liberty Press.

———. 1982. "Order Defined in the Process of Its Emergence," *Literature of Liberty*, 5 (4), Winter.

———. 1986. "The Relevance of Constitutional Strategy," *Cato Journal*, 6 (2), Fall.

Cagan, Phillip. 1965. *Determinants and Effects of Changes in the Money Stock, 1875-1960*, New York: National Bureau of Economic Research.

Cagan, Phillip, and Anna Schwartz. 1991. "The National Bank Note Puzzle Reinterpreted," *Journal of Money, Credit, and Banking*, 23 (3), August, part 1.

Caldwell, Bruce, ed. 1990. *Carl Menger and His Legacy in Economics*, annual supplement 22 to *History of Political Economy*, Durham: Duke University Press.

———. 1991. "Ludwig M. Lachmann: A Reminiscence," *Critical Review*, 5 (1), Winter.

Calomiris, Charles W., and R. Glenn Hubbard. 1989. "Price Flexibility, Credit Availability, and Economic Fluctuations: Evidence from the United States, 1894-1909," *Quarterly Journal of Economics*, 104 (3), August.

Champ, Bruce A., Neil Wallace, and Warren E. Weber, 1992. "Resolving the National Bank Note Paradox," *Federal Reserve Bank of Minneapolis Quarterly Review*, 16 (2), Spring.

Christ, Carl. 1989. "Review of Selgin's *The Theory of Free Banking*," *Market Process*, 7 (1), Spring.

Clower, Robert W. 1967. "A Reconsideration of the Microfoundations of Monetary Theory," reprinted in Walker, ed. (1984).

———. 1969. "Intro to *Monetary Theory: Selected Readings,*" reprinted in Walker, ed. (1984).

———. 1970. "Foundations of Monetary Theory," reprinted in Walker, ed. (1984).

Coase, Ronald H. 1937. "The Nature of the Firm," *Economica,* 4, November.

Cooke, Thornton. 1903. "Branch Banking for the West and South," *Quarterly Journal of Economics,* 18.

Cordato, Roy. 1986. "An Analysis of Externalities in Austrian Economics," unpublished Ph.D. dissertation, George Mason University.

———. 1989. "Subjective Value, Time Passage, and the Economics of Harmful Effects," *Hamline Law Review,* 12 (2), Spring.

Corey, Lewis. 1930. *The House of Morgan,* New York: G. Howard Watt.

Cowen, Tyler. 1991. "The Costs of Inflation Reexamined," working paper, Department of Economics, George Mason University.

Cowen, Tyler, and Richard Fink. 1983. "Order Analysis and Economic Science," unpublished manuscript, George Mason University.

———. 1985. "Inconsistent Equilibrium Constructs: The Evenly Rotating Economies of Mises and Rothbard," *American Economic Review,* 75 (4), September.

Cowen, Tyler, and Randall Kroszner. 1987. "The Development of the New Monetary Economics," *Journal of Political Economy,* 95 (3), June.

Cukierman, Alex, and Allan H. Meltzer. 1986. "A Positive Theory of Discretionary Policy, the Cost of Democratic Government, and the Benefits of a Constitution," *Economic Inquiry,* 24, July.

Dallmayr, Fred, and Thomas A. McCarthy. 1977. *Understanding and Social Inquiry,* Notre Dame: University of Notre Dame Press.

Darwin, Charles. 1859. *The Origin of Species,* Modern Library edition, New York: Random House.

Davidson, Paul. 1978. *Money and the Real World,* 2nd ed., London: Macmillan.

Dawkins, Richard. 1976. *The Selfish Gene,* New York: Oxford University Press.

Debreu, Gerard. 1959. *The Theory of Value,* New York: John Wiley.

Demsetz, Harold. 1982. "Barriers to Entry," *American Economic Review,* 72 (5), December.

Dolan, Edwin, ed. 1976. *The Foundations of Modern Austrian Economics,* Kansas City: Sheed and Ward.

Dowd, Kevin. 1989. *The State and the Monetary System,* Oxford: Philip Alan.

———, ed. 1992. *The Experience of Free Banking,* London: Routledge.

Dyer, Alan W. 1989. "Making Semiotic Sense of Money as a Medium of Exchange," *Journal of Economic Issues,* 23 (2), June.

Ebeling, Richard. 1987. "Cooperation in Anonymity," *Critical Review*, 1 (4), Fall.

———. 1988. "Expectations and Expectations Formation in Mises's Theory of the Market Process," *Market Process*, 6 (2), Fall.

Ely, Bert. 1988. "The Big Bust: The 1930-33 Banking Collapse—Its Causes, Its Lessons," in *The Financial Services Revolution: Policy Directions for the Future*, edited by Catherine England and Thomas Huertas, Boston: Kluwer Academic.

Engineer, Merwan, and Dan Bernhardt. 1991. "Money, Barter, and the Optimality of Legal Restrictions," *Journal of Political Economy*, 99 (4), August.

Fehl, Ulrich. 1986. "Spontaneous Order and the Subjectivity of Expectations: A Contribution to the Lachmann-O'Driscoll Problem," in Kirzner, ed. (1986).

Fehtke, Gary, and Richard Jackman. 1984. "Optimal Monetary Policy, Endogenous Supply, and Rational Expectations," *Journal of Monetary Economics*, 13 (2), March.

Fink, Richard H. 1984-85. "General and Partial Equilibrium in Bork's Antitrust Analysis," *Contemporary Policy Issues*, 3, Winter.

Frankel, S. Herbert. 1977. *Two Philosophies of Money*, New York: St. Martin's Press.

Friedman, Milton. 1968. "The Role of Monetary Policy," *American Economic Review*, 58 (1), March.

———. 1977. "Nobel Lecture: Inflation and Unemployment," *Journal of Political Economy*, 85.

Friedman, Milton, and Anna J. Schwartz. 1963. *A Monetary History of the United States, 1867-1960*, Princeton, N.J.: Princeton University Press.

———. 1970. *Monetary Statistics of the United States*, New York: Columbia University Press.

Frisby, David. 1978. "Introduction to Georg Simmel's *Philosophy of Money*," in Simmel (1978).

Fromm, Erich. 1960. "Foreword" to *Looking Backward* by Edward Bellamy, New York: New American Library.

Froyen, Richard T. 1986. *Macroeconomics*, 2nd ed., New York: Macmillan.

Gadamer, Hans-Georg. 1966. "Man and Language," in Gadamer (1976).

———. 1967. "On the Scope and Function of Hermeneutical Reflection," in Gadamer (1976).

———. 1976. *Philosophical Hermeneutics*, translated and edited by David E. Linge, Berkeley: University of California Press.

———. 1981. *Reason in the Age of Science*, translated by Frederick G. Lawrence, Cambridge: MIT Press.

———. 1985. *Truth and Method*, New York: Crossroads.

Garrison, Roger. 1985. "Intertemporal Coordination and the Invisible Hand: An Austrian Perspective on the Keynesian Vision," *History of Political Economy,* 17 (2), Summer.

———. 1987. "Full Employment and Intertemporal Coordination: Reply," *History of Political Economy,* 19 (2), Summer.

Glasner, David. 1989. *Free Banking and Monetary Reform,* Cambridge: Cambridge University Press.

Goodhart, C.A.E. 1965. "Profit on National Bank Notes, 1900-13," *Journal of Political Economy,* 73, October.

———. 1988. *The Evolution of Central Banks,* Cambridge: MIT Press.

Gorton, Gary. 1985. "Clearinghouses and the Origin of Central Banking in the United States," *Journal of Economic History,* 45 (2), June.

Gorton, Gary, and Donald J. Mullineaux. 1987. "The Joint Production of Confidence: Endogenous Regulation and Nineteenth Century Commercial-Bank Clearinghouses," *Journal of Money, Credit, and Banking,* 19 (4), November.

Gould, Stephen Jay. 1980. *The Panda's Thumb,* New York: W. W. Norton.

Grathoff, Richard, ed. 1978. *The Theory of Social Action: The Correspondence of Alfred Schutz and Talcott Parsons,* Bloomington: Indiana University Press.

Greenbaum, Stuart I., and Anjan V. Thakor. 1989. "Bank Reserve Requirements as an Impediment to Signaling," *Economic Inquiry,* 27, January.

Hahn, Frank. 1970. "Some Adjustment Problems," *Econometrica,* 38 (1), January.

———. 1973. *On the Notion of Equilibrium in Economics,* Cambridge: Cambridge University Press.

Hamowy, Ronald. 1987. *The Scottish Enlightenment and the Theory of Spontaneous Order,* Carbondale, Ill: Southern Illinois University Press.

Haupert, Michael. 1991. "Investment in Name Brand Capital: Evidence from the Free Banking Era," *American Economist,* 35 (2), Fall.

Hayek, F. A. 1928. "Intertemporal Price Equilibrium and Movements in the Value of Money," in *Money, Capital and Fluctuations: Early Essays,* edited by Roy McCloughry, Chicago: University of Chicago Press, 1984.

———. 1935a. "The Nature and History of the Problem," in Hayek (1948).

———. 1935b. "The State of the Debate," in Hayek (1948).

———, ed. 1935. *Collectivist Economic Planning,* Clifton, N.J.: Augustus M. Kelley.

———. 1937. "Economics and Knowledge," in Hayek (1948).

———. 1940. "The Competitive Solution," in Hayek (1948).

———. 1944. *The Road to Serfdom,* Chicago: University of Chicago Press.

———. 1945. "The Use of Knowledge in Society," in Hayek (1948).

———. 1948. *Individualism and Economic Order,* Chicago: University of Chicago Press.

———. 1952a. *The Sensory Order,* Chicago: University of Chicago Press.

———. 1952b. *The Counter-Revolution of Science,* Indianapolis, Ind.: Liberty Press.

———. 1967a. "Notes on the Evolution of Systems of Rules of Conduct," in *Studies in Politics, Philosophy, and Economics,* Chicago: University of Chicago Press.

———. 1967b. "The Theory of Complex Phenomena," in *Studies in Politics, Philosophy, and Economics,* Chicago: University of Chicago Press.

———. 1967c. "Rules, Perception and Intelligibility," in *Studies in Politics, Philosophy, and Economics,* Chicago: University of Chicago Press.

———. 1973, 1977, 1979. *Law, Legislation, and Liberty,* vols. 1-3, Chicago: University of Chicago Press.

———. 1978a. "Competition as a Discovery Procedure," in *New Studies in Politics, Philosophy, Economics and the History of Ideas,* Chicago: University of Chicago Press.

———. 1978b. "The Errors of Constructivism," in *New Studies in Politics, Philosophy, Economics and the History of Ideas,* Chicago: University of Chicago Press.

———. 1978c. *The Denationalisation of Money,* 2nd ed., London: Institute for Economic Affairs.

———. 1978d. "The Pretence of Knowledge," in *New Studies in Politics, Philosophy, Economics and the History of Ideas,* Chicago: University of Chicago Press.

———. 1989. *The Fatal Conceit: The Errors of Socialism,* edited by W. Bartley III, Chicago: University of Chicago Press.

Hicks, Sir John. 1935. "A Suggestion for Simplifying the Theory of Money," reprinted in *AEA Readings in Monetary Theory,* New York: The Blakiston Company 1951.

———. 1946. *Value and Capital,* 2nd ed., Oxford: Clarendon Press.

Higgs, Robert. 1987. *Crisis and Leviathan: Critical Episodes in the Growth of American Government,* New York: Oxford University Press.

High, Jack C. 1983-84. "Knowledge, Maximizing, and Conjecture: A Critical Analysis of Search Theory," *Journal of Post-Keynesian Economics,* Winter.

———. 1986. "Equilibration and Disequilibration in the Market Process," in Kirzner, ed. (1986).

———. 1990. *Maximizing, Action and Market Adjustment,* Munich: Philosophia Verlag.

Hilferding, Rudolf. 1981. *Finance Capital,* London: Routledge and Kegan Paul.

Hobbes, Thomas. 1968. *Leviathan,* edited with an introduction by C. B. Macpherson, New York: Penguin Books.

Hodgson, Geoffrey M. 1989. *Economics and Institutions,* Philadelphia: University of Pennsylvania Press.

Holland, A. Steven, and Mark Toma. 1991. "The Role of the Federal Reserve as 'Lender of Last Resort' and the Seasonal Fluctuation of Interest Rates," *Journal of Money, Credit, and Banking*, 23 (4), November.

Hoff, Trygve J.B. 1981. *Economic Calculation in the Socialist Society*, Indianapolis, Ind.: Liberty Press.

Horwitz, Steven. 1989. "Keynes' Special Theory," *Critical Review*, 3 (3/4), Summer/Fall.

——. 1990a. "Competitive Currencies, Legal Restrictions and the Origins of the Fed: Some Evidence from the Panic of 1907," *Southern Economic Journal*, 56 (4), January.

——. 1990b. "A Subjectivist Approach to the Demand for Money," *Journal des Economistes et des Etudes Humaines*, 1 (4), December.

——. 1991. "The Political Economy of Inflation: Public and Private Choices," *Durell Journal of Money and Banking*, 3 (4), November.

——. 1992. "Monetary Exchange as an Extra-Linguistic Social Communication Process," *Review of Social Economy*.

Horwitz, Steven, and Howard Bodenhorn. 1991. "A Property Rights Approach to Free Banking," working paper, St. Lawrence University.

Horwitz, Steven, and G. A. Selgin. 1987. "Interstate Banking: The Reform That Won't Go Away," *Policy Analysis 97*, Cato Institute, Washington, D.C., December 15.

Hume, David. 1961. *A Treatise of Human Nature*, Garden City, N.Y.: Dolphin Books.

Humphrey, Thomas. 1984. "On Nonneutral Relative Price Effects in Monetarist Thought: Some Austrian Misconceptions," reprinted in Humphrey, *Essays on Inflation*, 5th ed., Richmond, VA: Federal Reserve Bank of Richmond, 1986.

Husserl, Edmund. 1964. *The Phenomenology of Internal Time Consciousness*, translated by Janes S. Churchill, Bloomington: Indiana University Press.

Hutt, William H. 1956. "The Yield from Money Held," in *On Freedom and Free Enterprise: Essays in Honor of Ludwig von Mises*, edited by Mary Sennholz, Princeton, N.J.: Van Nostrand.

——. 1977. *The Theory of Idle Resources*, Indianapolis, Ind.: Liberty Press.

James, John A. 1976. "The Conundrum of the Low Issue of National Bank Notes," *Journal of Political Economy*, 84 (2), April.

Jevons, William Stanley. 1969. *Money and the Mechanism of Exchange* 23rd ed., London: Kegan Paul.

Johnson, Gregory R. 1990. "Hermeneutics: A Protreptic," *Critical Review*, 4 (1/2), Winter/Spring.

Jones, Robert A. 1976. "The Origin and Development of Media of Exchange," *Journal of Political Economy*, 84 (4), August.

Jonung, Lars. 1985. "The Economics of Private Money: The Experience of Private Notes in Sweden, 1831-1902," paper presented at the Monetary History Group Meeting, London, September 27.

Kevelson, Roberta. 1988. *The Law as a System of Signs*, New York: Plenum Press.

Keynes, John Maynard. 1930. *A Treatise on Money*, vols. 1 and 2, London: Macmillan.

——. 1936. *The General Theory of Employment, Interest, and Money*, New York: Harcourt, Brace.

——. 1937. "The General Theory of Employment," reprinted in *The Collected Writings of John Maynard Keynes*, vol. 14, edited by Donald Muggridge, London: Macmillan, 1973.

King, Robert G., and Charles I. Plosser. 1986. "Money as the Mechanism of Exchange," *Journal of Monetary Economics*, 17 (1).

Kirchner, Christian. 1988. "The New Institutional Economics Applied to Monetary Economics: Comment," *Journal of Institutional and Theoretical Economics*, 144 (1), February.

Kirzner, Israel M. 1973. *Competition and Entrepreneurship*, Chicago: University of Chicago Press.

——. 1979. *Perception, Opportunity, and Profit*, Chicago: The University of Chicago Press.

——, ed.. 1982. *Method, Process, and Austrian Economics*, Lexington, Mass.: D. C. Heath.

——. 1985a. "The Perils of Regulation: A Market Process Approach," in *Discovery and the Capitalist Process*, Chicago: University of Chicago Press.

——. 1985b. "Review of *The Economics of Time and Ignorance,*" *Market Process*, 3 (2), Fall.

——, ed. 1986. *Subjectivism, Intelligibility, and Economic Understanding*, New York: New York University Press.

——. 1989a. "Welfare Economics: A Modern Austrian Perspective," in *Man, Economy and Liberty: Essays in Honor of Murray N. Rothbard*, edited by Walter Block and Llewellyn Rockwell, Auburn: Ludwig von Mises Institute.

——. 1989b. *Discovery, Capitalism, and Distributive Justice*, New York: Basil Blackwell.

Klamer, Arjo, Donald McCloskey, and Robert Solow, eds. 1989. *The Consequences of Economic Rhetoric*, Cambridge: Cambridge University Press.

Klein, Benjamin. 1974. "The Competitive Supply of Money," *Journal of Money, Credit, and Banking*, 6 (4), November.

Knight, Frank H. 1971. *Risk, Uncertainty, and Profit*, Chicago: University of Chicago Press.

Kolko, Gabriel. 1963. *The Triumph of Conservatism*, New York: Free Press.

Kydland, Finn E., and Edward C. Prescott. 1977. "Rules Rather than Discretion: The Inconsistency of Optimal Plans," *Journal of Political Economy*, 85 (3), June.

Lachmann, Ludwig M. 1956. *Capital and Its Structure*, Kansas City: Sheed Andrews and McMeel.

——. 1971. *The Legacy of Max Weber*, Berkeley: Glendessary Press.

——. 1977. *Capital, Expectations and the Market Process*, edited by Walter Grinder, Kansas City: Sheed Andrews and McMeel.

——. 1985. "Review of *The Economics of Time and Ignorance*," *Market Process*, 3 (2), Fall.

——. 1986. *The Market as an Economic Process*, London: Basil Blackwell.

Laidler, David E. W. 1985. *The Demand for Money*, 3rd ed., New York: Harper and Row.

Laidler, David E. W., and Nicholas Rowe. 1980. "Georg Simmel's *Philosophy of Money*: A Review Article for Economists," *Journal of Economic Literature*, 18, March.

Lange, Oscar. 1936. "On the Economic Theory of Socialism," in *On the Economic Theory of Socialism*, edited by Benjamin Lippincott, New York: McGraw-Hill, 1964.

Langlois, Richard. 1986. "Rationality, Institutions, and Explanation," in Langlois, ed. (1986).

——, ed. 1986. *Economics as a Process: Essays in the New Institutionalist Economics*, Cambridge: Cambridge University Press.

Langlois, Richard, and Roger Koppl. 1991. "Fritz Machlup and Marginalism: A Reevaluation," *Methodus*, 3 (2), December.

Laughlin, J. Lawrence. 1898. *Report of the Indianapolis Monetary Commission*, Chicago: University of Chicago Press.

Lavoie, Donald C. 1985a. *National Economic Planning: What is Left?* Cambridge, Mass.: Ballinger.

——. 1985b. *Rivalry and Central Planning*, Cambridge: Cambridge University Press.

——. 1986a. "The Market as a Procedure for the Discovery and Conveyance of Inarticulate Knowledge," *Comparative Economic Studies*, 28 (1), Spring.

——. 1986b. "Euclideanism versus Hermeneutics: A Reinterpretation of Misesian Apriorism," in Kirzner, ed. (1986).

——. 1987. "The Accounting of Interpretations and the Interpretation of Accounts: The Communcation Function of 'the Language of Business,'" *Accounting, Organizations, and Society,* 12 (6), December.

——. 1989. "Economic Chaos or Spontaneous Order? Implications for Political Economy of the New View of Science," *Cato Journal,* 8 (3), Winter.

——. 1990. "Understanding Differently: Hermeneutics and the Spontaneous Order of Communicative Processes," in Caldwell, ed. (1990).

——, ed. 1991. *Hermeneutics and Economics,* Boston: Routledge.

Leijonhufvud, Axel. 1968. *On Keynesian Economics and the Economics of Keynes,* New York: Oxford University Press.

——. 1981a. "Effective Demand Failures," in *Information and Coordination,* Oxford: Oxford University Press.

——. 1981b. "Costs and Consequences of Inflation," in *Information and Coordination,* Oxford: Oxford University Press.

——. 1981c. "The Wicksell Connection," in *Information and Coordination,* Oxford: Oxford University Press.

Livingston, James. 1986. *Origins of the Federal Reserve System: Money, Class, and Corporate Capitalism, 1890-1913,* Ithaca: Cornell University Press.

Lucas, Robert E. 1976. "Econometric Policy Evaluation: A Critique," reprinted in *Studies in Business Cycle Theory,* Cambridge, Mass.: MIT Press, 1981.

——. 1977. "Understanding Business Cycles," reprinted in Lucas (1981).

Lutz, Friedrich A. 1969. "On Neutral Money," in *Roads to Freedom: Essays in Honor of F. A. Hayek,* edited by E. Streissler, London: Routledge and Keegan Paul.

Madison, Gary B. 1988. "Hermeneutical Integrity," *Market Process,* 6 (1), Spring.

——. 1990. "How Individualistic Is Methodological Individualism?" *Critical Review,* 4 (1/2), Winter/Spring.

Mandeville, Bernard. 1970. *The Fable of the Bees,* New York: Penguin Classics.

Marx, Karl. 1906. *Capital* v. 1, New York: Random House Modern Library.

——. 1964. *The Economic and Philosophic Manuscripts of 1844,* edited with an introduction by Dirk J. Struik, New York: International Publishers.

——. 1971. *The Grundrisse,* translated and edited by David McLellan, New York: Harper Torchbooks.

McCloskey, Donald N. 1983. "The Rhetoric of Economics," *Journal of Economic Literature,* 31, June.

——. 1985. *The Rhetoric of Economics,* Madison: University of Wisconsin Press.

McKenzie, Richard. 1988. *The American Job Machine,* New York: Universe Books.

Menger, Carl. 1892. "On the Origin of Money," *Economic Journal,* 2.

——. 1981. *Principles of Economics,* New York: New York University Press.

———. 1985. *Investigations into the Method of the Social Sciences with Special Reference to Economics*, New York: New York University Press.

Miron, Jeffrey A. 1986. "Financial Panics, the Seasonality of Interest Rates, and the Founding of the Fed," *American Economic Review*, 76 (1), March.

Mises, Ludwig von. 1920. "Economic Calculation in the Socialist Commonwealth," in *Collectivist Economic Planning*, edited by F. A. Hayek, Clifton, N.J.: Augustus M. Kelley, 1935.

———. 1966. *Human Action: A Treatise on Economics*, Chicago: Henry Regnery.

———. 1976. *Epistemological Problems of Economics*, New York: New York University Press.

———. 1980. *The Theory of Money and Credit*, Indianapolis, Ind.: Liberty Press.

———. 1981. *Socialism: An Economic and Sociological Analysis*, Indianapolis, Ind.: Liberty Press.

———. 1983. *Nation, State, and Economy: A Contribution to the Politics of our Time*, translated by Leland Yeager, New York: New York University Press.

———. 1985. *Theory and History*, Auburn, Ala.: Ludwig Von Mises Institute.

———. 1990. "The Suitability of Methods of Ascertaining Changes in Purchasing Power for the Guidance of International Currency and Banking Policy," in *Money, Method, and the Market Process*, edited by Richard M. Ebeling, Norwell, Mass.: Kluwer Academic.

Mittermaier, Karl. 1986. "Mechanomorphism," in Kirzner, ed. (1986).

Mullineaux, Donald J. 1987. "Competitive Monies and the Suffolk Bank System: A Contractual Perspective," *Southern Economic Journal*, 53 (4), April.

———. 1988. "Competitive Monies and the Suffolk Banking System: Reply," *Southern Economic Journal*, 55 (1), July.

Murrell, Peter. 1983. "Did the Theory of Market Socialism Answer the Challenge of Ludwig von Mises?" *History of Political Economy*, 15 (1), Spring.

Nagatani, Keizo. 1978. *Monetary Theory*, Amsterdam: North-Holland.

Niehans, Jurg. 1971. "Money and Barter in General Equilibrium with Transaction Costs," *American Economic Review*, 61 (5), December.

———. 1978. *The Theory of Money*, Baltimore: Johns Hopkins University Press.

Nozick, Robert. 1974. *Anarchy, State and Utopia*, New York: Basic Books.

O'Driscoll, Gerald P. 1977. *Economics as a Coordination Problem*, Kansas City: Sheed Andrews and McMeel.

———. 1986. "Money: Menger's Evolutionary Theory," *History of Political Economy*, 18 (4), Winter.

O'Driscoll, Gerald P., and Mario J. Rizzo. 1985. *The Economics of Time and Ignorance*, London: Basil Blackwell.

Oh, Seonghwan. 1989. "A Theory of a Generally Acceptable Medium of Exchange and Barter," *Journal of Monetary Economics*, 23 (1), January.

Ostroy, Joseph M. 1973. "The Informational Efficiency of Monetary Exchange," *American Economic Review*, 63 (4), September.

Ostroy, Joseph M., and Ross M. Starr. 1974. "Money and the Decentralization of Exchange," *Econometrica*, 42, November.

Pareto, Vilfredo. 1971. *Manual of Political Economy*, translated by Ann S. Schwier, New York: Augustus M. Kelley.

Parthemos, James. 1988. "The Federal Reserve Act of 1913 in the Stream of U.S. Monetary History," *Federal Reserve Bank of Richmond Economic Review*, 74 (4), July/August.

Perlman, Morris. 1971. "The Roles of Money in an Economy and the Optimum Quantity of Money," *Economica* n.s., 38 (151), August.

Phelps, Edmund S., ed. 1970. *Microeconomic Foundations of Employment and Inflation Theory*, New York: W. W. Norton.

Polanyi, Michael. 1958. *Personal Knowledge: Towards a Post-Critical Philosophy*, Chicago: University of Chicago Press.

———. 1969. *Knowing and Being*, edited by Marjorie Grene, Chicago: University of Chicago Press.

Polanyi, Michael, and Harry Prosch. 1975. *Meaning*. Chicago: University of Chicago Press.

Poteat, William H. 1985. *Polanyian Meditations: In Search of a Post-Critical Logic*, Durham: Duke University Press.

Prendergast, Christopher. 1986. "Alfred Schutz and the Austrian School of Economics," *American Journal of Sociology*, 92 (1), July.

Prychitko, David L. 1988. "Marxism and Decentralized Socialism," *Critical Review*, 2 (4), Fall.

———. 1990. "Toward an Interpretive Economics: Some Hermeneutical Issues," *Methodus*, 2 (2), December.

———. 1992. "Ludwig Lachmann and the Interpretive Turn in Economics: Praxeological or Phenomenological Hermeneutics?" paper presented at the American Economics Association meetings, New Orleans, January.

Rabinow, Paul, and William M. Sullivan, eds. 1986. *Interpretive Social Science: A Reader*, 2nd ed., Berkeley: University of California Press, 1986.

Read, Leonard. 1975. "I, Pencil," in *Free Market Economics: A Basic Reader*, compiled by Bettina Bien Greaves, Irvington-on-Hudson, N.Y.: Foundation for Economic Education, 1975.

Rector, Ralph. 1987. "Has Market Coordination Been Replaced?" *Critical Review*, 1 (4), Fall.

Ricoeur, Paul. 1971. "The Model of the Text: Meaningful Action Considered as a Text," reprinted in Dallmayr and McCarthy (1977).

Roberts, Paul Craig. 1971. *Alienation and the Soviet Economy*, Albuquerque: University of New Mexico Press.

Roberts, Paul Craig, and Matthew A. Stephenson. 1973. *Marx's Theory of Exchange, Alienation and Crisis*, Stanford: Hoover Institution Press.

Robertson, Dennis. 1963. *Lectures on Economic Principles*, London: Collins Press.

Rockoff, Hugh. 1974. "The Free Banking Era: A Re-examination," *Journal of Money, Credit and Banking*, 6 (2), May.

Rolnick, Arthur J., and Warren E. Weber. 1983. "The Free Banking Era: New Evidence," *American Economic Review*, 73 (5), December.

Rothbard, Murray N. 1956. "Toward a Reconstruction of Utility and Welfare Economics," in *On Freedom and Free Enterprise*, edited by Mary Sennholz, Los Angeles: Van Nostrand.

——. 1962a. "The Case For a 100 Percent Gold Dollar," in Yeager, ed. (1962).

——. 1962b. *Man, Economy and State*, Los Angeles: Nash.

——. 1963. *America's Great Depression*, New York: Richardson and Snyder.

——. 1984. "The Federal Reserve as a Cartelization Device: The Early Years 1913-1930," in Siegel, ed. (1984).

Rutland, Peter. 1985. *The Myth of the Plan*, LaSalle, Ill.: Open Court Press.

Samuelson, Paul. 1947. *Foundations of Economic Analysis*, Cambridge: Harvard University Press.

Say, Jean Baptiste. 1971. *A Treatise on Political Economy*, New York: Augustus M. Kelley.

Schotter, Andrew. 1986. "The Evolution of Rules," in Langlois, ed. (1986).

Schuler, Kurt. 1988. "Free Banking: A Bibliographic Essay," *Humane Studies Review*, 6 (1), Fall.

——. 1992. "The World History of Free Banking," in Dowd, ed. (1992).

Schutz, Alfred. 1967. *The Phenomenology of the Social World*, Evanston: Northwestern University Press.

Schweber, Silvan. 1977. "The Origin of the *Origin* Revisited," *Journal of the History of Biology*, 10 (2), Fall.

Selgin, G. A. 1987a. "The Yield on Money Held Revisted: Lessons for Today," *Market Process*, 5 (1), Spring.

——. 1987b. "The Stability and Efficiency of Money Supply Under Free Banking," *Journal of Institutional and Theoretical Economics*, 143 (3), September.

——. 1988a. "Accommodating Changes in the Relative Demand for Currency: Free Banking vs. Central Banking," *Cato Journal*, 7 (3), Winter.

———. 1988b. *The Theory of Free Banking: Money Supply Under Competitive Note Issue*, Totowa, N.J.: Rowman and Littlefield.

———. 1992. "Free Banking in Foochow," in Dowd, ed. (1992).

Selgin, G. A., and Lawrence H. White. 1987. "The Evolution of a Free Banking System," *Economic Inquiry*, 25, July.

———. 1988. "Competitive Monies and the Suffolk Bank System: Comment," *Southern Economic Journal*, 55 (1), July.

Shackle, G.L.S. 1973. *An Economic Querist*, Cambridge: Cambridge University Press.

———. 1982. "Means and Meaning in Economic Theory," *Scottish Journal of Political Economy*, 29 (3), November.

———. 1986. "The Origination of Choice," in Kirzner, ed. (1986).

Sheffrin, Steven M. 1983. *Rational Expectations*, Cambridge: Cambridge University Press.

Siegel, Barry N., ed. 1984. *Money in Crisis: The Federal Reserve, the Economy, and Monetary Reform*, Cambridge, Mass.: Ballinger.

Simmel, Georg. 1905. "How is History Possible?" *On Individuality and Social Forms*, edited by Donald N. Levine, Chicago: University of Chicago Press, 1971.

———. 1908. "How is Society Possible?" in *On Individuality and Social Forms*, edited by Donald N. Levine, Chicago: University of Chicago Press, 1971.

———. 1978. *The Philosophy of Money*, Boston: Routledge and Kegan Paul.

Simons, Henry C. 1936. "Rules Versus Authority in Monetary Policy," *Journal of Political Economy*, 44 (1), February.

Smith, Adam. 1976. *An Inquiry into the Nature and Causes of the Wealth of Nations*, edited by Edwin Cannan (1904), Chicago: University of Chicago Press.

Smith, Barry. 1990. "On the Austrianness of Austrian Economics," *Critical Review*, 4 (1/2), Winter/Spring.

Smith, Vera. 1990. *The Rationale of Central Banking*, Indianapolis, Ind.: Liberty Press.

Sowell, Thomas. 1980. *Knowledge and Decisions*, New York: Basic Books.

Spadaro, Louis M., ed. 1978. *New Directions in Austrian Economics*, Kansas City: Sheed Andrews and McMeel.

Sprague, O.M.W. 1977. *History of Crises Under the National Banking System*, Fairfield, N.J.: Augustus M. Kelley.

Starr, Ross M. 1972. "The Structure of Exchange in Barter and Monetary Economies," *Quarterly Journal of Economics*, 83 (2), May.

Stigler, George J., and Gary S. Becker. 1977. "De Gustibus Non Est Disputandum," *American Economic Review*, 67 (1), March.

Stonier, Alfred, and Karl Bode. 1937. "A New Approach to the Methodology of the Social Sciences," *Economica* n.s., 2, November.

Thomsen, Esteban. 1989. "Prices and Knowledge: A Market Process Perspective," unpublished Ph.D. dissertation, New York University.

Timberlake, Richard H. 1984. "The Central Banking Role of Clearinghouse Associations," *Journal of Money, Credit, and Banking,* 16 (1), February.

Tobin, James. 1983. "Monetary Policy: Rules, Targets, and Shocks," *Journal of Money, Credit, and Banking,* 15 (4), November.

Vaughn, Karen. 1980. "Economic Calculation Under Socialism: The Austrian Contribution," *Economic Inquiry,* 18, October.

———. 1990. "The Mengerian Roots of the Austrian Revival," in Caldwell, ed. (1990).

———. 1992. "The Problem of Order in Austrian Economics: Kirzner vs. Lachmann," *Review of Political Economy,* 4 (3).

Wagner, Richard E. 1977. "Economic Manipulation for Political Profit: Macroeconomic Consequences and Constitutional Implications," *Kyklos,* 30.

Walker, Donald, ed. 1984. *Money and Markets,* Cambridge: Cambridge University Press.

Wallace, Neil. 1983. "A Legal Restrictions Theory of the Demand for 'Money' and the Role of Monetary Policy," *Quarterly Review,* Federal Reserve Bank of Minneapolis, Winter.

———. 1988. "A Suggestion for Oversimplifying the Theory of Money," *The Economic Journal,* 98 (390), Conference edition.

Walras, Leon. 1977. *Elements of Pure Economics,* New York: Augustus M. Kelley.

Warner, John DeWitt. 1895. "The Currency Famine of 1893," *Sound Currency,* 2 (6), February.

Warneryd, Karl. 1990. "Conventions: An Evolutionary Approach," *Constitutional Political Economy,* 1 (3), Fall.

Warnke, Georgia. 1987. *Gadamer: Hermeneutics, Tradition and Reason,* Stanford: Stanford University Press.

Weber, Max. 1968. *Economy and Society,* Berkeley: University of California Press.

Weinsheimer, Joel C. 1985. *Gadamer's Hermeneutics: A Reading of Truth and Method,* New Haven: Yale University Press.

Weinstein, James. 1968. *The Corporate Ideal in the Liberal State 1900-1918,* Boston: Beacon Press.

Weintraub, E. Roy. 1985. *General Equilibrium Analysis: Studies in Appraisal,* New York: Cambridge University Press.

Wells, Donald R. 1987. "Banking Before the Federal Reserve: The U.S. and Canada Compared," *The Freeman*, 37 (6), June.

White, Eugene Nelson. 1983. *The Regulation and Reform of the American Banking System: 1900-1929*, Princeton, N.J.: Princeton Univeristy Press.

———. 1990. "Free Banking During the French Revolution," *Explorations in Economic History*, 27 (3), July.

White, Lawrence H. 1984. *Free Banking in Britain*, Cambridge: Cambridge University Press.

———. 1986. "The Secularly Growing Shortage of Banknotes in the United States 1865-1913," unpublished manuscript, New York University.

———. 1987. "Accounting for Non-interest Bearing Currency: A Critique of the 'Legal Restrictions' Theory of Money," *Journal of Money, Credit, and Banking*, 19 (4), November.

Wicksell, Knut. 1950. *Lectures in Political Economy*, v. 2: Money, London: Routledge and Kegan Paul.

Wiebe, Robert H. 1962. *Businessmen and Reform*, Chicago: Ivan R. Dee.

Williamson, Oliver. 1985. *The Economic Institutions of Capitalism*, New York: Free Press.

Witt, Ulrich. 1989. "Emergence and Dissemination of Innovations—Some Problems and Principles of Evolutionary Economics," unpublished manuscript, University of Freiburg.

Yeager, Leland B., ed. 1962. *In Search of a Monetary Constitution*, Cambridge: Harvard University Press.

———. 1968. "Essential Properties of the Medium of Exchange," *Kyklos*, January/March.

———. 1973. "The Keynesian Diversion," *Western Economic Journal*, 16.

———. 1982. "Individual and Overall Viewpoints in Monetary Theory," in Kirzner, ed. (1982).

———. 1986. "The Significance of Monetary Disequilibrium," *Cato Journal*, 6 (2), Fall.

Yugoff, A. 1929. *Economic Trends in Soviet Russia*, New York: Richard R. Smith.

About the Book and Author

This book deals with the origin and functions of money and banking, emphasizing the role both play in the promotion of economic order. Developing the insights of Hayek and others of the Austrian tradition, Professor Horwitz argues that an appreciation of the spontaneous evolutionary processes that produce and maintain our monetary institutions should make us skeptical of attempts to plan or regulate the production of money.

Horwitz offers a much broader perspective on financial institutions than can be found in the traditional literature. Of special interest are his argument for a completely deregulated "free banking" system and what amounts to a revisionist history of the end of the National Banking System and the origins of the Federal Reserve System.

This original and insightful study is an important book for specialists in monetary institutions, in particular proponents of free banking, as well as followers of the Austrian paradigm of economic analysis and other critics of neoclassical theory.

Steven Horwitz is assistant professor of economics and Dana Fellow at St. Lawrence University, Canton, New York. He is the author of numerous articles on monetary economics and the Austrian School. His research has appeared in *Review of Social Economy*, *Southern Economic Journal*, and *Critical Review*. He is also a contributing editor of *Critical Review* and an academic advisor to the Heartland Institute.

Index